7-14-94

To Garth,

Happy to know you enjoy Tim's films too!

Best Wishes,

David Rother

TIM HOLT

by David Rothel

Published by
Empire Publishing, Inc.
P. O. Box 717, Madison, NC 27025
(910) 427-5850

Also by David Rothel
    Who Was That Masked Man?: The Story of The Lone Ranger
    The Singing Cowboys
    The Great Show Business Animals
    Those Great Cowboy Sidekicks
    The Gene Autry Book
    The Roy Rogers Book
    Lash LaRue, The King of the Bullwhip
    Allan "Rocky" Lane, Republic's Action Ace
    An Ambush of Ghosts

Author
Casa Vaquero
7254 Bridle Path Way
Sarasota, Florida 34241

Tim Holt copyright © 1994 by David Rothel

ISBN 0-944019-13-7
Library of Congress Catalog Card Number 94-71493

Manufactured in the United States

1 2 3 4 5 6 7 8 9 10

COVER PAINTING
by
Ivan Jesse Curtis
Old West Art Productions
17122 Avenue 288
Exeter, California 93221

CONTENTS

Acknowledgments

Dedication

A Few Words Before Saddling Up . . .

Foreword by Burt Kennedy

1. Milestones and Minutiae in a Man's Life   13
2. You Can Know a Man by What He Says   37
3. Getting His Foot in the Stirrup — The Early Films (1928-1943)   45
4. Earning His Spurs — The Pre-War Western Series (1940-1943)   61
5. The Mature Cowboy Star — The Post-War Western Series (1947-1952)   85
6. Just a Sideline — The Other Films (1946-1971)   133
7. You Can Know a Man by His Family — Reminiscences   141

    Jennifer Holt, sister   141
    Jack Holt, son   155
    Byranna Holt, daughter   167
    Jay Holt, son   167
    Berdee Holt, Tim's widow   174

8. You Can Know a Man by the Company He Keeps — More Reminiscences   182

    Richard Martin, sidekick   182
    Nan Leslie, leading lady   193
    Walter Reed, actor   199
    Robert Clarke, actor   202
    Myrna Dell, actress   209
    William Phipps, actor   209
    John Doucette, actor   211
    Gail Davis, leading lady   211
    Harry Carey, Jr., actor   212
    Ann Rutherford, actress   213
    Budd Boetticher, schoolmate and director   214
    Orson Welles, director   216

9. A Tim Holt Scrapbook   219

    Comic Books   219
    Memorabilia   229
    Clippings and Photos   233

Into the Sunset   281

Selected Bibliography   282

Filmography Index   283

About the Author   285

ACKNOWLEDGMENTS

There are many people who provided assistance, interviews, photographs, information of all sorts, and encouragement during the many months I spent researching the life and times of Tim Holt. I am deeply grateful to them and just hope that I can recall all of their names as I compose this page.

My deep bow of thanks to the following for the many ways in which they helped me prepare this book:

Bill Black	Boyd Magers
Budd Boetticher	Richard Martin
Marilyn and Harry Carey, Jr.	Mike Marx
Robert Clarke	Les Mason
Bobby Copeland	Nick Nicholls
Gail Davis	House Peters, Jr.
Myrna Dell	William Phipps
John Doucette	Walter Reed
Johnny Efirt	Ann Rutherford
Grady Franklin	Bill Sasser
Berdee Holt	Ed Shatterly
Bryanna Holt	Wayne Short
Jack Holt	Ken Taylor
Jay Holt	Norvia Torine
Jennifer Holt	Virginia Vale
Dave Holland	Tinsley E. Yarbrough
Nan Leslie	Valery Anne Zurn

Ivan Jesse Curtis was kind enough to let us use his extraordinary painting of Tim Holt for the cover of this book.

Although I did not confer directly with Buck Rainey during the development of this book, his fine volume, *The Fabulous Holts,* was of enormous help to me as I began my research on Tim.

Chuck Thorton's book on Tim's films, *The Western Adventures of Tim Holt,* was also a deep well of information regarding the credits and plots of Tim's Western films. Chuck was also kind enough to share his huge collection of Tim Holt photos with me.

I want to extend my thanks and appreciation to Don Key, Rhonda Lemons, Debra DeLancey, and the staff of Empire Publishing, Inc. for doing such a fine job of overseeing the publication of this book.

And, finally, to the person whom I may have inadvertently overlooked, I offer an especially heartfelt "thank you" for your anonymous contribution.

DEDICATED

to

The Family of Tim Holt

A FEW WORDS BEFORE SADDLING UP...

During the last few years I became very intrigued with Tim Holt's films as they found new life on the TNT and American Movie Classics cable channels and, to a degree, on home video. Over time I have had the opportunity to videotape them and to view all of them repeatedly. I had previously seen some of the post-war films, of course, when I was a kid going to the Saturday matinees of so long ago, but I don't think I had ever seen any of his pre-war Westerns, and I was delighted to discover how enjoyable they are and how effectively this bright young actor claimed the mantle of Western film star — he was made for the assignment.

As I viewed these films and also Tim's non-Western films, I began to feel that I wanted to explore them even further by talking with some of the people who had been associated with them — specifically some of the actors who had worked with Tim during the making of the films. I was curious about their behind-the-scenes activities while filming on the Western street at the RKO Ranch in Encino or going on location at Lone Pine, the Jack Garner Ranch in Idyllwild, and elsewhere. How did Tim interact with other people on the set — cast and crew? What did they think of him? In the research for this book I attempted to get the answers to these and other related questions.

And then, of course, there was my curiosity about Tim Holt himself. What kind of a guy was he? What made him tick? Buck Rainey had delved into this subject, of course, in his fine book, but I wanted to find out more — especially more about those twenty-one years after he left Hollywood and made his home in Oklahoma. What was his life like in Oklahoma — "where the wind comes sweeping o'er the plains." What kind of husband and father was this former film cowboy star who had experienced two failed marriages prior to his arrival in the Sooner state? Why did he then seem to shun the industry that had provided him with a successful and lucrative career for some fifteen years? Tim's family provided many of the answers to these questions, and I think you'll find their comments very insightful.

I have enjoyed my year or so researching the life and career of Tim Holt; he's been a fascinating subject. I had considerable respect for the man before I began my research, and it has only grown during this time I have spent learning more about him.

Most of us were kids when we first saw Tim up there on the silver screen. He gave us many hours of movie thrills and adventure while subtly teaching us right from wrong in that somewhat simpler era of the 1940s and '50s. This book is my thank you to him.

David Rothel
Casa Vaquero
Sarasota, Florida
September, 1993

Director/screenwriter Burt Kennedy (right) is seen here at the 1992 Golden Boot Awards ceremony with Tim Holt's children — Bryanna, Jay, and Jack — after presenting them with Tim's posthumous award. Mr. Kennedy's extensive directing credits include *THE ROUNDERS* (1965, screenplay also), *THE WAR WAGON* (1967), *WELCOME TO HARD TIMES* (1967, screenplay also), *SUPPORT YOUR LOCAL SHERIFF* (1969), and *THE TRAIN ROBBERS* (1973, screenplay also). He gained his initial fame as a Western screenwriter for a trio of outstanding Randolph Scott films — *SEVEN MEN FROM NOW* (1956), *THE TALL T* (1957), and *COMANCHE STATION* (1960). Burt Kennedy was one of Tim's closest friends.

FOREWORD

I recently read a book titled *A Pictorial History of the West,* and in it they said: "Besides his many Westerns, Tim Holt gave creditable performances in two highly acclaimed films, Orson Welles' *The Magnificent Ambersons* and John Huston's *The Treasure of the Sierra Madre."* CREDITABLE, HELL!! Tim received the Best Performance Award from the National Board of Review for *Ambersons* and should have beeen nominated for Academy Awards for both *Ambersons* and *Treasure.* Tim Holt was, by all standards, a great actor — and a great friend. One story I must tell. When things got tough for Tim in the picture business, he packed up and rode out. Soon after he left, I was at a party and some know-it-all producer came up to me and said, "I understand Tim Holt is broke and had to leave town." I said, "Are you kidding? Tim owns the biggest ranch in Oklahoma. He can buy and sell this town." Within two weeks I was at another party, and some hot-shot came up to me and said, "Did you hear about Tim Holt? He struck oil and owns the biggest ranch in Texas!" I loved it. Like an ole cowboy once told me, "Don't let Hollywood get between you and the sun." Tim Holt never did. I loved him.

Burt Kennedy

Tim and a family dog — not Casey. (Photo courtesy of Jennifer Holt.)

Chapter 1
Milestones And Minutiae In A Man's Life

If you can answer most of the questions which follow, you certainly qualify as a Tim Holt authority. For most readers the information will serve as a quick overview of the cowboy star's life—some of it milestones, some of it minutiae—as the chapter title states. In later chapters many of the items touched on here will be explored in more depth by family, friends, and coworkers. So saddle up your easy chairs, and as Tim's sidekick Chito might say in his mangled English, "On the one hand in what follows there are the true facts about Tim; on the other hand there is the trivia for you to chew on in your thoughts, and on the third hand—wait a minute; my brain and mouth he is getting mixed up! Oh, just read, compadres, while I go see Chiquita and try to figure this out. Don't wait for me; Chiquita misses me like anything."

* * *

Q - When was Tim born and where did it take place?

A - Tim was born on February 5, 1919, in a house located on Hollywood Boulevard in Beverly Hills, California.

* * *

Q - Who were Tim's parents?

A - They were Jack and Margaret Wood Holt. Supposedly, Margaret fell instantly in love with Jack, a young film actor, at a garden party after only having viewed him from behind. It is said that she thought he had the most marvelous back of the head. They were married about a year after this first meeting. Tim was their first child.

* * *

Q - What family matters complicated the marriage of Tim's parents, Jack and Margaret?

A - Margaret's parents, wealthy and influential, were appalled that she would want to marry a lowly movie actor. Consequently, when she insisted, they disinherited her.

* * *

Q - Was Tim his given name?

A - No. His name at birth was Charles John Holt III, but his parents dubbed him Tim immediately.

* * *

Q - Didn't Tim have a stepsister?

A - Yes. Imogene was Margaret's child from a previous marriage. When Jack married Margaret, he legally adopted the girl.

* * *

Q - When did sister Jennifer come along?

A - She was born on November 10, 1920, but she wasn't known as Jennifer then. The name given to her at birth was Elizabeth Marshall. Jennifer became her professional name years later.

* * *

Q - What was the name of Tim's dog when he was a kid?

A - Casey.

* * *

Q - Tim often commented that the 1924 Fresno Rodeo was a very happy remembrance of his childhood. Why was that?

A - Jack Holt was the "King of the Rodeo" that year and Tim, only five years old, got to ride with his father in the parade as "Crown Prince."

* * *

Q - Where did Tim learn to be a cowboy?

A - When he was about eight years old, his father bought a cattle ranch in Fresno, California, and the family moved there. For the next few years Tim spent most of his time on the ranch. In addition, his father Jack was a big Western star in silent films, and Tim was mighty impressed with his father.

* * *

Q - Did Tim ever visit his dad on the set while he was making his films?

A - Of course. As a matter of fact, Tim's first appearance in a film occurred as a result of his frequent visitations on the set. When he was about nine years old, he appeared in one of his father's films, *THE VANISHING PIONEER*, playing his father's char-

A very young Tim playing with his blocks.
(Photo courtesy of Jennifer Holt.)

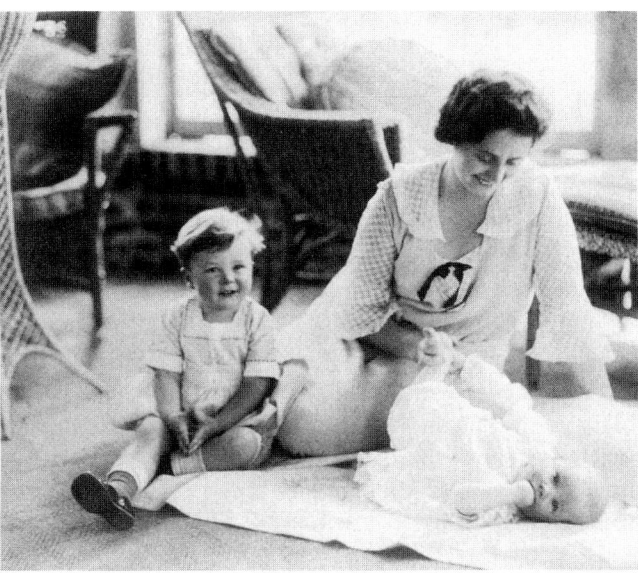

Young Tim, baby Jennifer, and their mother.
(Photo courtesy of Jennifer Holt.)

The Holt family of Beverly Hills. Tim is playing ball with his father Jack as mother Margaret looks on holding baby Jennifer. Imogene, Margaret's daughter from a previous marriage and adopted by Jack, sits next to her mother. (Photo courtesy of Jennifer Holt.)

Tim loved to visit his dad on film locations. Here (at about seven years of age), he got a chance to dress up like a real cowboy and ride with his dad. (Photo courtesy of Valery Anne Zurn.)

acter as a child.

* * *

Q - Wasn't Tim previously in one of his father's films entitled *RED RIVER VALLEY*?

A - Well, there is a lot of confusion on that matter. Tim mentions in an article he wrote about his father that when he was about four years old he appeared briefly in his father's film entitled *RED RIVER VALLEY*. The only problem is that his father never made a film by that title and nobody seems to know to what film Tim was referring.

* * *

Q - During Tim's childhood years was his home life happy and secure?

A - Only sporadically so. His parents' marriage was often strained and his mother was frequently "away." The reason given him was illness, but he was never certain that that was the case. When sister Jennifer was only seven years old, she went with her governess to live in Belgium for almost three years, while Tim remained at home in California. He was never close with his stepsister Imogene because she was some years older and was, more often than not, in boarding school. Imogene did not get along very well with her mother, so the boarding school arrangement worked best for them. In 1931 Tim's parents separated, and he chose to remain with his father. Jennifer and Imogene stayed with their mother, moving to Scarsdale, New York, for a short period of time and then moving to Santiago, Chile.

* * *

Q - Did Tim's parents divorce?

A - Well, technically no. Margaret sought a Mexican divorce in 1932 and asked for a large property settlement. Jack contested the divorce, and an item in the January 10, 1940, issue of the *New York Times* states the following:

> Los Angeles, Jan. 9 (AP)—On petition of Jack Holt, actor, a Mexican divorce obtained by Mrs. Margaret Wood Holt in 1932 was declared invalid today by a superior court judge. Mrs. Holt had filed an answer contending they were divorced. A property agreement was involved. The Holts were married in 1916.

There was no further divorce action taken by either side, and they remained married to each other for the rest of their lives.

* * *

Tim (at about eight years of age) and sister Jennifer pose for this family picture. Jennifer gave this photo to Valery Anne Zurn in appreciation of her work as Director of the Tim Holt Committee (which was instrumental in getting Tim inducted into the Cowboy Hall of Fame and other honors). (Photo courtesy of Valery Anne Zurn.)

Tim at fourteen years of age. (Photo courtesy of Chuck Thornton.)

Tim loved to hunt with his father on their ranch in Fresno, California. When this picture was taken, Tim was fifteen and on summer break before going to the Culver Military Academy in Indiana. (Photo courtesy of Chuck Thornton.)

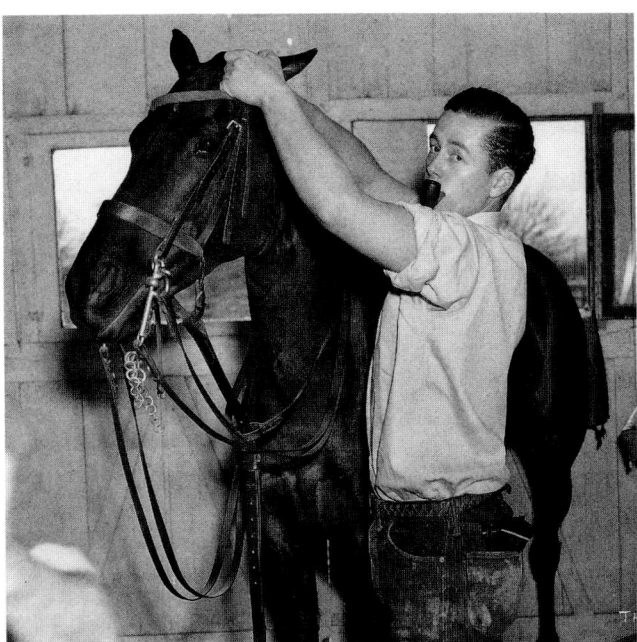

Tim acquired his love of polo from his father, who was an accomplished practitioner of the sport. Tim is seen here tacking up his favorite mount in preparation for a polo match. (Circa early 1940s.)

Tim and his first wife Virginia are pictured here; Tim's first son Lance is on the far right of the photo. The RKO publicity department caption for the picture is as follows: "Tim Holt, RKO Radio's young star who is currently appearing in *THE MAGNIFICENT AMBERSONS*, and his wife take time out between sets of tennis to relax on the grass in the gardens of their Pacific Palisades home, fifteen miles from Hollywood." It all sounds very Hollywood chic, doesn't it?

Q - Where did Tim go to high school?

A - He attended one year at Beverly Hills High School in California before transferring to the Culver Military Academy in Indiana. That's where he got most of his high school education.

* * *

Q - How did Tim do at Culver?

A - He graduated *cum laude* and was awarded the "Gold Spurs," their highest award for horsemanship. In addition, he participated succesfully in theatre activities and such sports as polo, boxing, tennis, and a little football (although his modest height and weight hindered him somewhat).

* * *

Q - Did Tim ever attend college?

A - Yes. He went to UCLA for two years.

* * *

Q - Where did Tim get his love for polo?

A - From his dad. Jack Holt's passion was polo, and he was one of the best players in the Hollywood circuit. He played with such excellent players as Will Rogers (considered the best of the Hollywood crowd), Doug Fairbanks, Walt Disney, and Hobart Bosworth—just to name a few. As soon as Tim got old enough, he took up the sport too and became a fine player.

* * *

Q - When and where did Tim get his first break in show business?

A - It was in 1936 while he was doing a play for the Westwood Theatre Guild called *Papa Is All,* a play about Pennsylvania Dutch people. During the run of the play, Tim tried to see producer Walter Wanger about the possibility of a screen test. Wanger knew Tim slightly through his polo playing and because of father Jack. It is not entirely clear whether Wanger actually saw Tim in *Papa Is All*, but he did arrange for a screen test and the success of it led to a personal contract with Walter Wanger and his first adult role in a movie, *HISTORY IS MADE AT NIGHT* (1937).

* * *

Q - Was it a good role?

A - Not very. If you blinked slowly, you missed him. (See Chapter 3 for details.)

* * *

Q - What was the first film in which he appeared that the audience could really take note of him?

A - His second film, *STELLA DALLAS*. Considering his relative lack of experience, it is amazing that he was given such an important role. (Again see

Tim was twenty-three when this publicity photo was taken in his Pacific Palisades home. The family pet and guardian pictured here is "Tell," a descendant of the famous Strongheart, a canine movie star during silent film years.

Chapter 3 for details.)

* * *

Q - Wasn't there any romance in the life of young Tim during these early years of his career?

A - Oh, yes. Tim enjoyed the company of many young ladies—in fact, rumor has it that he was quite a ladies' man—but he surprised his family in 1939 by eloping with a girl he had first met at a sorority dance while attending UCLA. Her name was Virginia Ashcroft, and she came from a wealthy family back East in New York.

* * *

Q - Did Tim and Virginia have any children?

A - Yes. Son Lance was born in 1940.

* * *

Q - Where did Tim and Virginia live during this time?

A - Between 1940 and 1943 Tim bought a beautiful house in Pacific Palisades and a small ranch in the San Fernando Valley. (One cannot help but wonder how he afforded all of this during the early years of

Q - When did Tim first become affiliated with the RKO studio?

A - *THE LAW WEST OF TOMBSTONE* (1938) was his first picture for the studio. At the time he was still under personal contract to producer Walter Wanger. Late in 1939 RKO bought Tim's contract from Wanger and signed him to a studio contract for his acting services.

* * *

Q - How many pictures did Tim make with director John Ford?

A - Although Tim was frequently thought of as being a member of the John Ford Company of Actors (so named because of Ford's penchant for using the same actors over and over again), Tim only appeared in two Ford films: *STAGECOACH* (1939) and *MY DARLING CLEMENTINE* (1946). Of course, they were two of Ford's biggest hits!

* * *

Q - What was the first film in which Tim had the starring role?

A - *THE ROOKIE COP* (1939). To be very accurate, Tim did not receive name-above-the-title billing (which generally signifies a star), and he did play second fiddle to the dog Ace during much of the picture. He was, however, the leading man in the production.

* * *

Q - What do Tim and Fred Astaire have in common?

A - No, not dancing skill. They both had the opportunity to woo Ginger Rogers in motion pictures—albeit Tim only did it once. The film was *FIFTH AVENUE GIRL* (1939), and in it Tim and Ginger fell madly in love—without benefit of a single dance step.

* * *

Q - How did Tim happen to get his first Western series with RKO?

A - During the early sound years of the 1930s, RKO never emphasized the Western in its yearly schedule of films, but it always had one B Western series in production. (During silent years the studio had been more prolific in its production of Westerns.) Cowboy stars Tom Keene and George O'Brien had carried the RKO banner throughout the 1930s with some assistance by Harry Carey in a few bigger-budgeted pictures. Keene continued to work for RKO frequently, but his star had faded and he was relegated to supporting roles, frequently as heavies, by the mid 1940s. O'Brien had been a popular star for many years, but by the late 1930s he was beginning to show his age and was squabbling with the studio over the renewal of his contract. RKO decided to gamble on its rising young contractee, Tim Holt, and gave him a chance to star in his own Western series as a cowboy hero.

* * *

Q - When Tim joined RKO in 1938, what was his only request?

A - He wanted to be given his dad's old dressing room at the studio.

* * *

Q - What was the name of Tim's horse in the pre-war series?

A - Duke. He was a saddlebred horse. When Tim returned from World War II service and was ready to start his Western series again, the horse suddenly died. That was when he got his palomino horse named Lightning.

* * *

Q - Was Tim an immediate hit in the Western series?

A - You bet! Within one year he was listed sixth in the poll of Top Money-Making Western Stars as determined by the *Motion Picture Herald* survey of movie exhibitors. Only Gene Autry, Bill Boyd, Roy Rogers, Charles Starrett, and Smiley Burnette were ahead of him.

* * *

Q - Who were Tim's sidekicks in his Western series?

A - He started out with Ray Whitley (who was known more for his Western singing and composing than acting) and squirrelly little Emmett Lynn. After four pictures Emmett left the series and was replaced by Lee "Lasses" White, who rode beside Tim and Ray Whitley for the next eight pictures. The final six entries in Tim's pre-war series featured Cliff "Ukelele Ike" Edwards as his comic sidekick. In the post-war series Tim had only one sidekick, Richard "Chito Jose Gonzales Bustamonte Rafferty" Martin.

* * *

Q - Who was Tim's best Western film sidekick?

A - Well, that calls for a very subjective evaluation, of course, but just about everyone seems to agree that Richard Martin was the most effective sidekick, and many feel that he was the best cowboy sidekick in the business, bar none! If you separate pre-war from post-war films, my choice would be the combination of Ray Whitley and Lee "Lasses" White,

Tim's pre-war series horse was a saddlebred named Duke. In this photo the horse's trainer seems to be getting the attention of Duke as Tim takes the horse into a rearing position.

Lightning was the name of the palomino horse that Tim rode in most of his post-war Western pictures.

Singer Ray Whitley and comic Lee "Lasses" White were Tim's sidekicks in eight Western features during 1941 and 1942. The scene here is from *THUNDERING HOOFS* (1942).

Emmett Lynn provided the comic hijinks in the first four features of Tim's pre-war Western series. He played the character of Whopper, which Chill Wills had originated in the George O'Brien series at RKO.

Richard "Chito" Martin was Tim's only post-war Western film sidekick, appearing in twenty-nine features with him. Many B Western fans feel that Martin was the best of the film sidekicks because he didn't play the sidekick role as broadly as most actors did.

Cliff "Ukelele Ike" Edwards was Tim's last pre-war series sidekick. They appeared together in six pictures during 1942 and 1943. In this scene from *SAGEBRUSH LAW* (1943) Tim seems none too sure that Ike's horse's tail disguise is going to work.

Emmett Lynn being edged out by just a smidgen. Cliff Edwards, again just my opinion, tried hard, but he was misplaced in Westerns.

* * *

Q - The character of Whopper was played by two of Tim's sidekicks. Did the character originate with Tim's series?

A - No. The Whopper character was first played by Chill Wills in the George O'Brien RKO series which preceded Tim's series. Whopper was played by Emmett Lynn and Lee "Lasses" White in Tim's films.

* * *

Q - Who was Tim's stunt double in his series?

A - Davey Sharpe was probably his most frequent double. Ben Johnson also worked as a stunt man on some of Tim's pre-war films before he became a star in his own right.

* * *

Q - Why did Tim shoot the final six pre-war films in fifty-four straight days of filming?

A - He was due to be inducted into the military service and RKO wanted to get the six scheduled pictures completed before that occurred. Tim's father jokingly claimed that his exhausted son had enlisted in the service just to escape the grueling schedule that RKO had set for him.

* * *

Q - How did Tim happen to be cast by Orson Welles in *THE MAGNIFICENT AMBERSONS*?

A - Welles studied John Ford's *STAGECOACH* before he began to make his first film, *CITIZEN KANE* (1941). Tim impressed Welles in his small role of the lieutenant, and he remembered Tim when he began work on *AMBERSONS*, his second film for *RKO*.

(There is more on this in Chapter 3.)

* * *

Q - The role of George Amberson Minifer was certainly an acting change of pace for Tim. Did he enjoy playing such a radically different character from what he was used to playing?

A - Yes. In fact, Tim commented throughout his later career that the role in *AMBERSONS* was his all-time favorite.

* * *

Q - What was Tim's standing at RKO at the time he enlisted in the service?

A - RKO saw Tim as one of its rapidly rising stars. In fact, in 1942 only Ginger Rogers received more fan mail than Tim at the studio.

* * *

Q - Jennifer Holt, Tim's sister, started her professional acting career in the early 1940s. Why was it that they never worked together in films?

A - There doesn't seem to be a clear-cut answer to the question. Jennifer has said at film festivals that she doesn't know why they never worked together. Occasionally, if pressed, she has added, "Well, he never asked me, and I could have used the work." After graduation from high school, Jennifer studied acting under the great Russian actress and teacher Maria Ouspenskaya for a year. Then at Ouspenskaya's suggestion she went to New Hampshire to study and perform with the Peterborough Players, where she appeared in such productions as *The Babbit, The Far Off Hills,* and a production of *Our Town,* which was supervised by the playwright, Thornton Wilder. Jennifer thought the stage was her true calling and hoped for a career that would include musical productions, since she loved singing and was studying voice. After a season at Peterborough, she went to New York to seek her fortune on Broadway but found the opportunities pretty scanty. After some months of frustration and

Tim and Alice Holt have been married since 1944 and live quietly near Santa Monica, California. They spend most of their time outdoors, raising Labrador retrievers, playing tennis or swimming. A keen judge of tobacco, Tim owns an enviable pipe collection, enjoys trying new brands of wood.

This photo and caption appeared in the June 1950 issue of *Movie Stars Parade*.

dwindling funds, she headed back to sunny California.

* * *

Q - How did Jennifer get her break in films?

A - While in Reno with Tim (he was appearing in a rodeo), Jennifer met Jerry Colona's agent, Bruce Geer, who indicated an interest in representing her

Jennifer Holt became a popular Western film heroine during the 1940s. She appeared with such Western stars as William "Hoppy" Boyd, Johnny Mack Brown, Tex Ritter, Eddie Dean, and Lash LaRue.

Tim is seen here in full dress uniform for the U. S. Army Air Force. He was in the service from late 1942 until December of 1945 and was a war hero, receiving many medals and citations. (Photo courtesy of Chuck Thornton.)

in films. Later, while negotiating a deal with producer Harry Sherman for Colona's services, Geer "sweetened" the deal by also getting Sherman to use Jennifer in one of his Hopalong Cassidy movies, *STICK TO YOUR GUNS* (1942). In the picture she was billed as Jacqueline Holt. Following the release of the film, Jennifer was signed to a contract by Universal Pictures and became a leading lady in Westerns (mostly) for the next six years. She appeared with some of the biggest Western stars— among them Johnny Mack Brown, Tex Ritter, Russell Hayden, Rod Cameron, Eddie Dean, and Lash LaRue.

* * *

Q - Didn't Tim's marriage to Virginia break up about the time he entered the service for World War II?

A - Yes. In a nasty divorce procedure she won total custody of son Lance and a court order that forbade Tim to have visitation rights because, as Virginia stated, it would be "upsetting" to him. Tim did not see Lance again until he was in his mid teens.

* * *

In October of 1943 Tim's picture was snapped in the famous Stork Club in New York City. The caption that was sent out with the photo stated the following: "Lt. Tim Holt of the U.S. Army Air Force is shown pictured at Sherman Billingsley's Stork Club in the company of charming Lyn Sheldon during Holt's recent leave from army chores. Lt. Holt also is the son of actor Jack Holt of the movies." That's Billingsley seated at the table behind Tim. No, I don't know who Ms. Sheldon is, but she sure is wearing a funny-looking hat. (Photo courtesy of Chuck Thornton.)

Q - Wasn't it while Tim was in the service that he met the woman who would become his second wife?

A - Yes. Tim spent some service time at Santa Ana Air Base in California. While there he met Alice Harrison, who worked in the base canteen. They fell in love and were married on June 24, 1944.

* * *

Q - In what branch of the service did Tim serve?

A- The U.S. Army Air Force. He trained at Victorville, California, (where Roy Rogers now has his museum) and was commissioned a second lieutenant upon completion of training. He first served as an instructor on the flight line and in ground school, but finally he was sent to the Pacific Theatre of the War where he served as a B-29 bombardier, flying many missions over Japan. While coming back from one of these missions, he spotted the mushroom cloud from the atomic bomb that was dropped on Hiroshima. He was truly a war hero, even experiencing a crash landing at Guam after having his plane badly damaged by Japanese gunfire on the day the war ended. As Tim recalled, "I was up in the sky somewhere over Guam, on my 22nd mission as a B-29 bombardier. Our plane was pretty well shot up with five and a half feet of the left wing missing and 175 bullet and flak holes in the fuselage. We managed to make a crash landing, and

Tim and his father are pictured here between scenes of the only film in which they appeared together as co-stars, *THE ARIZONA RANGER* (1948).

they told us that the war was over. They sure picked the right moment for that."

* * *

Q - Was Tim a highly decorated soldier?

A - Yes. He received a Presidential Citation with two clusters, the Pacific Defense Medal, the Asiatic Pacific Citation with three clusters, the Distinguished Flying Cross, Air Medal with three Clusters, and the Victory Medal. Not bad!

* * *

Q - When was Tim mustered out of the service?

A - On December 8, 1945. While he was happy to be out of the service, he was always proud of the contribution he was able to make during the crisis years of World War II.

* * *

Q - What was probably Tim's most-viewed film of all time?

A - Very likely it was a VD film he narrated while in the service for World War II. Just about every soldier who served in the military then and for years after the war saw the film.

* * *

Q - Did Jack, Jennifer, and Tim ever appear together professionally?

A - Yes, once. As mentioned earlier, Jack and Tim appeared together in *THE VANISHING PIONEER* (1928) when Tim was about nine years old. They also appeared together in *THE ARIZONA RANGER* (1948), one of Tim's post-war RKO films (and they were excellent together), and Jack had a cameo appearance with Tim in the flophouse scene of *THE TREASURE OF THE SIERRA MADRE* (1948). The only time the three Holts appeared together was on a CBS radio program in 1946 entitled "All-Star Theatre." This country-flavored show featured Western music by Foy Willing and the Riders of the Purple Sage and a dramatic sketch in which the Holts played three characters who were father, son, and daughter—not exactly a stretch for them.

* * *

Q - Speaking of *THE TREASURE OF THE SIERRA MADRE*, wasn't that Tim's most prestigious film?

A - Although he received several awards for *THE MAGNIFICENT AMBERSONS* in 1943, certainly

Tim featured his Lippizon stallion Sheik in his rodeo appearances for several years.

his greatest recognition came for *TREASURE*. It received an Oscar nomination for Best Film of the year, Walter Huston won the Best Supporting Actor Award for his role, and director John Huston won Oscars for Best Director and Best Screenplay. Yes, it was a prestigious film with which to be associated.

* * *

Q- Wasn't Tim nominated for Best Supporting Actor for *THE TREASURE OF THE SIERRA MADRE?*

A- No. There are at least two sources in print that state he was nominated, but they are in error.

* * *

Q - Was David Holt, an actor who appeared in a few films during the 1940s, any relation to Tim?

A - No, they are not related. It has been mistakenly reported that he was Tim's brother.

* * *

Q - Didn't Tim buy into a rodeo in the late 1940s?

A - Yes. He became a part owner of the Jennings-Lamarr Rodeo in 1947 and toured with the rodeo whenever he was not busy filming his RKO Western series. Tim loved rodeoing!

* * *

Q - What was the name of the Lippizon horse that Tim used in his rodeo?

A - The stallion was named Sheik. Tim used the horse for several years in his rodeo appearances. He retired Sheik in 1949 when the horse was sixteen years old. Tim wrote about the occasion of Sheik's last performance:

> That last appearance of his was in Texas on the Fourth of July. When he cantered into the ring that day, I made up my mind that I would end up his routine differently this time. Usually he goes through his maneuvers, his Spanish walk, Spanish trot, his "piaffe" (trot in place) and his other movements, and then we end up with a deep bow to the audience.
> On his last performance we did it differently. Instead of leading him into his bow, I walked him slowly around the ring while the band played taps. He seemed to sense the solemnity in the air as he paraded around, proudly wearing the maroon-and-gold cooler coat that his fans had presented to him that day, but he carried off the change in routine with never a falter nor a misstep.

* * *

Q - When did Tim's second marriage go on the rocks?

A - Although they weren't legally divorced until 1952, Tim and Alice publicly stated their separation in March of 1948, just after the national release of *THE TREASURE OF THE SIERRA MADRE*. It should be noted, however, that Tim's romance with leading lady Nan Leslie was well underway in 1947, so unofficially Tim and Alice had separated much

Tim's father, screen star Jack Holt, died in January of 1951. This shot of father and son was taken during the time that Tim was starring in *UNDER THE TONTO RIM* (1947).

earlier. Reportedly, Alice did not like the fact that Tim was on the road so much with his rodeo appearances or that he had decided that he now wanted to make Oklahoma his home. She very much preferred California. (Inexplicably, in the 1950 spring issue of *Western Stars*, Tim wrote lovingly of his relationship with Alice as if their marriage were rock solid.)

* * *

Q - Wasn't there a legal problem regarding Tim's divorce that caused him some difficulties?

A - There certainly was. In the November 20, 1951, issue of *The New York Times*, datelined Little Rock, Arkansas, and headlined "Actor Fined $200 for Perjury," it was stated:

> Tim Holt, movie actor, pleaded guilty today to committing perjury in an effort to obtain an Arkansas divorce and was fined $200. The charge grew out of testimony in Chancery Court here last month that he had fulfilled the ninety-day residence requirement in the state's divorce law. The actor, who plays cowboy roles, later said that he had believed his ownership of property in Arkansas qualified him under the law. His petition for divorce from Alice Harrison Holt was dismissed before a decree was entered.

* * *

Q - Wasn't it also in 1951 that Tim's father died?

A - Yes, but earlier in the year. Jack Holt passed away from a heart attack on January 18, 1951, at the age of sixty-two. The fine actor, who had made a fortune in Hollywood over a period of almost four decades, had fallen onto hard times during the last years of his life. Acting mostly in supporting or heavy roles in B Westerns after the war years, Jack died all but penniless.

* * *

Q - Did Tim ever get hurt while filming or while making his appearances with the rodeo?

A - He suffered quite a few broken bones, sprains, and bruises that accompany the rough and tumble business of making Western films and riding horses, but one of his worst "hurtin'" situations took place while he was making MY DARLING CLEMENTINE for director John Ford. He broke seven ribs during an accidental horse fall and had to be airlifted from Monument Valley, Utah, to Tucson, Arizona, to be patched up and then returned to the valley for the completion of filming.

* * *

Q - What was a typical budget for a Tim Holt Western?

A - That's a tough one because various budgets have been mentioned in print over the years. Tim claimed to biographer Buck Rainey that his pictures were budgeted in the $80,000 to $90,000 range. In the book The RKO Story the author (who had access to the RKO files) states that the budget for LAW OF THE BADLANDS (1951) was $98,000 and that it was the lowest Tim Holt budget since his series began after the war. It has been reported that Tim's personal yearly income for films, personal appearances, etc. during the post-war years was in the $65,000 range, which sounds somewhat low.

* * *

Q - In which of Tim's Westerns is there a bus visible in one scene?

A - That's GUNS OF HATE (1948). See Chapter 5

Nan Leslie, Pictured here with Tim and William Gould in a scene from WILD HORSE MESA, was Tim's leading lady in six consecutive films in 1947 and 1948. (Photo courtesy of Chuck Thornton.)

for details. In interviews Tim referred to the film in which this occurred as *DYNAMITE PASS* (1950) and said that the scene was reshot. If Tim was accurate in his comments, then it happened twice and was not reshot in the case of *GUNS OF HATE*, because a bus is certainly in the scene.

* * *

Q - Did Tim ever kiss the heroine in his Westerns?

A - Hardly ever! He always seemed uneasy and shy around the lady folk in his pictures. In a few scenes Chito even kidded Tim for not kissing his girl in public (see *PISTOL HARVEST*, 1951). As if to demonstrate that he really liked to romance girls, in *ROAD AGENT* (1952) Tim unexpectedly (and with little plot motivation) planted a big kiss on leading lady Noreen Nash, much to the surprise of Chito.

* * *

Q - Who were Tim's most frequent leading ladies?

A - There were a number of actresses who appeared twice as Tim's leading lady (Marjorie Reynolds, Joan Barclay, Martha Hyer, Noreen Nash, Jane Nigh, and Linda Douglas), but only two actresses were Tim's leading lady in more than two films. Nan Leslie was in six straight films during 1947 and 1948; Joan Dixon was in five films during 1951 and 1952.

* * *

Q - Did Tim do any television work after he ended his Western series for RKO in 1952?

A - Yes, but very little. He made a pilot a year or so after he finished the Western series for a TV series entitled *Adventure in Java*. Charles Bronson, just getting started in the acting business, was to be his co-star. The series didn't sell, but later it was revised and produced as a syndicated series entitled *Soldiers of Fortune*, starring John Russell and Chick Chandler. For a short time in the late 1950s he hosted a local Saturday morning series in Oklahoma City called *The Tim Holt Western Theatre*. Over the years there were a few infrequent one-shot TV appearances (*The Ken Murray Show*, *The Virginian*), but Tim pretty much resisted the temptation to go into the medium.

Lovely young starlet Joan Dixon was Tim's leading lady in five films during 1951 and 1952. The scene here is from *HOT LEAD* (1951). How about that flashy jacket Tim is wearing!

* * *

Q - Didn't Tim make an educational film for the National Rifle Association?

A - Yes, actually two short films during the 1950s. An article in *Who's Who in Western Stars* (1954) states the following about the NRA films:

> Tim Holt, now touring near Oklahoma City in the heart of the southwest rodeo territory, has long been concerned with the problem of teaching children the proper method of handling different types of firearms. An old hand knows that "Bang, bang, you're dead," spoken in play by a young'un who has just sneaked his Dad's .30-.30 shotgun from the back of a storage closet, may be the first words in a life-long tragedy. With this in mind, Tim recently completed a matched pair of TV films called *Shooting Straight with Tim Holt*. These educational films aim to amuse junior gun-toters while instructing them in safety methods, so that they may live to be the new builders of the old West.

* * *

Q - Did Tim make any more theatrical films after his Western series concluded?

A - Oh, yes, although many fans wish that he hadn't. He made THE MONSTER THAT CHALLENGED THE WORLD in 1957, which was a pretty good science fiction film, but the two stinkers that most fans wish did not exist are THE YESTERDAY MACHINE (1962) and THIS STUFF'LL KILL YA! (1971), independently produced low-budget pictures which Tim apparently made on a lark as a friendship gesture and which never got much release in the country. (There is more on these films in Chapter 6.)

* * *

Q - When did Tim meet the woman who was to become his last wife?

A - He first met Berdee Stephens around 1947 when he was in Oklahoma for a rodeo appearance. After his separation from Alice, he started seeing Berdee on a regular basis, and they were married in 1952.

* * *

Q - Did Tim and Berdee Holt have any children?

A - Yes, there were three born within three years. Charles John Holt IV was born on May 30, 1958. He has always been called Jack. Tim's only daughter, Bryanna, was born on May 15, 1959. Jay Perry Holt was born the next year on July 11, 1960.

* * *

(The personal interviews in Chapter 7 with Berdee and the three children cover the major events of the final twenty years of Tim's life, and so they will not be discussed here.)

* * *

Q - When did Tim die and what was the cause of his death?

A - Tim died on February 15, 1973, of cancer.

* * *

Q - Where is Tim buried?

A - In an unmarked grave in the Memory Lane Cemetery in Harrah, Oklahoma. The grave is unmarked because a couple of times the marker placed there by the family was stolen.

* * *

Q - In what ways has Tim been honored since his death?

A - In early 1975 Tim's close Oklahoma friend Carl Knox came up with the idea of dedicating the annual Harrah, Oklahoma, *Frontier Days* celebration to Harrah's most famous citizen, Tim Holt. With the cooperation of the city fathers, the arrangements were made to celebrate September 13, 1975, as *Tim Holt Memorial Day,* and it was so designated by Oklahoma Governor David L. Boren. The Holt family was delighted and lent their support to the occasion. As part of the celebration, a street in Harrah was to be redesignated as "Tim Holt Drive." Celebrities who knew and/or had worked with Tim were invited to attend or, if that was not possible, they were asked to send letters expressing their remembrances of and feelings for Tim. The letters and other mementos that arrived were later given to Tim's family. Mrs. Holt has been kind enough to share some of the letters with me for this book.

SCREEN ACTORS GUILD

7750 Sunset Boulevard/Hollywood, California 90046
(213) 876-3030/Cable SAGHOLLY

NATIONAL OFFICERS
DENNIS WEAVER, PRESIDENT
KATHLEEN NOLAN, 1ST VICE PRESIDENT
...

TIM HOLT MEMORIAL DAY
HARRAH, OKLAHOMA

Attn: Carl Knox
4524 N.W. 46th Street
Oklahoma City, Okla. 73122

Gentlemen:

The Screen Actors Guild, which represents all actors in the motion picture Industry—some 30,000 in number, is delighted to compliment the City of Harrah for its recognition of our member, Tim Holt.

Tim Holt was a hero of his time; the embodiment of the best of Hollywood; and an individual beloved by his colleagues as a professional artist. His human characteristics are still remembered and cherished by all.

We congratulate the City on this occasion. Our best wishes for a most successful TIM HOLT MEMORIAL DAY.

Sincerely,

Dennis Weaver
Dennis Weaver
President

Chet Migden
Chester L. Migden
National Executive Secretary

/jcm

August 13, 1975

DEPARTMENT OF THE AIR FORCE
HEADQUARTERS OKLAHOMA CITY AIR LOGISTICS CENTER (AFLC)
TINKER AIR FORCE BASE, OKLAHOMA 73145

13 September 1975

TO: Residents
Harrah, Oklahoma

I am pleased to represent the United States Air Force and Tinker Air Force Base, and join in the ceremony to pay tribute to the late TIM HOLT, a native of your community and a former member of our armed forces.

The reknowned western screen star's roles have left an excellent image of true entertainment. Likewise, his talents and showmanship were used in many training films for the armed forces. As a Major in the U. S. Army Air Corps during World War II, his dedication and concern for his Country earned him numerous awards and medals.

I am honored to be a part of Harrah's "Tim Holt Memorial Day."

Sincerely,

F. E. Heanue
F. E. HEANUE, JR
Colonel, USAF
Chief, Aircraft Division

(Photo courtesy of Bill Sasser.)

August 27, 1975

As Tim Holt's co-star, Smokey, in twelve of his feature-length "B" Westerns for R.K.O., my memories of Tim are happy and fresh. Not only was he a person easy to get along with, but his resourcefulness in acting earned him the respect of all who worked with him. He was a darned good horseman, too! He was well-coached by his father, Jack Holt, who was a skilled horseman as well as a gentleman.

It gives me great pleasure to know that he is being honored at this time by his friends, family, fellow actors, fans and The National Cowboy Hall of Fame. The honor was well-deserved.

With the highest regard and fondest memories of my friend, Tim Holt,

RAY WHITLEY

Ray Whitley

Harry Carey, Jr.
4957 Matilija Avenue
Sherman Oaks, California 91403

August 25, 1975

TO THE PEOPLE OF HARRAH OKLAHOMA AND CARL KNOX

Like Tim Holt I am also the son of a famous father. How much that had to do with the ups and downs of Tim's film career I have no idea.....any more than I do of my own. I never worked with Tim but my dad did and I had the good fortune to speak to him on the phone just a few weeks before his death. It's only natural for me to think of Tim first, as a hell of a horsebacker but it is more fair really for me to say that I don't believe Hollywood ever really acknowledged the fact that he was a fervent and fine convincing performer. I have missed him since he left our industry. To me he was a shining star in our Western sky.
May God bless him and may all of us who follow never forget Tim Holt.

Fondest regards,

Harry Carey Jr.
Harry Carey Jr.

SKY KING YOUTH RANCHES
of
AMERICA, INC.

August 27, 1975

Mr. Carl Knox
4524 N. W. 46th Street
Oklahoma City,
Oklahoma 73122

Dear Mr. Knox:

It is an honor for me to be asked to contribute a testimonial letter in memory of Tim Holt.

It is a fitting and proper thing you and the state of Oklahoma are doing.

It is interesting to note that some of the greatest names in the entertainment world, and most particularly in western films, were Oklahomans. Tom Mix and Will Rogers come readily to mind, and, of course, there have been many others.

I have had occasion to visit Oklahoma many times and toured extensively with the Carson & Barnes Circus. As you probably know, Hugo, Oklahoma is their winter quarters.

It was my privilege to know Jack Holt, Tim's father, and Jennifer, his sister. She and I worked together on several occasions.

When Orson Welles was casting for "The Magnificent Ambersons" I was up for the same part as Tim. Needless to say, he got the role and did a fine job.

Tim was cast in the same heroic mold as were so many other western stars of that era. It is a shame that so many of them are no longer with us.....however, I'm sure that whatever trail they ride in spirit, they will pull up and wish you "Godspeed" in your endeavor.

Kindest personal regards,

Kirby Grant

P. O. BOX 4098 • WINTER PARK, FLORIDA 32793 • PHONE (305) 339-4339

STUNTMEN'S ASSOCIATION
4810 WHITSETT AVENUE - NORTH HOLLYWOOD, CALIFORNIA 91607
(213) 766-4334 - AFTER 5: 462-2301

August 22, 1975

Mr. Carl Knox
4524 N. W. 46th Street
Oklahoma City, Oklahoma 73122

Dear Sir:

We were recently informed of the "Tim Holt Memorial Day" to be held on September 13, 1975.

We, of the Stuntmen's Association of Motion Pictures, wish to commend you for the recognition of a man who contributed so much to our industry. Many of the members of our group, including myself, had the pleasure of working with Tim on many occasions.

We salute you for this very deserving tribute to an exceptionally talented gentleman.

Sincerely,
STUNTMEN'S ASSOCIATION

Henry Wills
President

HW:jw

Henry Wills

Stuntmen's Association of Motion Pictures, Incorporated

IRON EYES CODY
2013 GRIFFITH PARK BLVD.
LOS ANGELES, CALIFORNIA 90039
PHONE: 661-0160

Sept. 10, 1975

Mr. Carl Knox
4524 N.W. 46th Street
Oklahoma City, Oklahoma 73122

Dear Mr. Knox:

Thank you for your kind invitation for the Tim Holt Memorial Day, Saturday, September 13, 1975, sponsored by the City of Harrah, Oklahoma and you. I regret I will be unable to attend due to another commitment.

I knew and worked with Tim in many a picture and he was a fine actor and came from a wonderful family. I wouldn't want to have worked with a better person than he was. My personal opinion is that he stole the picture "Sierra Madre." He helped a lot of actors when they had problems, gave them work and money. He was a gentleman at all times. He is greatly missed here by all his friends.

I am very pleased to see this fine gentleman receive the recognition he deserves, and am truly sorry I will not be there to join in the honors.

At various functions I present the Great Spirit Prayer in voice and sign language and I would appreciate it if someone would read it in my absence. It is a very old prayer which I have altered to fit my signs.

Again thanking you, I remain,

Sincerely yours,

Iron Eyes Cody

CLAYTON MOORE
Box 3797
Incline Village, Nevada 89450

September 11, 1975

City Council
Harrah
Oklahoma

IN MEMORY OF TIM HOLT

I am sure the name TIM HOLT will be remembered forever.

I am very honored to have known and worked in the motion picture business with Tim. Harrah, Oklahoma -- you too must be very proud of him!

Most sincerely,

Clayton Moore
THE LONE RANGER

CM:rs

SUNSET CARSON

Post Office Box 3751, Carroll Reece Station
Johnson City, Tennessee 37601
615-477 3062

September 10, 1975

Mr. Carl Knox
4524 NW 46th Street
Oklahoma City, Oklahoma, 73122

Dear Mr. Knox;

Memory of Tim Holt stirs deep emotions in all who knew him. Most significantly are respect for the warm human kindness Tim radiated, humility for having been so fortunate as to have enjoyed the Acting Profession he so aptly served, profound admiration of the man himself, and, affection for a good friend.

Many people live quietly and un-noticed, while others go to great length to be spectacular. Tim was an example of quiet greatness. He did not strive to be spectacular, but the way that the natural warmth of his personality influenced all who passed his way is far from un-noticed.

Tim's talent, kindness, and genuine sincerity will be deeply missed by all of us so fortunate as to have been his friends.

I sincerely offer my best wishes and kindest regards to the family, friends, and countless fans of this fine American on this Memorial occasion.

With kindest regards,

Sunset Carson

SC/bt

DONALD BARRY
4729 FARMDALE AVE.
NO. HOLLYWOOD, CALIF. 91602
766-2867

8/25/75

Dear Mr Knox;

It is a wonderful feeling to know that the City of Harrah and you are doing so much to keep the memory of Tim Holt alive.

It was with tremendous pride that I called him "Friend". His contribution to the happiness of the citizens of the world will be hard to top.

I wish it were possible to be there in person, but I assure you I will be there in spirit.

I know that God will smile on you for what you are doing and Tim will be at his side.

Bless you
Don "Red" Barry

Dear Mr. Knox;

Thank you for the invitation to the Tim Holt Memorial Day. Tim Holt is a fond memory to me -- I had the pleasure of having him as guest on -- "All Star Western Theater" appearing with him was his Father - Mr. Jack Holt and his sister -- Jennifer Holt.

It was from Mr. Jack Holt that I got the idea of forming the musical, singing group the - "Riders of the Purple Sage".

Mr Tim Holt will always remain in our fondest memories as well as his entire family.

My Best,
Foy Willing

P.S. - I recieved this letter today - thought you might like to see it.

Foy Willing

Duncan Renaldo .. Rancho Don Amigo
974 Debra Drive
SANTA BARBARA, CALIF. 93110
PHONE (805) 687-0966

August 29, 1975

To the Tim Holt Memorial Day
City of Harrah, Oklahoma

Dear Amigos:

In behalf of all of us in the Motion Picture Industry I want to send you our grateful thanks for your magnificent gesture in dedicating this day of September 13, 1975 as THE TIM HOLT MEMORIAL DAY.

The Holt family contributed a great deal to the evolution of The American Motion Picture. Tim's father, Jack Holt, his sister Jennifer and Tim delighted the world and particularly our own people with their excellent and powerful performances.

In his private life, Tim was a fine young man, an example of a dedicated AMERCAN CITIZEN in every respect.

Due to my poor health, I am sorry I cannot be there in person at the dedication, but my heart is with you.

May The Good Lord Bless you all.

Sincerely,

Duncan Renaldo

"Cisco Kid"

SEPT. 4, 1975

DEAR CARL:

IN REFFERENCE TO TIM HOLT.

AS A COWBOY I ENJOYED HIM VERY MUCH. I NEVER KNEW HIM THAT WELL
EXCEPT FOR MEETINGS AT SOCIAL FUNCTIONS AND SO FORTH BUT WHAT I SAW
I LIKED AS HE WAS ALWAYS A GENTLEMAN WITH ME.

AMONG US COWBOYS ACTORS OF WHICH I LIKE TO INCLUDE MYSELF,
JOHN WAYNE GOT AN OSCAR AND TIM WAS NOMINATED FOR ONE, WHICH IS
NOT TOO SHADY. THE ONLY COWBOY I KNOW THAT IS IN THE SAME
CATEGORY IS THAT HEAD AND HEAL ROPER THATS CONSIDERED A FAIR HAND
CALLED BEN JOHNSON, WELL THATS PRETTY FAIR COMPANY NO MATTER
HOW YOU SLICE IT. TIM WAS A HANSOME WITH SQUARE SHOULDERS
AND CAPABLE OF RIPPING A PRETTY WIDE SWATH IF NEED BE.
TIM GAVE ME MANY HOURS OF ENJOYMENT.
I UNDERSTAND DAVE SHARPE AND A LARGE GROUP WILL BE ON HAND
PLEASE GIVE ALL THE GUYS MY BEST AND DO GOOD BY TIM.

      SINCERELY

      JOCK MAHONEY
      ADVERTISING MANAGER

Johnny Bond

1001 NORTH LINCOLN STREET
BURBANK, CALIFORNIA 91506
213 - 848-7373   213 - 842-4488

August 27, 1975

RED RIVER SONGS, INC.
VIDOR PUBLICATIONS, INC.
LAREDO PUBLICATIONS

Mr. Carl Knox
4524 N. W. 46th St.
Oklahoma City, Okla. 73112

Dear Mr. Knox:

Thank you for yours of recent date. I welcome the news of a TIM HOLT MEMORIAL DAY and wish that it were possible for me to be there in person.

While I only met Tim one time when he and his father, Jack Holt visited Jennifer Holt on the movie set when we were filming a Universal Picture starring Johnny Mack Brown and Tex Ritter, I was and am a fan of his and enjoy his work whenever featured on TV. On the occasion in question, I filmed a short scene of the three Holts with my 8mm Movie Camera in color and am happy to say that it is still as good today as it was the day it came back from the developers.

I offer my undivided support to the Memorial and extend all of my best wishes for a successful event.

Thanks and regards.

      Sincerely,

      Johnny Bond

GEORGE O'BRIEN

9/13/75.

Tim Holt Memorial

As I say, Sincerely enjoyed knowing Tim & his father Jack Holt. Before W.W.II Tim spent much time at my Ranch and after Jack would join us. Tim & I were of the last Motion Picture before Hollywood active duty with U.S. Navy. In the summer of 1941. Regretably we can't turn back Calendars to renew old friendships. Stan Jones the famous music composer gives the answer in his hit song "Ghost Riders in the Sky." Perhaps we all will meet again some day that way.

George O'Brien

Harrah City Council
Harrah, Oklahoma 73045

Dear Sirs:

I have just learned of your plans for the Harrah Day celebration and the Tim Holt Memorial Day planned for September 13, 1975.

Tim was one of the finest people in his profession, well liked and always ready to help anyone that he could. He was instrumental in the careers of countless actors.

If at all possible, I would like to be there for your Tim Holt Day. If not, my best wishes to all of you planning a day to honor one of your own people.

      Very truly yours,

      Jim Bannon
      RED RYDER

Jim Bannon

For years many fans and friends wrongly assumed that Tim had been inducted into the National Cowboy Hall of Fame in Oklahoma City—perhaps because he had been an Oklahoma resident for so long. In 1990, in an effort to remedy this oversight by the Cowboy Hall of Fame, Valery Anne Zurn of Los Angeles, California, formed a loose-knit organization called the "Committee of Friends for Tim Holt's Induction into the Cowboy Hall of Fame for Western Performances for 1991." Despite the many problems inherent in organizing such a grassroots movement, Valery was able to enlist prominent show business personalities, various other "movers and shakers" in related fields, and Tim Holt fans to lobby for Tim's induction. Her efforts were successful and Tim was inducted at the March 23, 1991, Western Heritage Awards Ceremonies. Among those in attendance were the Holt family and Tim's film sidekick, Richard Martin.

Through Valery Anne Zurn's continued efforts another longstanding oversight was corrected. The Golden Boot Awards, an annual benefit for the Motion Picture and Television Fund, honors Western performers, directors, producers, and others who have through their artistry contributed to our Western film heritage. Although Jennifer Holt had been awarded a Golden Boot during one of the annual celebrations, Tim had never been so honored. At the Tenth Annual Golden Boot Awards on August 18, 1992, Tim's friend Burt Kennedy presented the award to Jack Holt, accepting for the Holt family who were in attendance.

In October of 1992 Tim was honored by the Lone Pine Sierra Film Festival in Lone Pine, California. Tim's family and many fans and friends (including film sidekick Richard "Chito" Martin) were in attendance as a Tim Holt film (*DYNAMITE PASS*) was shown and a Lone Pine thoroughfare was named "Tim Holt Street" in his honor. At the dedication son Jack unveiled the street sign and a framed portrait of Tim by artist Ivan Jesse Curtis was presented to Mrs. Holt. (The artist was gracious enough to let me use his beautiful painting for the cover of this book.)

*   *   *

Q - Tim's major film-making career ended over forty years ago. Is it likely that his films will still be viewed in another forty years with the respect and acclaim they currently hold?

A - One can only speculate, of course, but Tim's "classic" films such as *STAGECOACH, THE MAGNIFICENT AMBERSONS, MY DARLING CLEMENTINE,* and *THE TREASURE OF THE SIERRA MADRE* have so far only increased in appreciation and prestige with the passage of years. The same has been true of his B-Western series. The strong production values, excellent scripts, abundant action content, and interesting portrayals have caused the series to remain as palatable to present generations as it was to the kids and adults of the 1940s and 1950s. Evidence of this is the continued presentation of the films on such popular television cable channels as American Movie Classics and Ted Turner's TNT at a time when most other B Westerns are pretty hard to find on television.

*   *   *

Tim's grave in the Memory Lane Cemetery in Harrah, Oklahoma, is unmarked because a couple of times the marker placed there by the family was stolen. The X in this photo marks the location of the grave. (Photo courtesy of Norman T. Foster.)

The Holt family regularly places flowers on Tim's grave site. (Photo courtesy of Valery Anne Zurn.)

Harrah, Oklahoma, honored Tim in 1975 with "Tim Holt Drive." (Photo courtesy of Valery Anne Zurn.)

During the 1975 Harrah, Oklahoma, "Frontier Days" celebration Tim was honored with Tim Holt Memorial Day. Friends and celebrities came to pay their respects to Tim. Seen here in a parade car are ace stunt man (and Tim's frequent stunt double) Dave Sharpe, Mrs. Holt, and actor Ben Johnson. (Photo courtesy of Mrs. Holt.)

NATIONAL COWBOY HALL OF FAME

Contact: Dana Sullivant
Public Relations Director
(405) 478-2250

News Information

Goldwater, Browning, Holt, Drury, and Connors
To Be Inducted Into National Cowboy Hall of Fame

OKLAHOMA CITY---Former Arizona Senator Barry Goldwater, Arizona cattleman Ernest Browning, and actors Tim Holt, James Drury and Chuck Connors will be honored with induction into the National Cowboy Hall of Fame during the 1991 Western Heritage Awards ceremonies, honoring the year's winners in fourteen categories of literature, film and music, on Saturday, March 16.

The ceremonies will be broadcast on OETA, Oklahoma's PBS station, on Saturday, March 23 at 8:00 p.m. CST.

Goldwater and the late Ernest Browning will be inducted into the Great Westerners Hall of Fame, recognizing the accomplishments of more than 200 men and women whose lives exemplify the greatness of the American West. Drury, Connors, and the late Tim Holt will be honored with induction into the Great Western Performers Hall of Fame, which pays tribute to outstanding western actors. The trio will join thirty-two other individuals in the Western Performers Hall of Fame, including John Wayne, James Stewart, Barbara Stanwyck, and Tom Mix.

405/478-2250 • 1700 Northeast 63rd Street • Oklahoma City, Oklahoma 73111

Son Jack Holt looks admiringly at the street sign in Lone Pine, California, which honors his father. (Photo by Ken Taylor.)

On March 16, 1991, the Cowboy Hall of Fame Wrangler Award was presented to Tim Holt posthumously, his family accepting. Seen here are Jack (holding the award), Bryanna, and Jay Holt on the evening of the presentation. (Photo courtesy of Valery Anne Zurn.)

The Holt family was delighted that Tim's film sidekick was able to attend the Cowboy Hall of Fame induction of Tim. Pictured here are Tim's daughter Bryanna and Richard "Chito" Martin. (Photo courtesy of Valery Anne Zurn.)

The Holt family and friends pose for a picture at the 1992 Golden Boot Awards at which Tim was honored. (From left to right) Jay Holt, Valery Zurn (who spearheads the Tim Holt Committee), artist Ivan Jesse Curtis, Berdee Holt, Sean (a friend of Bryanna), Bryanna Holt, and Jack Holt. (Photo courtesy of Valery Anne Zurn.)

This pin with Tim's photo was the official badge for the 1992 Lone Pine Sierra Film Festival. (Photo by Ken Taylor.)

At the 1992 Lone Pine Sierra Film Festival Tim was honored by having a street named for him, and the Holt family was presented with a painting of Tim by artist Ivan Jesse Curtis, the same painting that adorns the cover of this book. Seen here at the presentation are son Jack Holt, grandson Shaeffer (Jay's boy), Tim's sister Jennifer, and Berdee Holt. (Photo by Ken Taylor.)

Chapter 2
You Can Know A Man By What He Says

"In the old days, when you had Gene Autry and Roy Rogers and Hoppy, you would see kids out on the front lawn playing. They identified themselves with those characters. Nowadays, kids don't have anybody to identify with. Clint Eastwood and Lee Marvin are two real good friends of mine, but I sure wouldn't want my kids identifying with them."

On not copying anybody else's style of acting: "Copies never have a chance. Acting is a lonely job, for every actor must be a law to himself."

On Hollywood: "I never did feel there was anything mystic about Hollywood. I never really did like it."

*   *   *

On when he and his rodeo partners came out on the short end of a financial split with rodeo sponsors after a series of sold out performances: "Let's schedule this town again next year. I want to find out how they do it."

Recalling a filming incident: "Chito and I were doing a chase down this little valley, and Chito hit a tree! I told him afterwards, 'Now, Chito, it's all right to go between two trees but don't try to go between one!'"

* * *

"When I signed my contract with RKO Studios, I asked just one favor; I asked them to give me the same dressing room my dad had occupied there for so many years. They granted my request and it's been a sort of permanent inspiration to me."

Tim's father, Jack Holt.

On advice he received from his dad: "My real film debut was in *STELLA DALLAS* with Barbara Stanwyck and John Boles. I remember dad giving me a sage and salty bit of advice at that time. He said, 'Don't ever be late on the set; they are paying you too much, anyway!' I've never forgotten his advice, and I've never been late."

On getting into a fight when he was young: "One Sunday morning I got into a fight with another kid right in front of Sunday School. He beat me up good. I went home, nursing my wounds, and dad said, 'Why did you pick a fight with him?' 'I didn't think he would fight back so hard,' I replied. Dad said to me quietly, 'They always do, son.'"

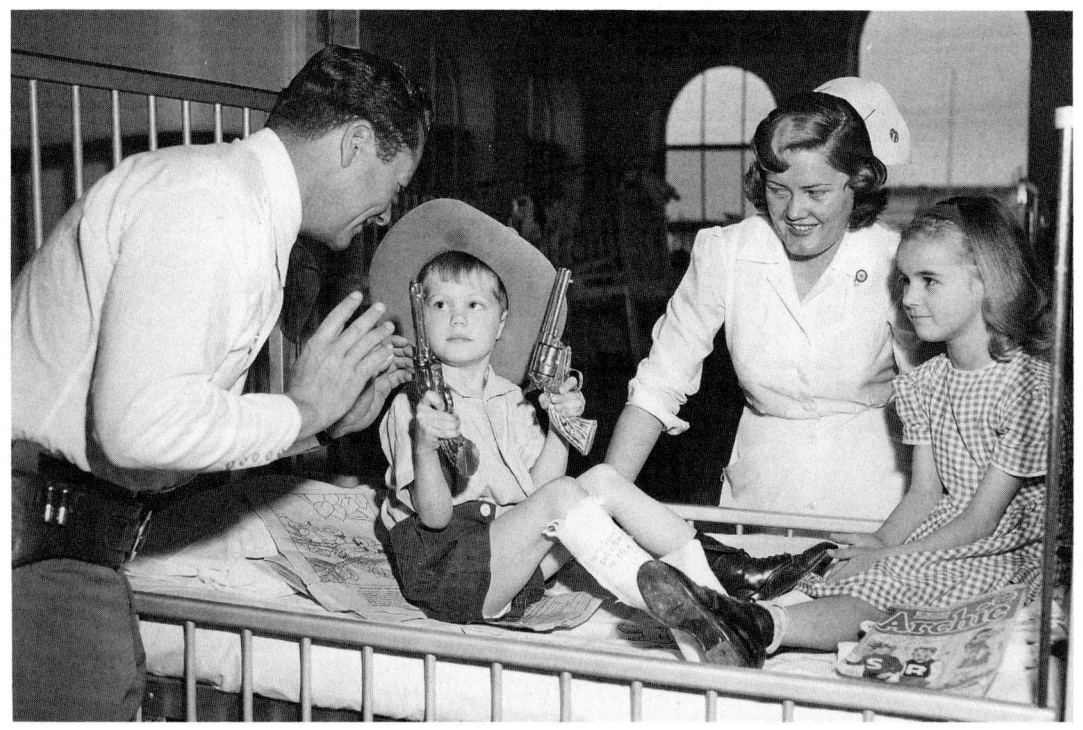

On visiting children's hospitals: "I never turn them down if it is humanly possible, not because of what I think I can do for them but because I know they will listen to me like an old friend, and I may be able to help them get well by providing an incentive or interest in life that they may have lacked."

On his love of Western pictures: "In Westerns, like the six I just finished, we try to implant courage and high ideals of citizenship and personal conduct in the minds of the kids who see them. We never use slang in our dialogue. They are good clean pictures. Westerns are just natural for me."

(Photo courtesy of Bill Sasser.)

Chapter 3
Getting His Foot In The Stirrup
The Early Films (1928-1943)

Tim was only nine years old when first he went before a movie camera for a role in his father's Zane Grey feature, *THE VANISHING PIONEER* (1928), but that was enough to make him contemplate following in his father's footsteps. Although Jack Holt did not necessarily push his son in the direction of a film career, there can be little doubt that he was proud to have his son enter the business that he had found so satisfying. But there undoubtedly was also some trepidation because of the roller-coaster nature of the business, and Jack was well-aware of that too.

Nine more years were to pass before the then eighteen-year-old Tim had his next opportunity to play a film role, the tiniest of bit parts in *HISTORY IS MADE AT NIGHT* (1937). He was now under personal contract to producer Walter Wanger who cast him in several of his own productions but also frequently loaned him to other studios for supporting roles that would give the boy valuable experience.

THE LAW WEST OF TOMBSTONE (1938) starring Harry Carey was a turning point for young Tim. His Tonto Kid role, a good/bad man modeled somewhat after the legendary (if not actual) Billy the Kid, was the kind of leading role that allowed him to show his capability as an action performer, demonstrate his natural flair for comedy, and reveal his vulnerable, somewhat shy romantic nature. In addition, the kid had shown that he could hold his own with veteran scene-stealer Harry Carey.

In 1939 Tim made six films for three different studios, and his roles ranged from small supporting parts to leading men. His role in *STAGECOACH* was certainly small, but he had the opportunity to work with director John Ford in a prestigious production which has come to be a classic. Tim's other "important" film (read A budget) for 1939 was *FIFTH AVENUE GIRL*, where he got to romance no less a star than Ginger Rogers (although the picture only received mediocre reviews and a tepid reception at the box office). His other films for the year were B programmers that provided him with roles in support of George O'Brien, Jackie Cooper and Leo Carrillo. *THE ROOKIE COP* was the only film in which Tim played the top role in the cast.

Late in 1940 Tim undertook his first Western series for RKO (which is covered in the next chapter), but prior to saddling up for that, he completed *LADDIE*, another B picture in which he was top featured; *SWISS FAMILY ROBINSON*, a big-budget adventure in which he played a strong supporting role as the oldest son of the shipwrecked family; and *BACK STREET*, another top-of-the-line film which he made at Universal on loan-out to the studio. In addition, he made the first two films in the aforementioned Western series. All in all, a rather busy year for the young actor.

Back during those years Hollywood tradition pretty much held that once you got typed as a B-Western star there was little opportunity to graduate to roles in A-budget pictures. The most notable exception to this rule, of course, was John Wayne— and he had the highly respected John Ford to help push him to the top. Tim was certainly another exception, and, like Wayne with director Ford, he could thank the perception and support of three top directors (Orson Welles, John Huston, and John Ford) for giving him the opportunity to take important roles in major productions. (The interesting and somewhat perplexing thing about Tim was that he kept returning to B Westerns of his own volition because he just liked making B Westerns.)

The first director to take Tim from his B-Western series was Orson Welles for his production of *THE MAGNIFICENT AMBERSONS* (1942), a film now ranked by international film critics as one of the finest ever made. Indirectly, Tim could thank John Ford for the opportunity to work in *AMBERSONS*. When novice director Welles was preparing for his first film, *CITIZEN KANE*, he repeatedly viewed and studied Ford's *STAGECOACH* to, as he put it, learn how to direct a film. Welles was very much taken by Tim's performance in the small role of the

Lieutenant and remembered it in 1942 when he was casting *THE MAGNIFICENT AMBERSONS*. (Tim's other A-picture ventures were in post-war films and will be dealt with in chapter 6.)

Tim's last non-Western effort before he went into the service for World War II was the startling and somewhat provocative film, *HITLER'S CHILDREN* (released in 1943 but made in 1942). The role of a young Nazi was certainly a stretch for the actor and a zillion miles away philosophically from the super-patriotic Tim. Now it was time for him to serve his country in its time of need. There would be time for more film making when it was over over there.

*   *   *

THE VANISHING PIONEER **1/2

60m. August 1928 Paramount Famous Lasky Corporation

Director	John Waters
Screenplay	John Goodrich and Ray Harris
	(from the novel by Zane Grey)
Titles	J. Johnson

CAST:
Jack Holt
Sally Blane
William Powell
Fred Kohler
Guy Oliver
Roscoe Karns
Tim Holt
Marcia Manon

PLOT: (According to the *Variety* review) A covered wagon sequence opens and closes 'The Vanishing Pioneer.' The irrigation gag and its complications, with a little cold love sequence thrown in, moves along pleasantly enough to send home the average audience, partial to westerns, partially satisfied.

When a nearby city decides that it needs the town's water supply, a thug member of the common council gets the assignment to look after the dickering. He finds the town sheriff to be one of the old boys and they work along lines accordingly.

Jack Holt plays a double part, that of the papa who steers the plains commuters right to the fodder land, and later as the son who balks the gyps by either filling them with lead or sending them to the gallows. Everybody shakes hands when Holt holds up his mother's apron. This is taken as the signal for the pioneers' sons to abscond.

Taken altogether, this will not be considered half bad by those who know nothing about westerners.

COMMENT: I trust that the film makes more sense than this review by some New York hack writer. Tim was about nine years old when he appeared briefly in this film in which his father starred. In the picture he plays the hero (Jack Holt) as a child.

HISTORY IS MADE AT NIGHT ***

97m. April 1937 United Artists

Producer	Walter Wanger
Director	Frank Borzage
Screenplay	Gene Towne and Graham Baker
Photography	Greg Toland
Musical Director	Alfred Newman

CAST:
Charles Boyer	Paul Dumond
Jean Arthur	Irene Vail
Leo Carrillo	Cesare
Colin Clive	Bruce Vail
Ivan Lebedeff	Michael
George Meeker	Norton
Lucien Prival	Detective Witness
Georges Renavent	Inspector Millard
George Davies	Maestro
Adele St. Mauer	Hotel Maid
Tim Holt	Unbilled

PLOT: Jean Arthur, attempting to flee the clutches of a clinging, vindictive husband, falls for head-waiter Boyer. Colin Clive, the spoil-sport husband, frames Boyer for a murder and even precipitates a Titanic-like disaster at sea in which Arthur and Boyer almost perish.

COMMENT: Tim is unbilled and only on screen a few seconds. In the disaster-at-sea finale, he is a ship's radio man who relays the SOS message from the ship in peril.

STELLA DALLAS ***

106m. August 1937 United Artists

Producer	Samuel Goldwyn
Director	King Vidor
Screenplay	Sarah Y. Mason and Victor Herman
	(Based on the novel by Olive Higgins Prouty)

Photography ....Rudolph Mate
Musical Director ....Alfred Newman

CAST:
Barbara Stanwyck ....Stella Dallas
John Boles ....Stephen Dallas
Anne Shirley ....Laurel Dallas
Barbara O'Neil ....Helen Morrison
Alan Hale ....Ed Munn
Marjorie Main ....Mrs. Martin
Edmund Elton ....Mr. Martin
George Walcott ....Charlie Martin
Gertrude Short ....Carrie Jenkins
Tim Holt ....Richard Grosvenor
Nella Walker ....Mrs. Grosvenor
Bruce Satterlee ....Con Morrison
Jimmy Butler ....Con Morrison (grown up)
Jack Egger ....John Morrison
Dickie Jones ....Lee Morrison
Laraine Day .... Unbilled girl at Soda Fountain
Lon McAllister ....Unbilled
Ann Doran ....Unbilled

PLOT: This is the classic soap-opera situation of the uncouth, uneducated mother (Stella Dallas) who sacrifices everything in her life for the welfare of her adoring daughter (Laurel)—even to the extent of ruthlessly sending her away as a young adult so that she can have opportunities in wealthy society circles where Stella would never fit in.

COMMENT: Tim plays the tennis-/polo-playing son of a wealthy family who falls in love with Laurel Dallas. In the conclusion of the film, Tim marries Laurel as Stella watches from a sidewalk window, self-sacrificing tears streaming down her face. The film holds up fairly well today except for the tacky clothes and make-up on Barbara Stanwyck, which seem a tad overdone to demonstrate her uncouthness. Little Dickie Jones (of later Western fame on the *Ranger Rider* and *Buffalo Bill, Jr.* TV series) is impressive in a small but showy role.

I MET MY LOVE AGAIN **1/2

77m. January 1938 United Artists

Producer ....Walter Wanger
Director Arthur Ripley, Joshua Logan, George Cukor
Screenplay ....David Hertz
(Based on the novel *Summer Lightning* by Allene Corliss)
Photography ....Hal Mohr
Musical Director ....Heinz Roemheld

CAST:
Joan Bennett ....Julie
Henry Fonda ....Ives
Dame May Whitty ....Aunt William
Alan Marshal ....Michael
Louise Platt ....Brenda
Alan Baxter ....Tony
Tim Holt ....Budge
Dorothy Stickney ....Mrs. Towner
Florence Lake ....Carol
Gene Hall ....Michael
Alice Cavenna ....Agatha

PLOT: The time is 1927. Shy Ives (Henry Fonda) and exciting Julie (Joan Bennett) seem to be heading toward the altar in the small Vermont town where they live when suddenly Julie runs off to Paris with Michael (Alan Marshal), a young writer who becomes an alcoholic and dies within a few years—paying the price for living wildly in the roaring 1920s. Julie returns to find Ives now a biology professor who is being romantically pursued by one of his students, Brenda (Louise Platt). In time Ives ditches the amorous student, and he and Julie rekindle the fires of romance that once burned so brightly.

COMMENT: This was designed to be a typical "woman's film" of the 1930s—an uplifting soap opera. One critic called it "pretty gooey." Leonard Maltin felt that "the acting surpasses the script." Tim doesn't have much to do in the film but does it well. He is a pleasant young college student who has romantic inclinations toward Louise Platt (who, unfortunately for Tim, is after Henry Fonda).

GOLD IS WHERE YOU FIND IT ***

90m. February 1938 Warner Brothers Color

Producer ....Hal B. Wallis
Director ....Michael Curtiz
Screenplay .... Warren Duff, Robert Buckner
(Based on a story by Clements Ripley)
Photography ....Sol Polito
Musical Director ....Max Steiner

CAST:
George Brent ....Jared Whitney
Olivia De Havilland ....Serena Ferris
Claude Rains ....Colonel Ferris
Margaret Lindsay ....Rosanne Ferris
John Litel ....Ralph Ferris
Tim Holt ....Lance Ferris
Barton MacLane ....Slag Minton
Henry O'Neill ....Judge
Marcia Ralston ....Molly Featherstone
George E. Hayes ....Enoch Howitt

Sidney Toler .... Harrison McCoy
Willie Best .... Joshua
Russell Simpson .... McKenzie

PLOT: The picture takes place thirty years after Sutter struck gold in California, a time when most of the mines are now owned by corporations. Jared (George Brent) is a mining engineer who has been sent from San Francisco to supervise the mining and to do what he can to resolve the fight between mining interests and the wheat-growers in the valley. Jared meets Serena (Olivia De Havilland), daughter of the leading planter (Claude Rains), after saving her brother Lance (Tim Holt) in a barroom brawl. As one might guess, Jared and Serena soon fall in love, complicating the miners'/wheat-growers' problem that must be resolved by Jared before the picture can go to closing credits.

COMMENT: The film was a follow-up to *GOD'S COUNTRY AND THE WOMAN*, which had been a hit for Warner Brothers the previous year. Tim, as Olivia De Havilland's younger brother, has another picture role in which he can gain some experience and be a "sturdy subordinate," as *Variety* put it.

SONS OF THE LEGION **

60m. September 1938 Paramount

Producer .... Stuart Walker
Director .... James Hogan
Screenplay .... Lillie Hayward, Lewis Foster, Robert F. McGowan
Photography .... Charles Schoenbaum
Musical Director .... Boris Morros

CAST:
Donald O'Connor .... Butch Baker
Billy Lee .... Billy Lee
Billy Cook .... David Lee
Evelyn Keyes .... Linda Lee
Elizabeth Patterson .... Grandmother Lee
Tim Holt .... Steven Scott
Lynne Overman .... Charles Lee
William Frawley .... Uncle Willie Lee
Richard Tucker .... State Commander
Johnnie Morris .... Mickey
Wally Albright .... Harold
Benny Bartlett .... Red O'Flaherty
Edward Pawley .... Gunman Baker
Lucille Ward .... Margaret
Ronnie Page .... Boy

PLOT: The story deals with the founding of the Sons of the American Legion, an organization that was formulated to help teach the Legion's values to the youth of 1938. Father Charles Lee (Lynne Overman) is reluctant to help in the organizing because he was dishonorably discharged from the army and is hiding the fact from his two boys who want to join the legion. After he catches an escaped convict in a car chase and shows "the straight and narrow" to a street-smart hood, the dishonorably discharged army vet/father is vindicated and is a hero in the eyes of his boys and the townspeople.

COMMENT: The reviewer for *Variety* wrote, "in a word, this one is pretty terrible." Tim, again in a supporting role, is one of the youths attempting to organize the Sons of the American Legion organization in his hometown. He even finds a few moments to romance Evelyn Keyes during the brief sixty-minute running time.

THE LAW WEST OF TOMBSTONE **1/2

72m. November 1938 RKO

Producer .... Cliff Reid
Director .... Glenn Tryon

The lovesick Tonto Kid (Tim) tells Jose that beautiful Nitta (Jean Rouverol) gives him the "gallopin' flitter-flutters." The scene is from *THE LAW WEST OF TOMBSTONE*.

Screenplay .John Twist and Clarence Upson Young
Photography ....J. Roy Hunt
Musical Director ....Roy Webb

CAST:
Harry Carey ....Bill Parker
Tim Holt..The Tonto Kid
Evelyn Brent......................................Clara Martinez
Jean Rouverol ....Nitta Moseby
Clarence Kolb...Sam Kent
Allan Lane ....Danny
Esther Muir ....Mme. Mustache
Bradley Page ....Doc Howard
Paul Guifoyle ....Bud McQuinn
Robert Moya...Chuy
Ward Bond ....Mulligan
George Irving..Mort Dixon
Monte Montague............................Clayt McQuinn
Bob Kortman ....Unbilled
Kermit Maynard ....Unbilled

PLOT: Borrowing from other classic Western tales, this film presents Harry Carey as a sort of Judge Roy Bean type who becomes mayor and judge in the little town of Martinez, Arizona. He befriends the Tonto Kid (Tim), a young hold-up man (who might remind one of Billy the Kid) and has him help rid the area of the McQuinn gang (a family of hoodlums not unlike the Clanton's of OK Corral infamy) that has manipulated water rights to its own advantage.

COMMENT: An oddity among Westerns, the film is played primarily for comedy. It has a little of the flavor of *DESTRY RIDES AGAIN*, which would be produced the next year. Tim is appealing as the good/bad youthful gunfighter who falls hard for Carey's daughter and decides to go straight. As Tim's Tonto Kid so aptly puts it, "She gives me the gallopin' flitter-flutters." The film uses the RKO Ranch for street scenes and the Walker Ranch for many of the wide-open-spaces shots.

STAGECOACH ****

97m. March 1939 United Artists

Producer ....Walter Wanger
Director ....John Ford
Screenplay ....Dudley Nichols
(Based on Ernest Haycox's story "Stage to Lordsburg")
Photography ....Bert Glennon
Musical Director ....Boris Morros

CAST:
Claire Trevor..Dallas
John Wayne ....The Ringo Kid
John Carradine...Hatfield
Thomas Mitchell ....Dr. Josiah Boone
Andy Devine...Buck
Donald Meek....................................Samuel Peacock
Louise Platt ....Lucy Mallory
Tim Holt.............................Lieutenant Blanchard
George Bancroft ....Sheriff Curly Wilcox
Berton Churchill ....Henry Gatewood
Tom Tyler..Hank Plummer
Chris Pin Martin ....Chris
Elvira Rios ....Yakima, his wife
Francis Ford ....Billy Pickett
Yakima Canutt ....White Scout
Chief Big Tree ....Indian Scout
Jack Pennick..........................Jerry, the bartender
Joseph Rickson ....Luke Plummer
Vester Pegg..Ike Plummer

PLOT: A disparate group of travelers (prostitute, gambler, drunken doctor, crooked banker, whiskey salesman, pregnant woman, and revenge-seeking outlaw) are on the stage to Lordsburg. At first the story is propelled by the social tensions among the passengers but all that changes when Geronimo's Apaches attack the stage and put the passengers in physical peril until the cavalry arrives in the nick of time to save them. The final climax to the story pits the Ringo Kid against the Plummer boys in a shoot out on the streets of Lordsburg.

In *STAGECOACH* Tim plays Lieutenant Blanchard, a young cavalry officer who follows orders. (Photo courtesy of Bobby Copeland.)

Captain Sickels (Walter McGrail) and Lieutenant Blanchard (Tim) of the U.S. Cavalry receive word from the white scout (Yakima Canutt) about the rampaging Apaches. That's Chief Big Tree in the background and Harry Tenbrook at the telegraph.

The travelers are at Dry Fork and must decide if they will continue to Lordsburg without cavalry protection. This scene does not exist in the film but was released as a publicity photo. (Left to right) Donald Meek, John Wayne, Claire Trevor, Andy Devine, George Bancroft, Louise Platt, Tim Holt, John Carradine, Berton Churchill, Francis Ford, and Thomas Mitchell.

COMMENT: One of the all-time great Westerns, the film brought the genre back to prominence after years of mostly B Westerns in the marketplace. Tim has the small role of the dutiful cavalry lieutenant who has orders forbidding him to escort the travelers all the way to Lordsburg. Director John Ford provides Tim with a great on-horseback final camera shot as he separates from the regiment to wave a poignant good-bye to the departing stage and its passengers.

The movie was Ford's first to be filmed in Monument Valley, Utah. Other familiar locations utilized include Kernville, Dry Lake, Victorville, Fremont Pass, Calabasas, and Iverson's Movie Location Ranch in Chatsworth, California.

THE RENEGADE RANGER ***1/2

60m. September 1939 RKO

Producer	Bert Gilroy
Director	David Howard
Screenplay	Oliver Drake
	(From a story by Bennett Cohen)
Photography	Harry Wild
Musical Director	Roy Webb

CAST:
George O'Brien	Captain Jack Steele
Rita Hayworth	Judith Alvarez
Tim Holt	Larry Corwin
Ray Whitley	Happy
Lucio Villegas	Juan Capillo
William Royle	Ben Sanderson
Cecilia Callejo	Tonia Capillo
Neal Hart	Sheriff Joe Rawlings
Monte Monague	Monte
Bob Kortman	Idaho
Charles Stevens	Manuel
James Mason	Hank
Tom London	Red
Guy Usher	Major Jameson
Chris Pin Martin	Felipe
Hank Bell	Barfly
Jack O'Shea	Henchman
Tom Steele	Unbilled
Ken Card	Unbilled

PLOT: Judith (Rita Hayworth) is the leader of a gang of border outlaws, and Captain Steele (George O'Brien), a Texas Ranger, is sent to capture her. Larry Corwin (Tim Holt) is the hot-headed renegade Ranger of the title. He seemingly goes bad for a while and joins Judith's band, but he comes back into the Ranger fold by the end of the film. The conclusion also reveals that Rita and her men were led into a life of crime by a crooked tax collector.

COMMENT: This is an excellent, fast-moving Western film. The story was originally used for a Tom Keene feature produced in 1932 under the title of COME ON, DANGER. In 1942 Tim starred in still another version of the story, using the original title of COME ON, DANGER. Locations utilized for the picture include the RKO Ranch and Iverson's Movie Location Ranch.

SONG:
"Move Slow, You Little Doggies" by Ray Whitley.

THE SPIRIT OF CULVER **

89m. March 1939 Universal

Producer	Burt Kelly
Director	Joseph Santley
Screenplay	Nathanael West and Whitney Bolton
	(Based on a story by George Green,
	Tom Buckingham, and Clarence Marks
Photography	Elwood Bredell
Musical Director	Charles Previn

CAST:
Jackie Cooper	Tom Allen
Freddie Bartholomew	Bob Randolph
Tim Holt	Captain Wilson
Henry Hull	Doc Allen
Andy Devine	Tubby
Gene Reynolds	Carruthers
Kathryn Kane	June Macy
Jackie Moran	Perkins
Walter Tetley	Hank
Pierre Watkin	Captain Wharton
John Hamilton	Major White
Ed Brendel	Unbilled
Robert Keith	Unbilled
Milburn Stone	Unbilled

PLOT: Homeless Tom Allen (Jackie Cooper) is awarded an American Legion Post scholarship to Culver Military Academy. At first rebellious at the discipline imposed by the academy, he is gradually transformed into an enthusiastic plebe. During this same difficult time period, father Doc Allen (Henry Hull), who was reported killed in action during the war and was a recipient of the Congressional Medal, suddenly turns up in a veterans' hospital in a shell-shocked condition and is reunited with his son. As the son finds his place at Culver, Doc Allen gradually recovers in the V.A. hospital.

COMMENT: This was one of several "Spirit of..." films that were made in the late 1930s of middling quality. Tim provides strong support for Cooper and Freddie Bartholomew as the senior class officer at Culver and mentor to the plebes. Much of the film was shot on location at the Culver Academy in Indiana, which Tim attended when he was younger.

SONG:
"You Are the Words to a Song" is sung by Kathryn "Sugar" Kane.

THE ROOKIE COP **

60m. April 1939 RKO

Producer ....Bert Gilroy
Director ....David Howard
Screenplay ....Jo Pagano
(Based on a story by Guy K. Austin and Earl Johnson)
Photography ....Harry Wild

CAST:
Tim Holt ....Clem
Virginia Weidler ....Nicey
Janet Shaw .... Gerry
Frank M. Thomas ....Lane
Robert Emmett Keane ....Commissioner
Monte Montague ....Tom
Don Brodie..Frankie
Ralf Harolde..Joey
Muriel Evans ....Fern
Ace, the Wonder Dog...Ace
Ralph Stein ....Unbilled
Bob Lafferty ....Unbilled

PLOT: Tim is the rookie cop of the title who wants to use the canine skills of his pooch Ace to catch criminals. Unwisely, the police commissioner bans the use of the dog and lives to regret his ruling, of course. A crimewave immediately erupts in the city, and it seems that only Tim and his pal Ace can bring justice back to town.

COMMENT: This movie marked Tim's first leading role in a picture, albeit he was actually only featured in the cast. The film was designed to play to juvenile audiences, and reviewers commented that it would fit that bill nicely but might be a bit tedious for adults. The picture was produced on a shoestring budget, which one critic stated "couldn't cover the cost of a bag of dog bones."

THE GIRL AND THE GAMBLER **

62m. June 1939 RKO
Producer ....Cliff Reid
Director ....Lew Landers
Screenplay ..Joseph A. Fields and Clarence Upson Young
(Based on the play *The Dove* by Willard Mack)
Photography ....Russell Metty
Musical Director ....Aaron Gonzales

CAST:
Leo Carrillo..El Rayo
Tim Holt ....Johnny Powell
Steffi Duna ....Dolores
Donald MacBride ....Mike
Chris Pin Martin ....Pasqual
Edward Raquello ....Rudolfo
Paul Fix ....Charlie
Julian Rivero..Pedro
Frank Puglia ....Gomez
Esther Muir ....Madge
Paul Sutton ....Manuelo
Charles Stevens..Andres
Frank Lackteen ....Tomaso
Henry Rocquemore ....Unbilled

Leading lady Janet Shaw and Tim are posed here in a publicity photo for THE ROOKIE COP. (Photo courtesy of Chuck Thornton.)

PLOT: El Rayo (Leo Carrillo) is a dashing Mexican Robin Hood of 1912. Boasting of his ability at sexual conquest to his gang, El Rayo bets them that he can

This publicity photo of Tim was taken during the time he was co-starring in THE GIRL AND THE GAMBLER.

woo and win a beautiful dancer (Steffi Duna) and bring her back to the hideout. When he undertakes the task, however, he finds that she is in love with Johnny (Tim Holt), stick man at a gambling house dice table. Frustrated, El Rayo starts to bring them both back with him but finally relents near the border and turns the lovers loose.

COMMENT: *Variety's* reviewer didn't much care for the film, calling it "a lightweight piece, with a shoddy script failing to arouse audience interest except for brief moments." The best that can be said for it from Tim's point of view is that it provided him with more experience in film acting.

SONGS:
"La Gunga Timbalero"
"Mi Ultimo Adios"
Both songs are by Aaron Gonzales.

FIFTH AVENUE GIRL **1/2

83m. September 1939 RKO

Producer/Director .... Gregory La Cava
Screenplay .... Allan Scott
Photography .... Robert DeGrasse
Musical Director .... Robert Russell Bennett

CAST:
Ginger Rogers .... Mary Grey
Walter Connolly .... Mr. Borden
Verree Teasdale .... Mrs. Borden
James Ellison .... Mike
Tim Holt .... Tim Borden
Kathryn Adams .... Katherine Borden
Franklin Pangborn .... Higgins
Ferike Boros .... Olga
Louis Calhern .... Dr. Kessler
Theodore Von Eltz .... Terwilliger
Alexander D'Arcy .... Maitre D'Hotel
Bess Flowers .... Woman in Nightclub
Jack Carson .... Sailor in Park
Charles Lane .... Labor Representative
Harlan Briggs .... Labor Representative
Roy Gordon .... Board Member

PLOT: Poor, homeless Mary Grey (Ginger Rogers) is befriended by Mr. Borden (Walter Connolly), who hires her to pretend she is his mistress in order to make his wife (Verree Teasdale) jealous and, thus, more interested in him. It works, and in the process Mary falls for Connolly's son (Tim Holt).

COMMENT: Tim seems uncomfortable playing the spoiled-little-rich-boy in this social comedy. He smokes a pipe in the film, which he always did in real life. Here, however, the pipe seems to be an intrusive prop in some scenes. One wonders if he will remove it when he kisses the compliant Ginger.

LADDIE **1/2

69m. January 1940 RKO

Producer .... Cliff Reid
Director .... Jack Hively
Screenplay .... Bert Granet and Jerry Cady
   (Based on the novel by Gene Stratton-Porter)
Photography .... Harry Wild
Musical Director .... Roy Webb

CAST:
Tim Holt .... Laddie
Virginia Gilmore .... Pamela
Joan Carroll .... Sister
Spring Byington .... Mrs. Stanton
Robert Barrat .... Mr. Stanton
Esther Dale .... Bridgette
Miles Mander .... Mr. Pryor
Sammy McKim .... Leon
Joan (Leslie) Brodel .... Shelley
Martha O'Driscoll .... Sally
Rand Brooks .... Peter Dover

Young Laddie (Tim) has some plowing to do in this rustic scene from the film entitled *LADDIE*. Nobody seems to know who the fellow with the missing tooth and hair is — perhaps Hank. (Photo courtesy of Berdee Holt.)

Mary Forbes .... Mrs. Pryor
Peter Cushing .... Robert Pryor

PLOT: Laddie (Tim) is an Indiana farm boy who falls head over heels in love with Pamela (Virginia Gilmore), the daughter of his new neighbor, an English squire. Joan Carroll (as the kid sister) complicates the romancing of the young couple, adding humor to the situation.

COMMENT: This is another minor entry in Tim's film career, but, again, it provides valuable experience for the fledgling film star, and he's working with some pretty fine supporting actors here.

SWISS FAMILY ROBINSON ***1/2

92m. February 1940 RKO

Producer .... Gene Towne and Graham Baker
Director .... Edward Ludwig
Screenplay .... Walter Ferris and Towne Baker
    (Based on the novel by Johann David Wyss)
Photography .... Nicholas Musuraca

CAST:
Thomas Mitchell .... William Robinson
Edna Best .... Elizabeth Robinson
Freddie Bartholomew .... Jack Robinson
Terry Kilburn .... Ernest Robinson
Tim Holt .... Fritz Robinson

Tim played Fritz, the oldest of the three indolent sons of William Robinson (Thomas Mitchell) and his socially-inclined wife Elizabeth (Edna Best). This is a publicity photo from early in the film.

Fritz Robinson (Tim) finds gold coins on the scuttled ship that was to carry his family to Australia. Unfortunately, the coins have no value on the deserted island where they have been shipwrecked.

Tim played Charles Boyer's son in the tear-jerker drama *BACK STREET*, which also starred Margaret Sullavan. Sometime Western heroine Nell O'Day (right) played Tim's sister in the film.

Baby Bobby Quillan	Francis Robinson
Christian Rub	Thoren
John Wray	Ramsey
Herbert Rawlinson	Captain

PLOT: A London family is on a voyage to Australia when a tropical storm strikes the ship, and all hands and the captain are lost at sea; only the family and some animals survive on a deserted island. The family of city tenderfoots, led by the strong-willed father (Thomas Mitchell), learns to survive and actually thrive in the jungle wilderness, the experience binding the family closer together than they have ever been. Ultimately, when a rescue ship finally arrives, the family decides to remain on the tropical paradise.

COMMENT: Considering the overall quality of this film and the good reviews it received, it is surprising that it lost $180,000 for the studio when it was released. Tim played oldest son Fritz of the Robinson family and received excellent reviews for this performance. It was shortly after this film that Tim began work on his own starring Western series for the studio.

BACK STREET ****

89m. February 1941 Universal

Producer	Frank Shaw
Director	Robert Stevenson
Screenplay	Bruce Manning and Felix Jackson
	(Based on the novel by Fannie Hurst)
Photography	William Daniels

CAST:

Charles Boyer	Walter Saxel
Margaret Sullavan	Ray Smith
Richard Carlson	Curt Stanton
Frank McHugh	Ed Porter
Tim Holt	Richard Saxel
Frank Jenks	Hary Niles

Esther Dale	Mrs. Smith
Samuel S. Hinds	Felix Darren
Peggy Stewart	Freda Smith
Nell O'Day	Elizabeth Saxel
Kitty O'Neil	Mrs. Dilling
Nella Walker	Corinne Saxel
Cecil Cunningham	Mrs. Miller
Marjorie Gateson	Mrs. Adams
Dale Winter	Miss Evans

PLOT: According to the *Variety* reviewer, Margaret Sullavan meets young banker Charles Boyer and the pair engage in a sincere romance which shatters when she fails to meet him at a riverboat departure, where he had made preparations for a surprise marriage. The pair meet again in New York five years later, and their love affair is intimately resumed without benefit of clergy, due to his marriage bonds. For a quarter of a century Miss Sullavan is content to remain in the background of Boyer's life, happy to counsel and encourage him to great success. The tragic ending has Boyer dying of a stroke while on a European financial mission.

COMMENT: *BACK STREET* was a very popular and profitable film in 1941. Tim played the son of Charles Boyer in the film and again received excellent reviews for his performance.

THE MAGNIFICENT AMBERSONS ****

88m. July 1942 RKO

Producer	Orson Welles
Director	Orson Welles, Freddie Fleck, Robert Wise
Screenplay	Orson Welles
(Based on the novel by Booth Tarkington)	
Photography	Stanley Cortez, Russell Metty,

Tim and Agnes Moorehead are seen here in one of the dramatic scenes from *THE MAGNIFICENT AMBERSONS*. The somber and shadowed Amberson mansion (as devised under the direction of Orson Welles) becomes almost as important to the film as the characters who live there.

The role of the spoiled and insufferable George Amberson Minifer was certainly a contrast from the likeable roles Tim was accustomed to playing. He is seen here in a surly, stubborn mood as his mother (Dolores Costello) stands in an archway of the Amberson mansion.

                                  Harry J. Wild
Musical Director .... Bernard Herrmann
                                  and Roy Webb

CAST:
Joseph Cotten .... Eugene Morgan
Dolores Costello .... Isabel Amberson Minafer
Anne Baxter .... Lucy Morgan
Tim Holt .... George Amberson Minifer
Agnes Moorehead .... Fanny Amberson
Ray Collins .... Jack Amberson
Richard Bennett .... Major Amberson
Erskine Sanford .... Benson
J. Louis Johnson .... Sam the Butler
Don Dillaway .... Wilbur Minafer
Charles Phipps .... Uncle John

PLOT: Set at the turn of the twentieth century, *THE MAGNIFICENT AMBERSONS* is the story of a wealthy Midwestern family that finds itself incapable of changing with the changing times. It is also the story of a failed love between the socially elite Amberson daughter Isabel (Dolores Costello) and the social commoner (but romantically desirable) Eugene Morgan (Joseph Cotten). Isabel dutifully marries a socially prominent but colorless suitor, Wilbur Minifer (Don Dillaway), and together they produce a hateful, spoiled wretch of a son named George (Tim Holt), who the whole town hopes will someday get his deserved comeuppance.

Years later when Wilbur dies, Isabel and Eugene (now a successful automobile manufacturer) initiate a tentative renewal of their earlier courtship, but the now adult George objects vehemently to the possibility of his mother consorting romantically with an automobile manufacturer whose product, he feels, threatens their whole way of life—life as it used to be and as George would like it to continue. George's objection effectively blocks his mother's romance and probably hastens her untimely death.

Karl Bruner (Tim), a member of the Nazi youth movement, is romantically involved with Anna Muller (Bonita Granville) but finds that she is intractable in her opposition to the Third Reich.

The collapse of the Amberson fortune and social position follows hard upon Isabel's death and leads to George's long-deserved comeuppance.

COMMENT: First the bad news: Many critics and the general public had little regard for THE MAGNIFICENT AMBERSONS when it was released in 1942. The studio thought so little of it that in Los Angeles it opened on a twin bill with a Lupe Velez MEXICAN SPITFIRE B picture. It is said to have lost $625,000 on its original release. And now the good news: During the last thirty years film critics and film aficionados from around the world have rediscovered THE MAGNIFICENT AMBERSONS and have proclaimed it one of the greatest films of all time. (Interestingly, the general public still pretty much ignores this marvelous film.)

Despite the fact that the reaction to the film was generally disappointing back in 1942, it did have its admirers and was nominated for Best Picture by the Motion Picture Academy. Also, Tim and Agnes Moorehead received Best Performance Awards from the Nation Board of Review, and Moorehead won the New York Film Critics Award for Best Female Performance. Many critics and the public were surprised by Tim's outstanding performance. One critic commented that he "completely captured the despicable character of the utterly selfish son." The role is certainly a highlight in Tim's film career, and many people feel that this performance even outshines the one he gave in THE TREASURE OF THE SIERRA MADRE.

HITLER'S CHILDREN **1/2

80m. March 1943 RKO

Producer .... Edward A. Golden
Director .... Edward Dmytryk
Screenplay .... Emmett Lavery
(Based on the book *Education for Death* by Gregor Ziemer)
Photography .... Russell Metty
Musical Director .... Roy Webb

CAST:
Tim Holt .... Karl Bruner
Bonita Granville .... Anna Muller
Kent Smith .... Professor Nichols
Otto Kruger .... Colonel Henkel
H. B. Warner .... The Bishop
Lloyd Corrigan .... Franz Erhart
Erford Gage .... Dr. Schmidt
Hans Conreid .... Doctor Graf
Nancy Gates .... Brenda
Gavin Muir .... Nazi Major

PLOT: The setting is wartime Germany and Karl (Tim), a devoted Nazi youth, falls in love with Anna (Bonita Granville) even though she has not shown the proper reverence and support for the Third Reich. Because of her love of freedom and anti-Nazi statements, Anna is to be forceably sterilized. Karl's love for the clear-thinking fraulein eventually undermines his loyalty to the Nazi cause and brings about his death by Nazi gunfire as he shouts "the truth" to the German youth.

COMMENT: Critics generally frowned upon this sensationalistic picture because of its ham-handed attempt to tell of the Nazi horrors through an "unconvincing boy-girl plot," as one critic put it. Another wrote that it was mostly "an excuse to film a catalogue of horrors visited upon girls—married or not—who refused to bear children for the Fuehrer." The public, however, took to the film unabashedly and made it the top-grossing RKO film to that time (think about that for a moment). The film was made for $205,000 and grossed over $3,355,000 in film rentals (Source: *The RKO Story*). The bosses at the studio were so happy with the success of the picture that they gave the director and screenwriter $5,000 bonuses.

Tim, personally, got mostly good reviews for his acting in the film, although one said that he played the Nazi youth "in deadpan bewilderment," whatever that means.

* * *

(Photo courtesy of Chuck Thornton.)

Chapter 4
Earning His Spurs
The Pre-War Western Series (1940-1943)

Tim had only toiled for a little over a year on the RKO back lot when the studio offered him a chance to star in his own Western series. He had acquitted himself well during this time in supporting roles in A and B features and leading roles in a few minor pictures, but he seemed to particularly shine when decked out in cowboy togs astride a horse, as in such popular outdoor adventures as *THE LAW WEST OF TOMBSTONE* with Harry Carey and *THE RENEGADE RANGER* starring George O'Brien—and O'Brien's imminent departure from the studio set the stage for Tim's future as a cowboy star for the studio.

George O'Brien had been a popular film actor since the silent days, appearing in such classics as *THE IRON HORSE* (1924), under the direction of his mentor, John Ford, and *SUNRISE* (1927), co-starring Janet Gaynor and directed by F. W Murnau.

Sound pictures did not lessen O'Brien's popularity with movie fans, and he continued to be a star in several film genres, but more and more he saddled up and rode the Western film range—in particular, for the Fox studio from 1931 through 1936. He made seventeen Westerns during those years, and they were as high in quality as any Westerns being turned out at that time.

In mid 1936 George O'Brien made a switch to RKO, partly because the studio promised him a sizable budget for a series of Westerns, and perhaps because he was getting a little restless at Fox after five years. According to writer Buck Rainey, O'Brien claimed in an interview that the budgets for his new RKO series were between $200,000 and $260,000, which sounds rather high for B Westerns of that time period (or any other, for that matter). O'Brien's first picture for the studio was a "special," *DANIEL BOONE*, and very likely did cost that much, and that perhaps explains O'Brien floating the above figures for his series. (Tim's pictures before the war cost well under $100,000, and there shouldn't have been that much difference in the two series.)

George O'Brien made twenty high quality and reasonably popular features for RKO between 1936 and 1940, and then, for reasons which have never been totally clear, he left the studio, and the mantle of RKO Western film star was passed to young Tim Holt. I suspect that there were several factors which came into play during this time of transition. The war situation with Germany and Japan was heating up and O'Brien would shortly reenter the Navy (he'd been an officer in years past) and serve throughout World War II. In addition, he was forty years old at this time and his popularity rested more with adults than with the kid audience to which the B Western was primarily directed. Add to all of this the fact that, indeed, his films undoubtedly would cost somewhat more to produce because he was pulling down a considerably higher salary than the youthful Holt could command.

(Photo courtesy of Bobby Copeland.)

Tim, on the other hand, seemed a natural for the Saturday matinee youth audience by the RKO studio brass; after all, he was only twenty-one himself and was the perfect "older brother" for every kid in the audience. In addition, he was a great horseman, could handle action scenes well and deliver his lines believably, and he was the son of a famous action/Western star—the Holt name was already well known on theater marquees.

So it all came together in the summer of 1940, and Tim Holt became RKO's Western film star until 1943, when he received word that he was to be inducted into the military service for World War II. During those three years Tim made eighteen Westerns of unusually high quality. The RKO studio had always turned out a product that was technically excellent—photography, sound, and direction were usually first rate. And while the scripts to Tim's first series were generally typical B-Western fodder, the extraordinarily appealing manner of the young star, his excellent supporting casts, fine direction, and the established production gloss of the studio all combined to produce films of which the studio (and all concerned) could be justly proud.

Especially noteworthy among the pre-war films are *WAGON TRAIN, ALONG THE RIO GRANDE, THE BANDIT TRAIL, DUDE COWBOY,* and *LAND OF THE OPEN RANGE*. They meet the criteria established in the preceding paragraph (including strong scripts), and they certainly rank in the upper echelon of the best B-Western action films ever made—and Tim was just beginning to hit his stride when he had to leave the series for duty in World War II.

* * *

WAGON TRAIN ****

62 m. October 1940

Producer	Bert Gilroy
Director	Edward Killy
Screenplay	Morton Grant
	(from a story by W. C. Tuttle)
Photography	Harry Wild
Musical Director	Paul Sawtell

CAST:

Tim Holt	Zack Sibley
Ray Whitley	Ned
Emmett Lynn	Whopper
Martha O'Driscoll	Helen Lee
Malcolm McTaggart	Coe Gardner
Cliff Clark	Matt Gardner
Ellen Lowe	Amanthy
Wade Crosby	O'Follard
Ethan Laidlaw	Pat Hayes
Monte Montague	Curt
Carl Stockdale	Wilkes
Bruce Dane	Player
Glenn Strange	Stage Driver
Harry Harvey	Unbilled

PLOT: Tim is leading a wagon train of supplies to Pecos, just as his murdered father had done in years past. After contending with the rugged landscape, savage Indians, and looting outlaws, Tim finally discovers that store owner Matt Gardner (Cliff Clark) killed his father and has been responsible for all the trouble he has had getting the supplies through.

COMMENT: Tim takes over the RKO Western reins from George O'Brien with this film, and a grand start it is. The picture has the look and feel of a big-budget Western. The scripting and characterizations are way beyond the simplistic situations and characters usually found in B Westerns. Tim looks dashing and handsome in a buckskin shirt with fringe and uses his boyish smile effectively in scenes with leading lady Martha O'Driscoll. Don't miss this one; it's one of Tim's best films.

SONGS:
"Why, Shore"
"A Girl Just Like You"
"Farewell"
All songs were written by Ray Whitley and Fred Rose.

(Lobby card courtesy of Johnny Efird.)

THE FARGO KID **1/2

63m. December 1940

Producer	Bert Gilroy
Director	Edward Killy

Crooked businessman Cy Kendall (center) attempts to hire Tim, mistaking him for the outlaw Deuce Mallory, as henchman Ernie Adams looks on. (Photo courtesy of Chuck Thornton.)

Screenplay ...... Morton Grant and Arthur V. Jones
(from a story by W. C. Tuttle)
Photography .... Harry Wild
Musical Director .... Paul Sawtell

CAST:
Tim Holt .... The Fargo Kid
Ray Whitley .... Johnny
Emmett Lynn .... Whopper
Jane Drummond .... Jennie Winters
Cyrus W. Kendall .... Nick Lane
Ernie Adams .... Butch Cleveland
Paul Fix .... Deuce Mallory
Paul Scardon .... Caleb Winters
Glenn Strange .... Sheriff
Mary McLaren .... Sarah Winters

PLOT: Tim is mistaken for the well-known outlaw Deuce Mallory and is hired by Nick Kane (Cyrus W. Kendall), a crooked businessman, to kill a homesteader so that he can get his ore-rich land. Tim thwarts Kane's plan and also captures the real Deuce Mallory.

COMMENT: Tim spends most of the movie with a big boyish grin on his face—even when there is little or no motivation for it. It would appear that the

Tim (The Fargo Kid) has romantic eyes for the homesteader's daughter, Jane Drummond, during this calm-before-the-storm moment in THE FARGO KID.

Even a threatened fist to the mouth will not wipe that grin off Tim's face or make him provide the information that Ernie Adams (left) wants. Boss crook Cy Kendall (right) observes his henchman in action in this scene from THE FARGO KID.

director (or someone in authority) felt there was a lot of appeal in that grin—and there was—but it's almost a constant throughout the entire film and, at times, it makes him appear somewhat demented. The whole film, in fact, seems to be an experiment to see if they could play the story for comedy but still maintain a sincerity in the action department. It doesn't quite come off successfully, and the technique was dropped in the next film in Tim's series. The film is a remake of the 1928 FBO film MAN IN THE ROUGH and the 1933 RKO film THE CHEYENNE KID, starring Tom Keene. The RKO Ranch and Iverson's Ranch were used for location filming.

SONGS:
"On the Crazy Ole Trails Ahead"
"Twilight on the Prairie"
Both songs were by Ray Whitley and Fred Rose.

ALONG THE RIO GRANDE ***1/2

61m. February 1941

Producer .... Bert Gilroy
Director .... Edward Killy
Screenplay ...... Arthur V. Jones and Morton Grant
(from a story by Stuart Anthony)
Photography .... Frank Redman
Musical Director .... Paul Sawtell

CAST:
Tim Holt .... Jeff
Ray Whitley .... Smokey
Betty Jane Rhodes .... Mary Loring
Emmet Lynn .... Whopper
Robert Fiske .... Doc Randall
Hal Taliaferro .... Sheriff
Carl Stockdale .... Joe Turner
Slim Whitaker .... Pete
Monte Montague .... Kirby
Ruth Clifford .... Dance Hall Girl
Harry Humphrey .... Pop Edwards

PLOT: Tim and his two pals, Whopper and Smokey, avenge the murder of their friend and boss, Pop Edwards (Harry Humphrey), by joining the outlaw gang of Doc Randall (Robert Fiske) that committed the crime. Eventually, with a little help from the sheriff (Hal Taliaferro), they bring the murderers to justice.

COMMENT: Helped by another excellent script by Jones and Grant, Tim and his supporting cast make this a very fine episode in the series. Leading lady Betty Jane Rhodes is particularly effective and, in addition, sings two songs in a pleasant and appealing manner. This is the first time that Ray Whitley plays his ongoing role of Smokey. Frankie Marvin, who usually shows up in bit parts in Gene Autry films, sits in on guitar in Whitley's musical aggregation. The RKO Ranch, Walker Ranch, and Andy Jauregui Ranch are used for locations in the film.

SONGS:
"Along the Rio Grande"
"My Grand Pap"
"Old Monterey Moon"
All songs were written by Ray Whitley and Fred Rose.

Bad guy Monte Montague gets a grilling from Tim, Emmett Lynn, and Ray Whitley in this tense moment from *ALONG THE RIO GRANDE*. (Photo courtesy of Chuck Thornton.)

(Photo courtesy of Chuck Thornton.)

The going has gotten tough for Tim and his friends Emmett Lynn (top) and George Melford in this climactic shoot-out scene from *ROBBERS OF THE RANGE*. (Photo courtesy of Chuck Thornton.)

(Photo courtesy of Chuck Thornton.)

ROBBERS OF THE RANGE ***

61m. April 1941

Producer ....Bert Gilroy
Director ....Edward Killy
Screenplay ......Morton Grant and Arthur V. Jones

(from a story by Oliver Drake)
Photography .... Harry Wild
Musical Director .... Paul Sawtell

CAST:
Tim Holt .... Jim Drummond
Virginia Vale .... Alice Tremaine
Ray Whitley .... Smokey
Emmett Lynn .... Whopper
LeRoy Mason .... Rankin
Howard Hickman .... Roy Tremaine
Ernie Adams .... Greeley
Frank LaRue .... Higgins
Ray Bennett .... Sam Daggett
Tom London .... Monk Saunders

Ed Cassidy .... Sheriff
Bud Osborne .... Blackie
George Melford .... Colonel Lodge
Malcolm McTaggart .... Curly Yantis
Harry Harvey .... Deputy Bill Brady
Hank Worden .... Unbilled

PLOT: Nefarious land agents, working as advance men for railroad interests, provide the villainy in the story by trying to cheat ranchers out of their land. Tim, one of the ranchers in the area, is framed for the murder of a neighbor by the land sharks and loses his ranch. In an attempt to right the wrong that has been done to him and other ranchers, he goes undercover with the outlaw gang led by Rankin (LeRoy Mason). Tim and his pals Whopper and Smokey capture a couple of Rankin's henchmen and force one of them to confess to a judge the evil doings of the outlaw leader and his men.

COMMENT: This is a good entry in Tim's series. Ernie Adams is particularly effective as LeRoy Mason's slick, but ultimately weak, henchman. The RKO Ranch and Walker Ranch are used for location work in the film.

SONGS:
"The Railroad's Coming to Town"
The song was written by Ray Whitley and Fred Rose.

CYCLONE ON HORSEBACK   ***

60m. June 1941

Producer .... Bert Gilroy
Director .... Edward Killy
Screenplay .... Morton S. Parker
(from a story by Tom Gibson)
Photography .... Harry Wild
Musical Director .... Paul Sawtell

CAST:
Tim Holt .... Stan Bradford
Marjorie Reynolds .... Mary Corbin
Ray Whitley .... Smokey
Lee "Lasses" White .... Whopper
Harry Worth .... Cobb Wayne
Dennis Moore .... Jeff Corbin
Eddie Dew .... Pete
Monte Montague .... Outlaw
Slim Whitaker .... Sheriff
Max Wagner .... Jamison
John Dilson .... Mr. Williams
Lew Kelley .... John Madison

PLOT: Tim and his pals Smokey and Whopper

RIDE 'EM, COWBOY!
—and Tim does just that as he sends a corral-full of connivin' coyotes high-tailin' for cover in a rugged romance of the rough-and-ready west.

TIM Holt IN CYCLONE ON HORSEBACK

with MARJORIE REYNOLDS
RAY WHITLEY and his Six-Bar Cowboys
LEE (LASSES) WHITE

RKO RADIO PICTURES

(Photo courtesy of Chuck Thornton.)

Leading lady Marjorie Reynolds and Tim are beginning to "notice" each other between bickering moments in the film. That's Lee "Lasses" White eavesdropping behind Tim.

arrive in the town of Valley City with a herd of horses meant for Jeff Corbin (Dennis Moore), an engineer who must meet a deadline for establishing the telephone line to the town or lose his contract for the job. Villain Cobb Wayne (Harry Worth) wants to see Corbin lose the contract, so he attempts to sabotage the stringing of the line by every means possible. Tim and his friends thwart Wayne and his thugs and help Corbin to meet the deadline.

COMMENT: Marjorie Reynolds is a feisty leading lady opposite Tim in this episode. The two of them also have some exceedingly humorous bantering regarding his much-delayed payment for the herd of horses he delivered to her brother (played by Dennis Moore). This was one of the few times that a studio "green set" was used in a Tim Holt film (the line camp of the telephone company). Lee "Lasses" White made his first appearance as Whopper in this picture, a role he would play in eight films in the Holt series. Locations used in the film include the RKO Ranch and Corriganville. One chase scene was shot right on the spot where Fort Apache was constructed in the late 1940s. Another scene is played at Robin Hood Lake in Corriganville.

SONGS:
"Bangtail"
"Tumbleweed Cowboy"
"Blue Nightfall"
The songs were written by Ray Whitley and Fred Rose.

SIX-GUN GOLD   ***

57m. August 1941

Producer .... Bert Gilroy
Director .... David Howard
Screenplay .... Norman S. Parker
.... (from a story by Tom Gibson)
Photography .... Harry Wild
Musical Director .... Paul Sawtell

(Photo courtesy of Johnny Efird.)

(Photo courtesy of Chuck Thornton.)

(Photo courtesy of Chuck Thornton.)

CAST:
Tim Holt	Don Cardigan
Ray Whitley	Smokey
Jan Clayton	Penny
Lee "Lasses" White	Whopper
LeRoy Mason	Reynolds
Eddy C. Waller	Ben Blanchard
Fern Emmett	Jenny Blanchard
Davison Clark	Robinson
Harry Harvey	Vander
Slim Whitaker	Miller
Lane Chandler	Brad Cardigan
Jim Corey	Chuck

PLOT; Tim, Smokey, and Whopper arrive in Placer City to visit Tim's brother, who is the town marshal. They discover that an impostor is marshal (LeRoy Mason) and posing as Tim's brother Brad while holding him prisoner. It soon becomes apparent to Tim and his pals that the bogus marshal is stealing gold from the local miners. In relatively short order they corral the villains and free Tim's brother.

COMMENT: This is a fairly good entry in the Holt series. Emmett Lynn, who just a few months earlier was co-starring with Tim in this series, is seen here in a tiny bit part as a drunken stagecoach driver. Top stunt man Davey Sharpe doubles as Tim in this picture. Film locations include the RKO Ranch and Iverson's Ranch.

SONGS:
"Six-Gun Gold"
The song was written by Ray Whitley and Fred Rose.

THE BANDIT TRAIL   ****

60m. October 1941
Producer	Bert Gilroy
Director	Edward Killy
Screenplay	Norton S. Parker and Arthur T. Horman
Photography	Harry Wild
Musical Director	Paul Sawtell

CAST:

Tim Holt	Steve Haggerty
Ray Whitley	Smokey
Janet Waldo	Ellen
Lee "Lasses" White	Whopper
Morris Ankrum	Red Haggerty
Roy Barcroft	Joe Nesbitt
J. Merrill Holmes	Player
Eddie Waller	Tom Haggerty
Glenn Strange	Idaho
Frank Ellis	Al
Joseph Eggerton	Andrew Grant
Guy Usher	Mayor Blake
Jack Clifford	Player
Bud Osborne	Bartender
Terry Frost	Unbilled
John Merton	Unbilled

PLOT: Tim, returning home after a long period of time, learns that his father has been shot and killed during a foreclosure confrontation with a money-grubbing banker. In his grief and anger, Tim is led into bank robbery by his unscrupulous Uncle Red—an action which the young man soon regrets. Later, after becoming a marshal and hero in the distant town of Remington, Tim returns the stolen money to make amends and to pay whatever debt society will demand.

COMMENT: From a plot standpoint, this is a most unusual episode in the series. This is the only film where Tim is led into actual crime (bank robbery), however briefly, by another character in the story—in this case his corrupt uncle, who himself later repents and joins Tim for a final shoot out against the evil-doers.* Whopper and Smokey are also in on the robbery and are ready and eagerly willing to continue a life of crime until Tim meets the beautiful heroine and decides to go straight, and they decide to go straight with him. We are forced to accept the fact that the comic sidekicks have no moral sense of right or wrong (except that which rubs off from the hero), since they went along with the initial robbery just because they were pals (not because of any misguided righteous revenge such as Tim's character displayed), and they are happy to continue a life of crime as the plot unfolds.

There are lots of dudes in this scene where Tim borrows Whopper's gun in *DUDE COWBOY*. A really duded-up Ray Whitley looks on with Helen Holmes.

Leading lady Marjorie Reynolds (left) eyes Louise Currie as she takes a loving look at Tim in *DUDE COWBOY*. Lasses and Helen Holmes seem to have discovered each other too. (Photo courtesy of Chuck Thornton.)

Despite the moral questions raised in the previous paragraph, this is one of Tim's best and most interesting Western films. The characters are strong (especially Morris Ankrum as Tim's outlaw uncle), and the final shoot out is a dramatic standout of shear bravado (but very implausible) when Tim and his uncle trudge down the center of town (a perfect target), guns blazing every step of the way as they ravage the bad guys.

SONGS:
"The Bandit Trail"
The song was written by Ray Whitley and Fred Rose.

*Eleven years later in *ROAD AGENT* Tim and Chito become masked bandits, but the scriptwriter attempts to justify their crime, and the sheriff is extremely lenient.

DUDE COWBOY   ***1/2

59m.   December 1941

Producer .... Bert Gilroy
Director .... David Howard
Screenplay .... Morton Scott
                         (from his own story)
Photography .... Harry Wild
Musical Director .... Paul Sawtell

CAST:
Tim Holt .... Terry McVay
Marjorie Reynolds .... Barbara Adams
Ray Whitley .... Smokey
Lee "Lasses" White .... Whopper
Louise Currie .... Gail Sargent
Helen Holmes .... Miss Carter
Eddie Kane .... Gordon West
Eddie Dew .... French
Byron Foulger .... Frank Adams
Tom London .... Sheriff
Lloyd Ingraham .... Pop Stebbens
Glenn Strange .... Krinkle
Earle Hodgins .... Unbilled
Dennis Moore .... Unbilled
Hank Worden .... Unbilled
Harry Harvey .... Unbilled

PLOT   Tim, a Treasury agent assigned to find a

missing counterfeiter, is sent to the Silver Bar Dude Ranch when it is learned that phony money is being passed to winners at the gambling tables. It's finally revealed that the owners of the dude ranch have kidnapped the missing counterfeiter and are forcing him to print the funny money.

COMMENT: This is another exceptionally good episode in Tim's series. Excellent use is made of the Bronson Canyon location site in Los Angeles, where the villains hide the kidnapped counterfeiter. The printing operation takes place in the Bronson caves. In one exciting scene Tim escapes from the caves and rides up the steep slope of the canyon wall to the ridge above, an extremely tricky bit of riding. In the climax of the film, a herd of horses is stampeded through the caves. Corriganville is also utilized to good advantage in the film, particularly for chase scenes. At one point Tim eludes a posse by guiding his horse into the crevice rock formation not far from Robin Hood Lake (see page 171 of *An Ambush of Ghosts*).

SONGS:
"At the End of the Canyon Trail"
"Dude Cowboy"
"Silver Rio"
"Echo Singing in the Wild Wind"
All songs were written by Ray Whitley and Fred Rose.

RIDING THE WIND **1/2

60m. February 1942

Producer	Bert Gilroy
Director	Edward Killy
Screenplay	Morton Grant and Earl Snell
	(from a story by Bernard McConville)
Photography	Harry Wild
Musical Director	Paul Sawtell

CAST:

Tim Holt	Clay Stewart
Ray Whitley	Smokey
Mary Douglas	Joan Westfall
Lee "Lasses" White	Whopper
Eddie Dew	Henry Dodge
Ernie Adams	Jones
Earle Hodgins	Bert McLeod
Kate Harrington	Martha
Charles Phipps	Esra Westfall
Bud Osborne	Chuck
Karl Hackett	Tappan
Hank Worden	Player
Larry Steers	Jackson

PLOT: Tim and his fellow ranchers in the valley take action when one of the land owners (Eddie Dew) builds a dam across the only water way that supplies the area and wants to charge an exorbitant fee for water. Then, to really get his neighbors riled, he sabotages the windmills that they build to pump water from wells. In a stirring climax, Dew attempts to blow up the dam after legal papers are served on him which state that he must provide water to his neighbors. Tim stops him in a brutal fight at the dam site.

COMMENT: This is an average (but interesting) film in Tim's series. The final fight between Tim and Eddie Dew is especially effective as they play it out on the edge of a cliff at the dam site. The comedy of Lee "Lasses" White, however, is carried beyond the bounds of reason and appropriateness a couple of times, and it somewhat weakens the overall effect of the film—at least in the opinion of this reviewer.

SONGS:
"Ridin' the Wind"
"I'll Live Until I Die"
"Goin' on a Hayride Tonight"
All songs were written by Ray Whitley and Fred Rose.

LAND OF THE OPEN RANGE ***1/2

60m. April 1942

Producer	Bert Gilroy
Director	Edward Killy
Screenplay	Morton Grant
	(from a story by Lee Bond)
Photography	Harry Wild
Musical Director	Paul Sawtell

CAST:

Tim Holt	Dave Walton
Ray Whitley	Smokey
Janet Waldo	Mary Cook
Lee "Lasses" White	Whopper
Hobart Cavanaugh	Pinky Gardner
Lee Bonnell	Stuart
Roy Barcroft	Gil Carse
John Elliott	George Cook
Frank Ellis	Dode
Tom London	Tracy Briggs
J. Merrill Holmes	Sheriff Walton

PLOT: An old scoundrel seeks revenge on his community from the grave by leaving his sixty-four-thousand-acre ranch for homesteading with the stipulation that only ex-convicts can apply. Tim, a deputy

Tim and leading lady Frances Neal dismount from their horses to chat for a few minutes in COME ON DANGER. It's time for the kids to go get candy in the lobby. (Photo courtesy of Chuck Thornton.)

sheriff, is assigned to oversee the land rush and to keep the good citizens, the reformed ex-cons, and the ruffian ex-cons from having a confrontation. And all the while crooked lawyer Gil Carse (Roy Barcroft) is trying to acquire some of the choice land for himself so that he can control the water rights. Not to fear though, Tim gets it all straightened out in an hour of film time.

COMMENT: The film has special appeal because of its unusual plot and effective comedy. In addition to the clever ex-convict land rush plot situation, there is also a nicely staged scene where Tim gets into a foot race contest with a rider on horseback—and wins! The comedy scenes between Whopper and Pinky, an ex-con (Hobart Cavanaugh), are hilarious—especially the one where they are searched after lawyer Barcroft accuses them of stealing money from his office. Pinky, the actual thief, slips the wad of money to Whopper, who panics. Pinky then retrieves it from Whopper and finally sticks it in Barcroft's pocket—causing him extreme embarrassment when he discovers he has the stolen money on his person.

Locations used in the film include the RKO Ranch and Corriganville. Footage of the famous land rush scenes from CIMARRON is intercut effectively with new footage to give the film a much more expensive look than it's reported $49,000 budget.

SONGS:
"Land of the Open Range"
"KI-O"
The songs were written by Ray Whitley and Fred Rose.

COME ON DANGER **1/2

58m. June 1942

Producer .... Bert Gilroy
Director .... Edward Killy
Screenplay .... Norton S. Parker
          (from a story by Bennett Cohen)
Photography .... Harry Wild
Musical Director .... Paul Sawtell

Tim and his pals Ray Whitley and Lee "Lasses" White (right of unidentified player) stand ready to take action in this scene from THUNDERING HOOFS.

CAST:
Tim Holt	Jack Mason
Frances Neal	Ann Jordan
Ray Whitley	Smokey
Lee "Lasses" White	Whopper
Karl Hackett	Ott Ramsey
Malcolm McTaggart	Russ
Glenn Strange	Sloan
Evelyn Dockson	Aunt Fanny
Davison Clark	Captain Blake
John Elliott	Pop Saunders
Slim Whitaker	Sheriff
Kate Harrington	Maggie
Henry Rocquemore	Jed

PLOT: Tim, a Texas Ranger, is sent out to capture a gang of outlaws which is led by a beautiful young woman (Frances Neal). With the help (sometimes despite the interference) of his two sidekicks, Smokey and Whopper, Tim learns that the real culprit is an unscrupulous tax collector.

COMMENT: The film is a second remake of the same basic story. It was originally a Tom Keene film in 1932 (same title), then a George O'Brien feature with Tim in support (THE RENEGADE RANGER, 1939), and, finally, this version, which is probably not quite as good as the first two.

Tim is about to punch a bad guy who has been irritating leading lady Luana Walters. (Photo courtesy of Ed Shetterly.)

Confounded new-fangled fountain pens! Lasses just can't seem to learn how these new writin' utensils work. Tim and Ray Whitley have a good laugh as THUNDERING HOOFS BEGINS.

Ace stunt man Davey Sharpe shows up for a few seconds at the start of the film during a humorous fight sequence involving Smokey, Whopper, and a group in the saloon. Future film singing cowboy star Jimmy Wakely, strumming a banjo, joins Whitley and his musical backup for one song in the picture, "On the Trail Again." Locations used include the RKO Ranch and Corriganville.

SONGS:
"Come on, Danger"
"On the Trail Again"
"Old Bow-legged Jones"
All songs were written by Ray Whitley and Fred Rose.

THUNDERING HOOFS   ***

61m. July 1942

Producer .... Bert Gilroy
Director .... Lesley Selander
Screenplay .... Paul Franklin
Photography .... J. Roy Hunt
Musical Director .... Paul Sawtell

CAST:
Tim Holt .... Bill Underwood
Ray Whitley .... Smokey
Lee "Lasses" White .... Whopper
Luana Walters .... Nancy Kellogg
Archie Twitchell .... Stephen Farley
Gordon Demain .... Dave Underwood
Charles Phipps .... Player
Monte Montague .... Slick
Joe Bernard .... Hank
Frank Fanning .... Player
Fred Scott .... Dade Armstrong
Frank Ellis .... Outlaw
Bob Kortland .... Unbilled

PLOT: The legal profession takes its lumps again in this Tim Holt episode. A crooked lawyer (Archie Twitchell) tries to buy a struggling stage line cheaply so that he can resell it at a huge profit to a competing stage line owner, the father of Tim. When the lawyer's plan starts to go awry, he sabotages the line so that they will have to sell out to him at his price. Tim, not sure at first if his own father (Gordon Demain) might be in on the crooked deal, investigates the nefarious activities and exposes them in time to save the day, confirm that his father had nothing to do with the crookedness, and win the gratitude (and perhaps love) of the rival stage owner's daughter (Luana Walters).

COMMENT: Along with being a pretty good Tim Holt picture, it offers a trio of additional rewards for the eagle-eyed viewer. During a dance scene, the mustachioed leader of the musical aggregation is Fred Scott, a singing cowboy film star of the late 1930s. Playing fiddle in his group is an about-to-be recording and personal appearance star, Spade Cooley. And, most surprising of all, there among the dancers is Richard Martin sashaying around the floor with a pretty young lady on his arm. Yes, Tim's post-war Chito Jose Gonzales Bustamonte Rafferty sidekick! Chito never gets to say anything, and you have to look quickly or you'll miss him. And for the record, this was the last film in which Ray Whitley and Lee "Lasses" White would be Tim's sidekicks.

Director Lesley Selander dragged his cast all over the Hollywood area to film this feature. Among the locations used are the RKO Ranch, Corriganville, the Andy Jauregui Ranch, and Iverson's Ranch.

SONGS:
"Thundering Hoofs"
"Ramble On"
"As Along the Trail I Ride"
All songs were written by Ray Whitley and Fred Rose.

BANDIT RANGER **1/2

60m. September 1942

Producer ....Bert Gilroy
Director ....Lesley Selander

(Photo courtesy of Chuck Thornton.)

Tim catches lovely Joan Barclay as she descends somewhat less than gracefully from the stage after a bouncy ride. (Photo courtesy of Johnny Efird.)

Screenplay ... Bennett R. Cohen and Morton Grant
(From a story by Bennett R. Cohen)
Photography .... Nicholas Musuraca
Musical Director .... Paul Sawtell

Tim and heroine Joan Barclay pose in a romantic mood for this publicity shot for *BANDIT RANGER*. (Photo courtesy of Chuck Thornton.)

CAST:
Tim Holt	Clay Travers
Cliff Edwards	Ike
Joan Barclay	Sally Mattison
Kenneth Harlan	Art Kenyon
LeRoy Mason	Ed Martin
Glenn Strange	Frank Curtis
Jack Rockwell	Joe
Frank Ellis	Outlaw
Bob Kortman	Outlaw
Bud Geary	Outlaw
Dennis Moore	Frank Mattison
Russell Wade	Player
Tom London	Unbilled

PLOT: Tim, a young cattle rancher, comes upon a dying Texas Ranger who was coming to Trail City to investigate the rustling that has been plaguing all of the area ranchers. When Tim gets the body to town, he discovers that another man (LeRoy Mason) is impersonating the dead Ranger. Eventually it becomes clear that Mason is in cahoots with town

businessman Art Kenyon (Kenneth Harlan), the leader of the rustling scheme.

COMMENT: Cliff "Ukelele Ike" Edwards replaced Ray Whitley and Lee "Lasses" White as the sidekick foil for Tim starting with this feature—and it was a good deal for the studio. It only had to pay for one performer who could do the work of both Whitley and White. Ike handled the song department with vocal skill, and he had a definite flair for slapstick comedy. The catch was that Ike's persona seemed to beg for a New York vaudeville show rather than a period Western setting. He appeared extremely uncomfortable around horses, much less riding them, and he looked a bit peculiar in Western togs, but he was a game player and performed well in the six episodes he did with Tim. And these six pictures were cranked out in record time, since Tim had received his induction notice and had to report for military duty in late July of 1942. Tim worked without a day off between May 11th and July 17th so that RKO would have a year's worth of film product before he went into the service for the duration of World War II.

Corriganville was used extensively as the film location for *BANDIT RANGER*. Tim's ranch house in the film was the actual house in which Crash Corrigan lived at the time.

SONGS:
"I'm a Bad, Bad Man"
"Move Along, Little Dogie"
Both songs were written by Ray Whitley and Fred Rose.

PIRATES OF THE PRAIRIE ***

57m. November 1942

Producer ....Bert Gilroy
Director ....Howard Bretherton
Screenplay Doris Schroeder and J. Benton Cheney
(from a story by Berne Giler)
Photography ....Nicholas Musuraca
Musical Director ....Paul Sawtell

CAST:
Tim Holt ....Larry Durant
Cliff Edwards ....Ike

Nell O'Day	Helen Spencer
John H. Elliott	John Spencer
Roy Barcroft	Lou Harmon
Karl Hackett	Rufe Jackson
Edward Cassidy	Allen
Charles King	Blayton
George Morrell	Unbilled
Richard Cramer	Unbilled
Eddie Dew	Unbilled
Merrill McCormack	Unbilled
Reed Howes	Unbilled
Bud Geary	Unbilled
Lee Shumway	Unbilled
Russell Wade	Unbilled
Frank McCarroll	Unbilled
Artie Ortego	Unbilled

PLOT: Working undercover as a gunsmith, Deputy Marshal Tim goes to Spencerville to investigate the rustling of cattle, the looting and burning ranches, and the subsequent forced sale of the property to the head of the town vigilante committee, Lou Harmon (played by Roy Barcroft—'nuff said). Tim soon discovers that Harmon is buying up the land so that he can sell it at inflated prices to the incoming railroad.

COMMENT: Stunt man Davey Sharpe shows up briefly to double Tim in a fight. Though Ray Whitley is no longer appearing in the Holt series, his and Fred Rose's songs are still being performed in the films—now by Ukelele Ike.

SONGS:
"Grandpop"
"Where the Mountain Meets the Sunset"
Both songs were written by Ray Whitley and Fred Rose.

FIGHTING FRONTIER **1/2

57m. November 1942

Producer	Bert Gilroy
Director	Howard Bretherton
Screenplay	J. Benton Cheney and Norton S. Parker
	(from a story by Bernard McConville)
Photography	Jack Greenhalgh
Musical Director	Paul Sawtell

CAST:
Tim Holt	Kit Russell
Cliff Edwards	Ike
Ann Summers	Jeannie Halverson
Eddie Dew	Frank Walton
William Gould	Daniel Slocum

Tim and Ike take a break from their undercover work with the outlaws, and Ike sings, appropriately, "On the Outlaw Trail" in this scene from *FIGHTING FRONTIER*. That's popular character actor Tom London with his arm in a sling, in case you didn't recognize him.

Davison Clark	Judge Halverson
Slim Whitaker	Sheriff Logan
Tom London	Snap
Monte Montague	Pete
Jack Rockwell	Ira Jesup
Hank Bell	Unbilled
Steve Clark	Unbilled
Russell Wade	Unbilled
Bud Osborne	Unbilled

PLOT: It's a bit disconcerting to find Tim with a gang of stagecoach robbers as this episode begins, but we discover later that it's all a ruse. It seems he's working undercover for the governor to catch the mysterious, secret ringleader of the gang. The mystery angle, somewhat unusual in a B Western, is sustained until near the end of the film.

COMMENT: There's not quite as much action in this episode (Tim is locked up for about ten minutes of the fifty-seven), and the effect of the revelation of the mystery outlaw boss is dissipated somewhat due to the manner in which he is revealed—the abrupt blurting out of his name by a scared outlaw. Davey Sharpe doubles Tim again in this film. Oh, and someone on the production needs to check out the spelling of Tucson. The arrival/departure sign outside the stagecoach office reads "leave for Tuscon - Wed." Locations for the film include the RKO Ranch and the Iverson Ranch. There are some great shots of the Garden of the Gods area of Iverson's.

SONGS
"On the Outlaw Trail"
"The Edwards and the Drews"

Both songs were written by Ray Whitley and Fred Rose.

SAGEBRUSH LAW **

58m. April 1943

Producer	Bert Gilroy
Director	Sam Nelson
Screenplay	Bennett Cohen
Photography	Mack Stengler
Musical Director	Paul Sawtell

CAST:

Tim Holt	Tom Weston
Cliff Edwards	Ike
Joan Barclay	Sally Winters
John H. Elliott	Dole Winters
Roy Barcroft	Mark Carter
Ernie Adams	Landers
Edward Cassidy	Sheriff
John Merton	Burl Mason
Bud McTaggart	Foley
Karl Hackett	Roberts
Edmund Cobb	Doc Crandall
Bob McKenzie	Unbilled
Dick Rush	Unbilled
Cactus Mack	Unbilled
Ben Corbett	Unbilled
Frank McCarroll	Unbilled

PLOT: Tim's father, the town banker in Pinto Basin, is found dead, an apparent suicide, and is accused of embezzlement when a bank examiner goes over the books. Tim knows darned well that his father did not commit suicide (he was left handed and the gun that he was shot with was in his right hand) and that he would never take money from his own bank. With Roy Barcroft playing the father's bank partner, one doesn't have to look far for a possible suspect in chicanery.

COMMENT: While some of the action in the film plays very well, there are several scenes which are just totally illogical and hurt the overall effect of the

Tim explains to Ike that he has just received a telegram from his father, a banker, asking him to come at once. It looks as if there is trouble ahead for Tim in *SAGEBRUSH LAW*.

movie. For example, the villain hires a phony to play the bank examiner. A while later when Tim and Ike are out on the trail, they come upon a gravely wounded man who turns out to be the real examiner. Now, if you were the villain, wouldn't you make sure the real examiner is dead and not just wounded, *and* wouldn't you remove the body so that he would never be found? There is also an illogical conclusion set in the saloon as the baddies cave in too easily in a war of nerves set up by Tim and the good people of Pinto Basin. And, finally, in the climactic chase scene we have Barcroft fleeing on a stagecoach and shooting back at the oncoming Tim on horseback. Barcroft is less than ten feet away from Tim as our hero does a transfer onto the back of the stage, and still Barcroft can't hit him with a bullet. Davey Sharpe again doubles for Tim in the film.

SONGS:
"Crazy Old Trails"
"Rockin' Down the Cherokee Trail"
Both songs were written by Ray Whitley and Fred Rose.

THE AVENGING RIDER ***

55m. May 1943

Producer	Bert Gilroy
Director	Sam Nelson
Screenplay	Morton Grant
	(from a story by Harry O. Hoyt)
Photography	J. Roy Hunt
Musical Director	Paul Sawtell

CAST:

Tim Holt	Britt Marshall
Cliff Edwards	Ike
Ann Summers	Jean McLane
Davison Clarke	W. J. Grayson
Norman Willis	Red Hall
Earle Hodgins	Deputy
Edward Cassidy	Sheriff
Kenneth Duncan	Blackie
Bud McTaggart	Outlaw
Bud Osborne	Wade
Bob Kortman	Outlaw

Tim and Ike find it necessary to break out of jail to prove their innocence in *THE AVENGING RIDER*. Ike lures a deputy into the cell on the pretext that Tim is dying of blood poisoning. The unsuspecting and gullible lawman comes into the cell to investigate and gets pounced on by Tim.

Ike seems to be taking his role as the sidekick of "Mr. Justice" (Tim) rather seriously. Leading lady Barbara Moffett and Otto Hoffman look on. The scene is from RED RIVER ROBIN HOOD.

Guy Usher .... Unbilled
Lloyd Ingraham .... Unbilled
David Sharpe .... Unbilled

PLOT: Tim, with the help of his pal Ike, has to clear himself of the charge of murdering and robbing his partner in a gold claim. The real four criminals take a crooked banker into their plan and ask him to hide the gold they have stolen in his safe. They tear a five of spades card into five pieces, each take a piece, and agree to return later (when the heat is off) to claim their portion of the loot. If any of the four (other than the banker) cannot make it back personally, the piece of card will prove the bearer is an okay representative. (Sure, it's hokey and overly contrived, but it plays pretty well.) Tim, of course, gets onto the plan and eventually brings them to justice.

COMMENT: Ike is particularly good as a card shark/magician. A bit he has with Earle Hodgins (playing the dumbest deputy you have ever seen) is hilarious. And, it should be added, Hodgins all by himself is extremely funny as the befuddled deputy. Davey Sharpe again doubles Tim. Locations used for the film include the RKO Ranch and Iverson's Ranch. There are a couple of good shots of the Garden of the Gods area at Iverson's.

SONG:
"Minnie, My Mountain Moocher"
The song was written by Cliff Edwards.

RED RIVER ROBIN HOOD   **1/2

58m. July 1943

Producer .... Bert Gilroy
Director .... Lesley Selander
Screenplay .... Bennett Cohen
(from a story by Whitney J. Stanton)
Photography .... J. Roy Hunt
Musical Director .... Paul Sawtell

CAST:
Tim Holt .... Jim Carey
Cliff Edwards .... Ike
Barbara Moffett .... Carol Sterling
Eddie Dew .... Scott Yager
Otto Hoffman .... Sam Sterling
Russell Wade .... Chet Andrews
Tom London .... Sheriff
Earle Hodgins .... Deputy
Bud McTaggart .... Denver
Reed Howes .... Owens
Kenneth Duncan .... Rance
Bob McKenzie .... Unbilled
Jack Rockwell .... Unbilled
Jack Montgomery .... Unbilled
David Sharpe .... Unbilled

PLOT: Town businessman Scott Yager (Eddie Dew) has a phony old Spanish Land Grant paper which a judge (in the secret pay of Yager) states entitles him to take possession of all the land in the area or charge exorbitant rent for those choosing to remain on his land. Tim, in an attempt to help the stricken people, dons a black mask and cape, calls himself Mr. Justice, and fights for their rights—becoming a sort of Robin Hood as in the title.

COMMENT: Veteran actor Tom London plays an ineffectual (and somewhat comic) sheriff and Earle Hodgins is again a bumbling deputy, playing his scenes strictly for laughs and doing it quite well too. The problem is that with Ike also present for comedy (and playing his role very broadly) the film is top heavy in the comedic department. With so much levity, the effectiveness of the action heroics is somewhat diminished. Also, the "Mr. Justice" title comes across as rather sanctimonious and a bit hard to take. One of the most fascinating scenes in the film is a fight in a newspaper office between Tim and outlaw Bud McTaggart. During the staging of the fight, stunt man Davey Sharpe doubles *both* fighters. The RKO Ranch, Iverson's Ranch, and Corriganville are used for location work in the film, the last picture Tim made before he went into the service for World War II.

SONG:
"Twilight on the Prairie"
The song was written by Ray Whitley and Fred Rose.

Chapter 5
The Mature Cowboy Star
The Post-War Western Series (1947-1952)

During the years that Tim was serving in World War II, RKO didn't have a regular B-Western series in production. The closest thing to it was a package of five films very loosely based on Zane Grey novels. The first two—*NEVADA* (1944) and *WEST OF THE PECOS* (1945)—starred Robert Mitchum, a recent RKO contractee, who had in the preceding several years gained attention as a heavy in several Hopalong Cassidy pictures and then had made a big impression in the war epic, *THE STORY OF G. I. JOE*. Mitchum had no intention of limiting his career to B+ Westerns, and so he capitalized on his initial successes by moving into big-budget films in all genres.

The next three Zane Grey pictures starred film neophyte James Warren, who made little impression on Western fans in *WANDERER OF THE WASTELAND* (1945), *SUNSET PASS* (1946), and *CODE OF THE WEST* (1947) and very quickly faded from the motion picture scene.

When Tim got his military discharge on December 8, 1945, he headed back to Hollywood to get his film career back on track. He found that his old mentor, director John Ford, was prepping a film based on the legendary OK Corral gunfight between the Earp boys and the Clantons. Ford asked Tim to play Virgil Earp in a cast that would include Henry Fonda, Victor Mature, Linda Darnell, Cathy Downs, and Walter Brennan, among others. He planned to film the picture in Monument Valley on the Arizona-Utah border, the same location where Tim had first worked with Ford in *STAGECOACH* in 1939. It seemed like a great way to forget the travails of the war he had just experienced, so Tim signed on with Pappy Ford. The film was entitled *MY DARLING CLEMENTINE* and was released in November of 1946.

During this same time RKO was eager to reinstate Tim's B-Western series, but the studio decided to first finish up its option on the remaining entries in the Zane Grey series with Tim as star, since James Warren's episodes had been considered weak, and he was being dropped by the studio. Thus it was that Tim returned to the RKO lot and his second Western series for the studio.

First up were the three remaining Zane Grey titled films. I say "titled" because the film plots had nothing to do with the Grey stories; the studio simply used the titles—apparently for the marquee value of Zane Grey's name and the recognition factor of the novel titles.

The Zane Grey trio initiated Richard Martin's sidekick affiliation and personal friendship with Tim. Martin had played the character of Chito Jose Gonzales Bustamonte Rafferty in the two Mitchum Zane Grey films and one of the Warren features (*WANDERER OF THE WASTELAND*), after having created it for a 1943 war picture entitled *BOMBARDIER* with Pat O'Brien and Randolph Scott. The chemistry between Tim and Richard Martin was so good on and off the screen for those first three Grey films that they and the studio wished to continue the association in Tim's ongoing regular series.

The quality of Tim's post-war Western film series was among the best in the industry, and, to a great degree, it was due to Tim's new-found depth in his portrayal of the cowboy hero. The war years had had a profound effect on him, which was apparent in his acting. No more was he the callow, youthful cowboy with the big, silly grin on his face. Now he exuded a steady, serious, no-nonsense type of mature cowboy who was less impulsive, more contemplative, and somewhat "world weary." I suspect the acting reflected the real man, but it also made for an interesting cowboy hero on the silver screen.

From a "total production quality" standpoint (scripts, acting, direction, use of locations, cast sizes, musical scores, photography, etc.) the Tim Holt pictures really only had the Bill "Hopalong Cassidy" Boyd series as serious competition, in this writer's opinion. Many of Tim's films from the 1947-1949 period have the appearance of big-budget A West-

Steve Brodie (right) makes it clear to Tim that the feud between their families is still on in this scene from *THUNDER MOUNTAIN*. Leading lady Martha Hyer plays Brodie's sister in the film. (Photo courtesy of Johnny Efird.)

erns, and, indeed, the Grey films did have an increased budget.

The background music scores of the Tim Holt films certainly deserve special mention. They were particularly exciting and were very effective at highlighting, reenforcing and punctuating the activities on the screen—which all scores should do but frequently don't. For Tim's pre-war series Paul Sawtell composed and conducted the scores. While those scores were very good, it was in the post-war series, as Sawtell continued to compose the music and C. Bakaleinikoff began to conduct the actual scoring of the pictures, that the background music became (again, my opinion) the best in the B-Western business.

For the Western film fan who may want to first sample the post-war Holt films before viewing them all, I would recommend the following as some of the best: *THUNDER MOUNTAIN, WILD HORSE MESA, THE ARIZONA RANGER, GUNS OF HATE, GUN SMUGGLERS, BROTHERS IN THE SADDLE,* and *MASKED RAIDERS*. All of these films are from the 1947-1949 period, before television gave all B films a knockout punch from which they never recovered. The later films (1950-52) are also very well done, but budget restrictions began to show; for example, the more picturesque distant locations such as Lone Pine and the Garner Ranch near Palm Springs were no longer utilized, and cast sizes began to shrink. But from whatever period you choose a Tim Holt Western, you are not likely to be disappointed.

*   *   *

THUNDER MOUNTAIN ****

60m. June 1947

Producer	Herman Schlom
Director	Lew Landers
Screenplay	Norman Houston
(based on the novel by Zane Grey)	
Photography	Jack MacKenzie
Musical Director	C. Bakaleinikoff

CAST:

Tim Holt	Marvin Hayden
Martha Hyer	Elly Jorth
Richard Martin	Chito
Steve Brodie	Chick Jorth
Virginia Owen	Ginger Kelly
Jason Robards	Jim Gardner
Harry Woods	Carson
Richard Powers	Johnny Blue
Robert Clarke	Lee Jorth
Harry Harvey	Sheriff Bagly

PLOT: Tim, returning home from agricultural college, discovers that an old family feud with the Jorth family is still in progress and that the Jorths want to purchase land belonging to him, which is about to be lost to foreclosure for back taxes. A couple of slick operators in town (Harry Woods and Richard Powers) want to keep the feud boiling so that they can get the land. Tim and the Jorths don't know that the two swindlers have gotten advance notice that the land is to be the site for a new dam and is, therefore, very valuable.

COMMENT: Smartly written, directed, played, and photographed, this film, Tim's first series Western

The hacienda at the Anchor Ranch in Lone Pine, California, was a frequently used set. Strictly a facade, it served as Tim's ranch house in *THUNDER MOUNTAIN*. (See the Lone Pine chapter of *An Ambush of Ghosts* for more details on this fascinating location sight.

after the war, is a far more elaborate production than the typical B Western. And there is a new look to Tim and his surroundings. His Western clothing is very different from what he wore before the war, and he has a new horse, a palomino named Lightning. There is even a new sidekick, Richard Martin—although the two pals don't get to spend very much time together in this outing. Tim's youthful pre-war demeanor is now pretty much gone, and a new assured maturity is now apparent in his playing of the stalwart cowboy hero. But there is a strange new element that creeps into a few of his Westerns of this period—getting physical with his leading ladies. In this episode when feminine lead Martha Hyer takes a shot at him, he takes her over his knee and spanks her! He would use this strategy to deal with several recalcitrant heroines in future films.

The background music in the post-war films (though still composed by Paul Sawtell) is conducted by C. Bakaleinikoff and is much more exciting and dramatic than the pre-war music. The RKO Ranch Western street acquired a new saloon while Tim was off in the war, and it would be used in most of the future films. This was the first Tim Holt film to use the Alabama Hills of Lone Pine, a location he would return to frequently in his post-war films. The hacienda at the Anchor Ranch in Lone Pine was used as Tim's ranch in the film.

UNDER THE TONTO RIM ***1/2

61m. August 1947

Producer .... Herman Schlom
Director .... Lew Landers
Screenplay .... Norman Houston
(based on the novel by Zane Grey)
Photography .... J. Roy Hunt
Musical Director .... C. Bakaleinikoff

CAST:
Tim Holt .... Brad Canfield
Nan Leslie .... Lucy Dennison
Richard Martin .... Chito
Richard Powers .... Dennison
Carol Forman .... Juanita
Tony Barrett .... Roy Patton
Harry Harvey .... Sheriff
Jason Robards .... Captain McClain
Robert Clarke .... Hooker
Jay Norris .... Andy
Lex Barker .... Joe
Steve Savage .... Player
Bud Osborne .... Unbilled

PLOT: Tim, a stage owner in this episode, has his stage robbed of Wells Fargo money, a female passenger kidnapped, and his driver, a close friend, murdered. Vowing to see that justice is done, Tim and Chito visit an Arizona Ranger who tells them that the culprits are the Tonto Rim Gang, which has been committing many crimes in the area and that hole up in a mountainous area called the Tonto Rim. Tim goes undercover as an outlaw so that he can join the gang and help the sheriff bring them to justice.

COMMENT: Again the flavor of this excellent episode is more A Western than B Western. Future Tarzan Lex Barker, newly under contract to RKO, plays a small part as the sheriff's deputy. Tim has his holsters rigged with his left pistol butt forward for a cross draw and his right set for a standard draw. Unusual for a cowboy star, Tim smokes a cigarette

The RKO caption for this publicity photo reads, "Avenger Tim Holt, ignoring his wounded arm, uses some fast action to turn the tables on his captor, vicious badman Robert Clarke, in RKO Radio's adaptation from a Zane Grey Western, *UNDER THE TONTO RIM*" (1947). (Photo courtesy of Robert Clarke.)

From this publicity still one would think that Carol Forman was Tim's leading lady in *UNDER THE TONTO RIM* and not Nan Leslie. In fact, Carol played the role of Nan's Apache servant, and the posed shot above was strictly for publicity purposes. (Photo courtesy of Chuck Thornton.)

Tim, Chito, and the rest of the hands have been searching for a wild horse herd in the area. The boss is Jason Robards (right), and Nan Leslie (on wagon) is his daughter in this scene from WILD HORSE MESA. (Photo courtesy of Bobby Copeland.)

Villain Richard Powers has got himself caught in some barbed wire that he put up to catch and hold a wild stallion in this scene from WILD HORSE MESA. Tim and Nan Leslie obviously feel he got what he deserved. (Photo courtesy of Johnny Efird.)

while undercover as an outlaw. Also, there's an obvious continuity error to look for in the picture. When the outlaw gang comes into town to break their man out of jail, Lex Barker has a large tear in the seat of his pants during the outside gunfight. When he runs into the sheriff's office, the big tear is suddenly gone. Lone Pine is again used for the

Tim is ready to blaze away in this publicity shot from WILD HORSE MESA. Great-looking pair of chaps! (Photo courtesy of Chuck Thornton.)

outdoor locations, and the RKO Ranch is used for the town scenes.

WILD HORSE MESA ****

60m. October 1947

Producer	Herman Schlom
Director	Wallace A. Grissell
Screenplay	Norman Houston
	(based on the novel by Zane Grey)
Photography	Frank Redman
Musical Director	C. Bakaleinikoff

CAST:
Tim Holt	Dave Jordan
Nan Leslie	Susie Melhern
Richard Martin	Chito
Richard Powers	Slack
Jason Robards	Pop Melhern
Tony Barrett	Jim Horn
Harry Woods	Jay Olmstead
William Gould	Marshal
Robert Bray	Player
Richard Foote	Rusty
Frank Yaconelli	Player

PLOT: Tim and Chito work for Pop Melhern (Jason Robards) catching wild horses. After they have a large herd rounded up, Pop goes to Tuba City and sells the herd to Jay Olmstead (Harry Woods), an unscrupulous businessman. Olmstead then murders Pop, takes back the money he paid, and, with the signed bill of sale in hand, goes to claim the herd. Tim has his work cut out for him proving that Olmstead is a crook and murderer.

COMMENT: An excellent episode in the series, WILD HORSE MESA is the last of Tim's films to bear the Zane Grey imprint. In fact, only the titles (and not the stories) of the last three films had anything to do with the Grey novels, but the studio apparently felt the Grey name had value on the marquee. The Zane Grey titles must have some copyright or other contractual restrictions, because they are the only titles not released to cable TV on Ted Turner's TNT and American Movie Classics. The video copies in my possession, however, have the logo of the C&C Television Corporation, the company that was the original distributor of RKO pictures to television. Mysteries abound! Oh, yes, Davey Sharpe is back as Tim's stunt double for this film, and the filming was done at Lone Pine and the RKO Ranch.

Tim takes a punch at Tony Barrett in this scene staged in the Alabama Hills of Lone Pine, California. (Photo courtesy of Johnny Efird.)

WESTERN HERITAGE ***

61m. February 1948

Producer	Herman Schlom
Director	Wallace A. Grissell
Screenplay	Norman Houston
Photography	Alfred Keller
Musical Director	C. Bakaleinikoff

CAST:
Tim Holt	Ross Daggett

Tim and Chito have the drop on almost the whole gang of villains in this tense scene from *WESTERN HERITAGE*. In the left foreground are Tony Barrett, Harry Woods, and Robert Bray. (Photo courtesy of Bobby Copeland.)

Dance hall girl Lois Andrews arrives in town with the judge (Jason Robards) and with information that will expose the bad guys. Tim is there to greet them in this scene from *WESTERN HERITAGE*. (Photo courtesy of Chuck Thornton.

Nan Leslie..Beth Winston
Richard Martin ....Chito
Lois Andrews......................................Cleo Raymond
Tony Barrett...Trig McCord
Walter Reed ....Joe Powell
Harry Woods ....Arnold
Richard Powers ....Spade
Jason Robards ....Judge Winston
Robert Bray..Pike
Perc Launders ....Player

PLOT: An outlaw by the name of Arnold (Harry Woods) has hatched a scheme with his partner Spade (Richard Powers) to take possession of all the land in the area by means of a phony Spanish land grant. Tim and Chito work with the ranchers and townspeople to prove that the land grant paper is a forgery.

COMMENT: *WESTERN HERITAGE* is a very competently written, directed, and acted episode in Tim's series, but it is not one about which this reviewer can get particularly excited. Tim continues to wear his holster rigged with the left pistol butt reversed. He is riding a different horse in this feature—a chestnut

Tim and his army buddies, William Phipps (left) and Richard Benedict (right), are about to open the Arizona Rangers' headquarters in Longspur—much to the vexation of Tim's father.

Nan Leslie and Tim discuss their troubles in this scene from *THE ARIZONA RANGER*, which was staged in front of a Lone Pine Cabin that was utilized in several of Tim's films. This is the only photo I have found that shows the cabin (which I have come to call "the Lone Pine cabin").

quarter horse with four white stockings and a blaze face. It somewhat resembles Gene Autry's later Champion horse. Lone Pine and the RKO Ranch continue to be used for the location work.

SONG:
"If You Happen to Find My Heart, It's Yours" is sung

Steve Brodie (center) is Nan Leslie's abusive husband in *THE ARIZONA RANGER*. He gets his character name from the quirt that he's fondling menacingly in this scene. (Photo courtesy of Chuck Thornton.)

The Lone Pine cabin still exists today. With the assistance of Lone Pine resident (and fellow writer) Dave Holland, I was able to locate the cabin, which is just a little south and west of town. A relatively new house is located just a few hundred feet in front of the cabin, which is now used as a storage building.

by Lois Andrews. No composer credit is given in the film.

THE ARIZONA RANGER ★★★★

63m. May 1948

Producer ....Herman Schlom
Director ....John Rawlins
Screenplay ....Norman Houston
Photography ....J. Roy Hunt
Musical Director ....C. Bakaleinikoff

CAST:
Tim Holt	Bob Morgan
Jack Holt	Rawhide Morgan
Nan Leslie	Laura Butler
Richard Martin	Chito
Steve Brodie	Quirt Butler
Paul Hurst	Ben Riddle
Jim Nolan	Nimino Welch
Robert Bray	Jasper Todd
Richard Benedict	Gil
William Phipps	Mack
Harry Harvey	Peyton
Chuck Roberson	Unbilled

PLOT: When young Tim returns to his father's ranch from a tour of duty in Teddy Roosevelt's Rough Riders and informs his father he plans to become an Arizona Ranger, the old man tells him that the existing hang-outlaws-from-the-nearest-tree law works just fine and Tim should stay home and help him tend the ranch. Tim doesn't, of course, and sets up a chain of events that will at first alienate his father but will eventually bring them back together.

COMMENT: One of the best B Westerns ever made, the film—as with so many of these early post-war Holt features—plays like an action-packed, big-budget A Western. Both Tim and his father Jack get above-the-title billing, and they are excellent in this traditional Western action story which has the added strength of strong emotional conflict between father and son. The fact that the parts are played by a real father and son perhaps enhances the impact of their scenes together—and then, too, they are two extremely capable actors.

Tim is riding Lightning in this film and has reverted to the more traditional rigging of his pistol holsters, eliminating the cross draw with the left gun. The beautiful Lone Pine landscape is captured marvelously by J. Roy Hunt's camera. This is the first Holt film to utilize the Lone Pine Cabin (which still exists today; see accompanying photo); it's Steve Brodie's ranch in the picture. The Andy Jauregui Ranch serves as Jack Holt's ranch, and the RKO Ranch provides the Western street.

GUNS OF HATE ****

62m. July 1948

Producer	Herman Schlom
Director	Lesley Selander
Screenplay	Norman Houston and Ed Earl Repp
	(From a story by Ed Earl Repp)
Photography	George E. Diskant
Musical Director	C. Bakaleinikoff

CAST:
Tim Holt	Bob Banning
Nan Leslie	Judy Jason
Richard Martin	Chito
Steve Brodie	Morgan
Myrna Dell	Dixie Wyatt
Tony Barrett	Matt Wyatt
Jim Nolan	Sheriff Bradley
Jason Robards	Ben Jason
Robert Bray	Rocky
Marilyn Mercer	Mabel

PLOT: Ben Jason (Jason Robards) has found the Lost Dutchman Gold Mine, but an unscrupulous saloon owner (Steve Brodie) hears of Jason's find and murders him before he can get to file his claim. Tim and Chito happen upon the murder scene and are assumed to be the guilty parties by the dim-bulb sheriff. They soon break out of jail and bring the real culprit and his gang to justice.

The huge curved rock on my right is generally referred to as Gene Autry Rock because Autry filmed a memorable scene at this spot for his movie *BOOTS AND SADDLES*. Tim rides by the rock in a scene from *GUNS OF HATE*. In this writer's opinion, the Gene Autry Rock area provides one of the most breathtaking vistas in the entire country.

COMMENT: Another excellent film in the series, and one of the most beautiful because of the outstanding photography that shows off the Lone Pine area in winter. There is snow on the Sierra Mountains in the background and even patches of snow on the ground in the Alabama Hills location where it was shot.

The eagle-eyed viewer can spot a miscue in the filming of this picture. About midway through the film a posse chases Tim and Chito after they have escaped from jail. In one shot of the posse in the Alabama Hills, a bus can be seen traveling down the road in the background! You have to look closely because it quickly disappears behind some huge boulders. Right after the bus scene, Tim rides past "Gene Autry Rock" and then hides behind "Hoppy Rock" before he continues his ride past the Lone Ranger ambush area. If these comments don't quite make sense, check the Lone Pine chapter of *An Ambush of Ghosts*. The Lone Pine cabin from *THE ARIZONA RANGER* is used as Nan Leslie's ranch house. At the end of the film it is so windy outside the cabin that the closing dialogue has been shot in rear screen projection—a rarity in a Tim Holt film. (Also see the Richard Martin interview for his comments about the scene and Myrna Dell.)

Outstanding stunt man Dale Van Sickel doubles Steve Brodie in this film during a fight with Tim. Tim's always-conservative Western togs have gradually transformed into the even more rugged-looking Levi pants, a subdued Western shirt, and a Levi jacket. And, finally, Marilyn Mercer (apparently a Howard Hughes "starlet") has one line with Chito (He asks, "Are you Judy?" She says, "No. I'm Mabel," and walks on, never to be seen again). And for that she gets on-screen credit! It makes one wonder.

INDIAN AGENT   ***1/2

62m. December 1948

Producer	Herman Schlom
Director	Lesley Selander
Screenplay	Norman Houston
Photography	J. Roy Hunt
Musical Director	C. Bakaleinikoff

CAST:

Tim Holt	Dave Taylor
Noah Beery, Jr.	Red Fox
Richard Martin	Chito
Nan Leslie	Ellen Wheeler
Harry Woods	Carter
Richard Powers	Hutchins
Claudia Drake	Turquoise
Robert Bray	Nichols
Lee White	Inky
Bud Osborne	Sheriff
Iron Eyes Cody	Indian Scout

PLOT: Evil freight operator Carter (Harry Woods) has a deal with crooked Indian agent Hutchins (Richard Powers) to sell shipments of food intended for the Indians to others and then split the profits, leaving the Indians to starve. Tim and Chito become involved when a desperate Indian mother (Claudia Drake) leaves her hungry baby at Tim's ranch house.

COMMENT: This is another excellent film in the series and somewhat of an oddity since it deals with Indian matters. An examination of the Holt films reveals that not many of them involve Indian situations. Tim was reunited with Lee "Lasses" White in this picture. He last worked with Lasses in *THUNDERING HOOFS* in 1942 when Lasses was his sidekick Whopper.

The regular viewer of the Holt films begins to look for Ozzie's Restaurant and the Stampede Saloon the first time Tim rides into town (the RKO Ranch) in each episode. Even though the name of the town changes in each film, if you look closely, you can spot these particular establishments (almost across from each other). The out-of-town locations for the film were again at Lone Pine. The Anchor Ranch hacienda is the Indian agent's headquarters and the reservation. The Lone Pine cabin is used for Tim's ranch house in this episode.

A grim-looking Tim poses for this great publicity shot from *GUN SMUGGLERS* in the Alabama Hills of Lone Pine, California. (Photo courtesy of Chuck Thornton.)

GUN SMUGGLERS ****

61m. December 1948

Producer	Herman Schlom
Director	Frank McDonald
Screenplay	Norman Houston
Photography	J. Roy Hunt
Musical Director	C. Bakaleinikoff

CAST:

Tim Holt	Tim Holt
Richard Martin	Chito
Martha Hyer	Judy Davis
Gary Gray	Danny Reeves
Paul Hurst	Hasty Jones
Douglas Fowley	Steve Reeves
Robert Warwick	Colonel Davis
Don Haggerty	Sheriff

The whole gang of *GUN SMUGGLERS* has the drop on Tim in this scene. The two main varmints are Douglas Fowley (center) and Robert Bray (next to Tim). (Photo courtesy of Chuck Thornton.)

Frank Sully .... Corporal Clancy
Robert Bray .... Dodge
Harry Harvey .... Unbilled as doctor

PLOT: A gang of gunrunners led by Steve Reeves (Douglas Fowley) is stealing weapons from cavalry shipments. Steve's little brother Danny (Gary Gray) is a decoy for the gang. He stops the wagons on some pretext and then the gang ambushes the wagons. Tim and Chito come to the aid of their friend Sergeant Hasty Jones (Paul Hurst) when his detachment of wagons is ambushed, and they eventually bring the gang to justice and show the boy the error of his ways.

COMMENT: In the last film, *INDIAN AGENT*, the villain was Carter of the Carter Freighting Co. If you look carefully, you can still see a Carter Freighting Co. sign on one of the buildings in town. And speaking of the RKO Ranch Western street, a few buildings are shuffled a bit for this film to perhaps make us think we are in another town for the episode. A new building is used for the saloon,

Tim, Chito, and Martha Hyer come to the aid of Paul Hurst after his cavalry unit has been ambushed by the *GUN SMUGGLERS*. (Photo courtesy of Bobby Copeland.)

named the Bella Union Saloon. It is farther down the street than the Stampede Saloon and on the other side. And, oh yes, the Ozzie's Restaurant sign has been painted over too.

This is the first time that Tim is playing a character named Tim Holt, and, like Tim, he even smokes a pipe on screen—unusual for a cowboy movie star. Fine character actor Douglas Fowley, making his first appearance in a Holt film, is particularly effective as the leader of the smugglers. Paul Hurst, leading lady Martha Hyer, and young Gary Gray (brother of "Father Knows Best" son Billy Gray) also provide strong support. Frank McDonald, who directed many Autry and Rogers films, helms his only Holt film here and does an excellent job.

Lone Pine is again used for the location site. The Lone Pine cabin is used in the fourth straight film; this time it is the gun-smugglers' hideout.

BROTHERS IN THE SADDLE ★★★★

60m. February 1949

Producer .... Herman Schlom
Director .... Lesley Selander
Screenplay .... Norman Houston
Photography .... J. Roy Hunt
Musical Director .... C. Bakaleinikoff

CAST:
Tim Holt .... Tim Taylor
Richard Martin .... Chito
Steve Brodie .... Steve Taylor
Virginia Cox .... Nancy Austin
Carol Forman .... Flora Trigby
Richard Powers .... Nash Prescott
Stanley Andrews .... Sheriff
Robert Bray .... Poke Lynch
Francis McDonald .... Hoyt Parker
Emmett Vogan .... Judge Colter
Monte Montague .... Stage Driver

PLOT: Tim attempts to keep his younger brother Steve (Steve Brodie) from falling into a life of gambling and crime. Despite his best efforts, Steve kills

Virginia Cox is unaware of the gambling debts and violent temper of fiance Steve Brodie as they share one of the few gentle scenes in *BROTHERS IN THE SADDLE*. Richard Martin looks on happily as Tim puffs on his pipe. (Photo courtesy of Chuck Thornton.)

Tim is troubled by his brother's gambling losses, but Steve (right) will not be dissuaded from continuing. Richard Powers (left) is the slick card shark and Carol Forman is the floozy. The scene is from *BROTHERS IN THE SADDLE*. (Photo courtesy of Chuck Thornton.)

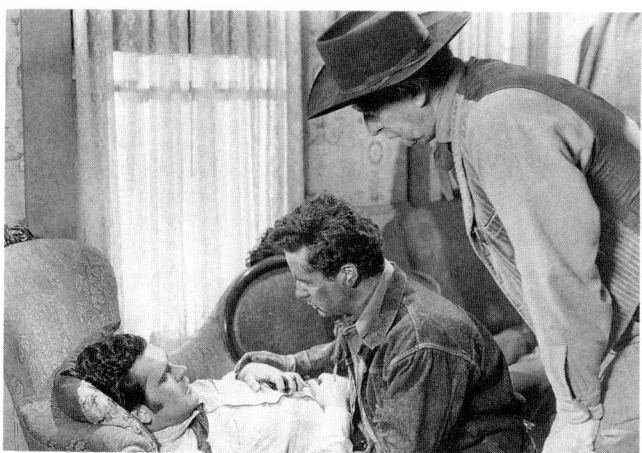

Tim's brother (played by Steve Brodie) has shot Chito in cold blood and fled. Tim looks after Chito as the sheriff, Stanley Andrews, looks on. The scene is from *BROTHERS IN THE SADDLE*. (Photo courtesy of Chuck Thornton.)

a card shark in self-defense but then murders the owner of the saloon/gambling hall in cold blood and flees. Later he also shoots Chito. Tim goes after his brother to bring him to justice.

COMMENT: Again, this outstanding Tim Holt film plays more like an A than a B western. The character development is considerably more complex—especially the love/hate relationship between Tim and his brother Steve (performed well by Steve Brodie). The action is grittier, as played out by Tim and Steve—especially their scene on a rock-strewn mountain precipice where they have a knuckle-busting fight that concludes with Steve pushing Tim off the mountain side, which nearly kills him. Later, in the climax, they have a brutal shoot out at the same rugged location. Steve has fled there after shooting Chito in cold blood. Tim, dirty, blood showing from a mouth wound suffered during the earlier cliff fall, follows Steve up into the pine-ridged mountain top. When the shoot out commences, Tim wounds Steve in the shoulder, but is himself wounded in the left hand from Steve's fire. Moments later, face to face, they both fire, both connect with their shots, and both fall (in a most dramatic fashion) as if shot dead. This type of bruising action is a long way from the typical "tidy" B Western shoot-'em-ups and is thrilling to watch.

The Stampede Saloon at the RKO Ranch is used again in this film as well as the Bella Union Saloon, which first appeared in *GUN SMUGGLERS*. Now the Bella Union is supposed to be in the Mexican town of Maringo, while the Stampede is in Lordsburgh, above the border—and in reality they're just up the street from one another. The gorgeous location used for this film is the Jack Garner Ranch in Idyllwild, California, west of Palm Springs. Tim shot several of his films at this location, and it is stunning!

Tim uses a bay horse in the first scene for some reason and then he makes a point of mentioning that he is switching to Lightning. No explanation is given. Lightning, by the way, gets to do the star horse thing of saving his master in this film. This is the first time the very spirited palomino has been required to do anything other than provide Tim with transportation.

RUSTLERS **1/2

61m. May 1949

Producer ....Herman Schlom
Director ....Lesley Selander
Screenplay ....Jack Natteford and Luci Ward
Photography ....J. Roy Hunt
Musical Director ....C. Bakaleinikoff

CAST:
Tim Holt..Dick McBride
Richard Martin ....Chito
Martha Hyer......................................Ruth Abbott
    Steve Brodie......................Mort Wheeler
    Lois Andrews ....Trixie Fontaine
    Harry Shannon ....Sheriff Harmon
    Addison Richards ....Frank Abbott
    Frank Fenton ....Carew
    Robert Bray......................................Hank
    Don Haggerty ....Rancher
    Monte Montague ....Player
    Stanley Blystone ....Player
    ~~Kenneth~~ Francis MacDonald ....Unbilled

(Photo courtesy of Chuck Thornton.)

PLOT: The Salt River Gang is terrorizing the area around Trail Cross by rustling cattle and then notifying the rancher whose cattle was stolen that he can have the herd back if he pays a ransom. In this way the rustlers don't have the problem of driving stolen cattle to a rail head, and it lessens their risk of being caught because they get the money and quickly leave the cattle at some designated place. Tim and Chito, a couple of out-of-work cowhands, become involved when Chito wins big at the gaming table of the local saloon and receives marked ransom money from the gambling/saloon boss, who is also the leader of the Salt River Gang.

COMMENT: RUSTLERS is one of Tim's lesser efforts from this very productive period in his career—a period that produced some of the best B Westerns ever made. For the second time in his postwar films, Tim becomes angry with the leading lady (this time for shooting his hat off) and takes her over his knee and spanks her—this time he does it standing up! It is such a strange thing to have

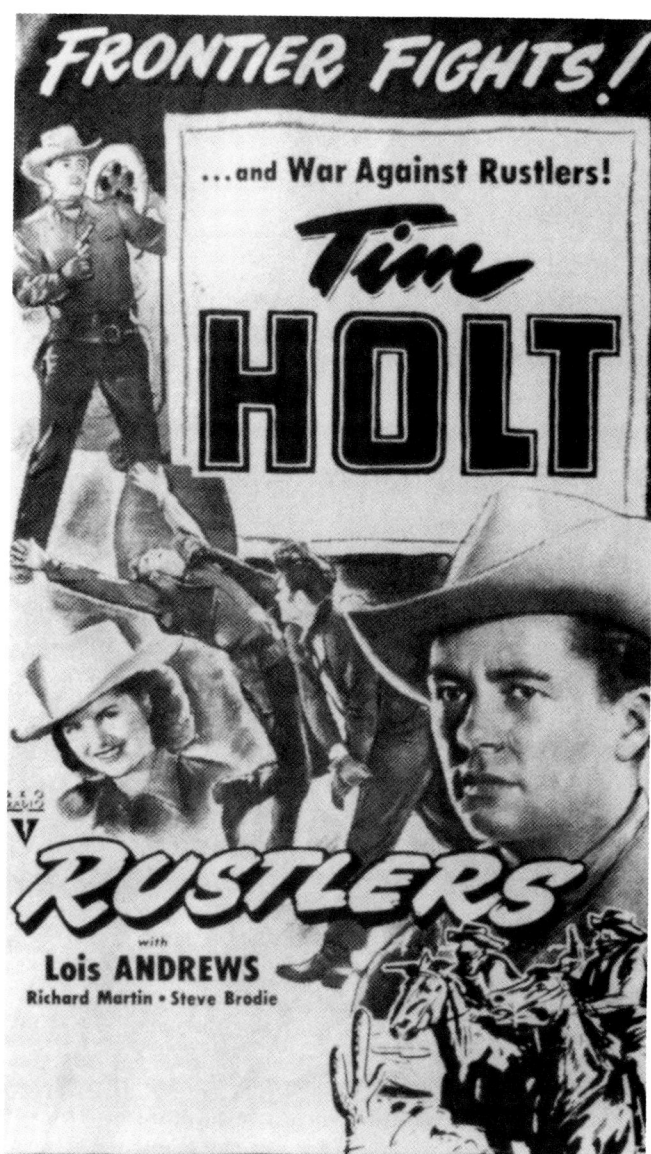

Director Lew Landers (right) and George McGonigle, property man, fixed up a gag sign for the entertainment of the cast and crew during the last day of shooting on *STAGECOACH KID*.

This rare and comically bizarre photo was secured from the original RKO archives and bears the following studio caption: NEW ROLE—Tim Holt stands in for his movie horse, Lightning, during some off-stage clowning between shots (or maybe it was during Lew Landers' party) of his current film, RKO Radio's *STAGECOACH KID*. The "driver" is Richard Martin.

the cowboy hero do, and it seems particularly out of place today in the 1990s with our awareness of the prevalence of sexual harrassment—or am I taking all of this too seriously?

The director used the "other end" of the RKO Ranch Western street in *RUSTLERS*. My guess is that he did it so that the town would not seem so familiar to regular viewers. The out-of-town location was again the beautiful tall pine country of the Jack Garner Ranch in Idyllwild, California.

SONG:
"She's Not Without a Lover Anymore" is sung by Lois Andrews.
No composer credit is given.

TIM HOLT in "STAGECOACH KID" with RICHARD MARTIN · JEFF DONNELL · JOE SAWYER · THURSTON HALL
Produced by HERMAN SCHLOM · Directed by LEW LANDERS · Story and Screen play by NORMAN HOUSTON

STAGECOACH KID **1/2

60m. June 1949

Producer	Herman Schlom
Director	Lew Landers
Screenplay	Norman Houston
Photography	Nicholas Musuraca
Musical Director	C. Bakaleinikoff

CAST:
Tim Holt	Dave Collins
Richard Martin	Chito
Jeff Donnell	Jessie Arnold
Joe Sawyer	Thatcher
Thurston Hall	Peter Arnold
Carol Hughes	Birdie
Robert Bray	Clint
Robert B. Williams	Parnell
Kenneth MacDonald	Sheriff

PLOT: Crooked ranch foreman Thatcher (Joe Sawyer) is swindling his absentee boss, Peter Arnold (Thurston Hall), out of cattle and money. When he learns that Arnold is returning to the ranch via stage, Thatcher sends two of his henchmen to dispose of the millionaire landowner. Tim and Chito, owners of the stage line, drive off the thugs. Not discouraged, Thatcher gets more devious in his plans to do away with Arnold. A sub plot deals with Arnold's rambunctious daughter (Jeff Donnell), who angrily accompanies him to Casco City on the stage and makes it clear that she wants nothing to do with the wild West. When they arrive in town, she flees from her father in disguise as a teenager (not at all believable) and plans to take the next stage back home. Her plan is foiled when she gets mixed up with the outlaws and with Tim and Chito.

COMMENT: For the second film in a row, Tim spanks his leading lady—this time following a rather rigorous wrestling match with her/him. Let me explain. At the time of the wrestling and spanking, Tim supposedly thinks that she is a spoiled teenage boy that he must teach a little discipline, but later on he acknowledges that he knew all the time that she was really a girl! The scriptwriters seemed to enjoy putting Tim into this type of situation; it certainly

Above—This shot from *STAGECOACH KID* was taken on the porch of the "Hoppy cabin" in Lone Pine, so named because Bill "Hopalong Cassidy" Boyd and his wife lived in the cabin when he came up to Lone Pine to film his Hoppy movies. The cabin frequently turned up in Western films as a ranch house, cabin, or outlaw hideout. In *STAGECOACH KID* it serves as Tim's ranch house.

wouldn't happen now with today's more liberated women. There are two other uncommon occurrences for a cowboy star in this film: he smokes a pipe in several scenes, and he gets kissed on camera by the leading lady at the fade out.

The Bella Union Saloon (down the street from the Stampede Saloon on the RKO Ranch Western street) is renamed the Stampede Saloon for this picture. (The original Stampede Saloon is never

Right—Here is a long shot of the Hoppy cabin as it appears today. You can see the porch where Tim and Chito are seated in the previous photo just to the left of the stone chimney that runs up the side of the building.

Tim and Chito have a run-in with a couple of land sharks (Robert Livingston and William Tannen) when they arrive in Santa Domingo to claim Chito's inheritance. (Photo courtesy of Bobby Copeland.)

utilized in this film.) The Hoppy cabin in Lone Pine (see *An Ambush Of Ghosts*, pages 64-66) is utilized as Tim's ranch house in this film, and the Anchor Ranch hacienda set is used as Arnold's ranch house (see *An Ambush Of Ghosts*, pages 70-80).

THE MYSTERIOUS DESPERADO ***

61m. September 1949

Producer	Herman Schlom
Director	Lesley Selander
Screenplay	Norman Houston
Photography	Nicholas Musuraca
Musical Director	C. Bakaleinikoff

CAST:
Tim Holt	Tim Holt
Richard Martin	Chito
Edward Norris	Ramon Bustamonte
Movita Castaneda	Louisa
Frank Wilcox	Elias Stevens
William Tannen	Bart Barton
Robert Livingston	John Jordan
Robert B. Williams	Whitaker
Kenneth MacDonald	Sheriff Anders
Frank Lackteen	Pedro
Leander Decordova	Padre

PLOT: Tim and Chito go to Santa Domingo to claim an inheritance due Chito from his deceased uncle. When they arrive, they discover that the uncle was murdered and his son Ramon (Edward Norris), who should inherit his father's valuable ranch, is accused of the crime. It soon becomes apparent that the public administrator (Frank Wilcox) and two real estate wheeler-dealers (Robert Livingston and William Tannen) are framing the son to get possession of the ranch.

COMMENT: In this film—and a pretty good outing it is—Tim plays a fellow named Tim Holt for only the

RKO put out this very misleading publicity shot of Tim and leading lady Movita Castaneda for the film *THE MYSTERIOUS DESPERADO*. The photo seems to suggest that Tim and Movita will be a romantic item in the film, but in actuality she plays the fiancee of the mysterious desperado of the title, Edward Norris. (Photo courtesy of Chuck Thornton.)

second time. The Lone Pine Anchor Ranch hacienda is used as the ranch house of Chito's murdered uncle, and, in a clever bit of deception, one of the entrances through the outer wall to the hacienda is used late in the film when Tim takes Chito to a mission after he has been wounded in the leg in a gunfight. The mission inside the hacienda entrance is, however, a real mission a long way from Lone Pine—the San Fernando Mission in San Fernando, California. The mission, which dates back to the 1700s, is a popular tourist attraction today. Tim also used the mission in his 1950 film entitled *BORDER TREASURE*. The Hoppy cabin in Lone Pine is used again, this time as Robert Livingston's ranch house. At the RKO Ranch Western street, the Stampede Saloon has been renamed the Willcox Saloon (see *MASKED RAIDERS* comment). And, finally, take notice of the especially exciting music score that supports the action in this film. Paul Sawtell's music and C. Bakaleinikoff's conducting make the Tim Holt background music scores the best in the business!

MASKED RAIDERS   ***1/2

60m. October 1949

Producer	Herman Schlom
Director	Lesley Selander
Screenplay	Norman Houston
Photography	George Diskant
Musical Director	C. Bakaleinikoff

CAST:

Tim Holt	Tim Holt
Richard Martin	Chito
Marjorie Lord	Gail Trevor
Gary Gray	Artie Trevor
Frank Wilcox	Corthell
Charles Arnt	Dr. Nichols
Tom Tyler	Trigg
Harry Woods	Sheriff Barlow
Houseley Stevenson	Uncle Henry
Clayton Moore	Matt
Bill George	Player
Jason Robards	Unbilled as the Ranger captain
Jay Kirby	Unbilled as a member of Diablo's gang

PLOT: Tim and Chito, Texas Rangers, are sent by their captain to Willcox, Texas, where the masked Diablo Kid and his gang have repeatedly been robbing the bank. Tim and Chito go undercover and soon discover that Diablo and the gang are robbing from the bank and giving the money to ranchers in the area who have bank foreclosures facing them—in other words, Diablo is a sort of Robin Hood. Tim discovers that the real villains are the bank owner and the town sheriff, who are working in cahoots to take over the ranch lands. And, big surprise, the Diablo Kid turns out to be a woman!

COMMENT: There is some evidence to indicate that this film may have been produced prior to *THE MYSTERIOUS DESPERADO*, the previously dis-

Tim and Chito are sent to Willcox, Texas, by their Texas Ranger captain (Jason Robards) to capture the masked Diablo Kid and his gang. The scene is from *MASKED RAIDERS*. (Photo courtesy of Chuck Thornton.)

Suspicious Uncle Henry (Houseley Stevenson) examines the dirt on Chito's boot to see if he and Tim are telling the truth about the area they came through to reach the ranch. Marjorie Lord and young Gary Gray are on the porch of her ranch house—in reality one of the ranch houses on the Jack Garner Ranch in Idyllwild, California.

Tim finally gets his hands on the Diablo Kid and discovers to his dismay that the outlaw leader is a woman—Marjorie Lord. The scene is from *MASKED RAIDERS*, which during production was entitled *TROUBLE IN TEXAS*.

cussed film. In DESPERADO the story takes place in the town of Santo Domingo, but the saloon in town has a sign that reads "Willcox Saloon." *MASKED RAIDERS*, it turns out, takes place in the town of Willcox, so the sign is appropriate for this film. Either the RKO art department was "jumping the gun" a bit by preparing for *RAIDERS* while *DESPERADO* was still being filmed, or it was a bit tardy in taking the sign down. Additionally, while most sources have *DESPERADO* listed first in Holt filmographies, the book entitled *The RKO Story* lists *MASKED RAIDERS* first.

Marjorie Lord (who later became Danny Thomas's wife in *The Danny Thomas Show* on TV) is excellent as the Diablo Kid in the film. Clayton Moore has a very small part as a member of Diablo's gang. This film was made just before Moore became the Lone Ranger in the TV series. There is some stock footage of Corriganville and Lone Pine used in the opening montage of the film, and then the Jack Garner Ranch in Idyllwild, California, is used for the rest of the film. One of the Garner ranch houses that was used in *RUSTLERS* is used again here for Harry Woods' ranch house.

RIDERS OF THE RANGE   ***

60m. February 1950

Producer	Herman Schlom
Director	Lesley Selander
Screenplay	Norman Houston
Photography	J. Roy Hunt
Musical Director	C. Bakaleinikoff

CAST:

Tim Holt	Kansas Jones
Richard Martin	Chito
Jacqueline White	Dusty Willis
Reed Hadley	Clint Burroughs
Robert Barrat	Sheriff
Robert Clarke	Harry Willis
Tom Tyler	Ringo Kid
William Tannen	Trump Dixon

(Photo courtesy of Johnny Efird.)

This three-way sign out in the middle of nowhere directs our *RIDERS OF THE RANGE*, Tim and Chito, the three miles to Cedar Hill—where trouble awaits them. (Photo courtesy of Chuck Thornton.)

This is the only film in which Lightning wore a bosal rather than a regular bridle and bit. As can be seen, the bosal looks more like a halter with a curved ring around the muzzle of the horse. The reins to guide the horse are attached to the bottom of the bosal. (Photo courtesy of Chuck Thornton.)

PLOT: Tim and Chito, two out-of-work cowpokes, befriend lady rancher Dusty Willis (Jacqueline White), who gives them a job on her ranch. Dusty is having trouble with her ne'er-do-well brother Harry (Robert Clarke), who has a three-thousand-dollar gambling debt he owes to saloon owner Clint Burroughs (Reed Hadley). Through a series of plot complications, Tim and Chito are charged with the murder of Burroughs and must break free of the accusing sheriff (Robert Barrat) to prove their innocence.

COMMENT: This is a fairly good entry in the series—almost non-stop action—but the plot is not as clearly focused as usual. There's a strange irony for Tom Tyler in the film. Eleven years before in *STAGECOACH*, Tyler, as Hank Plummer, was killed by John Wayne, who played the Ringo Kid. Now, in 1950, Tom Tyler gets to be the Ringo Kid, but he is again foiled—this time by Tim and Chito.

Tim uses a bosal on Lightning for this film (and only this film, as it turns out). A bosal is a halter-like bridle that does not utilize a bit in the horse's mouth. I can't remember ever seeing any other movie cowboy use a bosal in a film. The RKO Ranch Western street saloon has gone back to its usual name of Stampede Saloon in this film, and the spectacular scenery provided by the Jack Garner Ranch is once again utilized by producer Herman Schlom and director Leslie Selander. *RIDERS OF THE RANGE* reportedly lost fifty thousand dollars, a sad testimony to the inroads television was making on all motion pictures by 1950, but especially the B pictures.

STORM OVER WYOMING ***

60m. April 1950

Tim, Chito, and leading lady Noreen Nash attempt to hold off the bad guys in this lobby card scene from *STORM OVER WYOMING*. (Photo courtesy of Bobby Copeland.)

Richard Martin told me that the *STORM OVER WYOMING* scenes with sheep were shot in Agura, California. Basque shepherds from Spain tended the flock until it was ready for market. (Photo courtesy of Chuck Thornton.)

Producer	Herman Schlom
Director	Lesley Selander
Screenplay	Ed Earl Repp
Photography	J. Roy Hunt
Musical Director	C. Bakaleinikoff

CAST:

Tim Holt	Dave Saunders
Richard Martin	Chito
Noreen Nash	Chris Marvin
Richard Powers	Tug Caldwell
Betty Underwood	Ruby
Bill Kennedy	Jess Rawlins
Kenneth MacDonald	Robert Dawson
Holly Bane	Scott
Leo McMahon	Zeke
Richard Keane	Player
Don Haggerty	Marshal
Vince Barnett	Unbilled as telegraph operator

PLOT: Out-of-work cowhands Tim and Chito stop the lynching of Tug Caldwell (Richard Powers), the foreman of the Flying X Cattle Ranch, by Jess Rawlins (Bill Kennedy), the foreman of the Big M Sheep Ranch. Tim and Chito find themselves embroiled in a cattleman/sheepherder range war in Sundown Valley. Eventually it becomes clear that Rawlins is stirring up the feud to cover his own crooked operations.

COMMENT: Surprisingly, this is the only Tim Holt Western to deal with the traditional cattleman/sheepherder plot. Usually when you see a large herd of cattle or flock of sheep in a B-Western film, you can expect it to be stock footage that was inserted and that you will never see the actors and animals in the same shot. Not so in this film. The flock of sheep is used prominently and Tim and Chito can be seen riding around and through the flock repeatedly. The RKO Ranch was used for Western street scenes and the scenes with the sheep herd were filmed in Agura, California. (See the Richard Martin interview for his comments on this.)

RIDER FROM TUCSON **1/2

60m. June 1950

Producer	Herman Schlom
Director	Lesley Selander
Screenplay	Ed Earl Repp
Photography	Nicholas Musuraca
Musical Director	C. Bakaleinikoff

CAST:

Tim Holt	Dave Saunders
Richard Martin	Chito
Elaine Riley	Jane Whipple
Douglas Fowley	Bob Rankin
Veda Ann Borg	Gypsy
Robert Shayne	John Avery
William Phipps	Tug Bailey
Harry Tyler	Hard Rock Jones
Luther Crockett	Sheriff
Dorothy Vaughan	Mrs O'Reilly
Stuart Randall	Slim
Marshall Reed	Jackson

PLOT: Rodeo performers Tim and Chito are participating in the Tucson Rodeo when they get a telegram from their friend Tug Bailey (William Phipps) that he has struck it rich with a gold mine, is getting married, and wants Tim to be his best man at the wedding. When Tim and Chito arrive where Tug lives in Oro Grande, Colorado, they discover that the wedding has been called off and that Tug is plagued by claim jumpers who are attempting to kidnap him and then force him to tell where his rich claim is located. Tim and Chito come to the aid of Tug and soon deduce that the culprits are land developer John Avery (Robert Shayne) and his domineering wife Gypsy (Veda Ann Borg), the real brains and strength behind the skulduggery.

COMMENTS: Lovely Elaine Riley makes her only Tim Holt film appearance here. It was a fateful happenstance because she and Richard Martin fell in love and married shortly thereafter.

Some careless staging of scenes weakens the end of the film. Examples: Tim crouches behind a raised rock as several outlaws in a line ride by; then he leaps out and bulldogs one of them off his horse. The way the scene is staged, it seems obvious from the audience's vantage point that Tim would have been in plain view of those passing him as he hid at the rock. In addition, the outlaws behind the one who was bulldogged could have shot Tim a dozen times before he got to safety behind another rock. This type of careless filming was rare in a Tim Holt film and a surprising faux pas by excellent director Lesley Selander.

The RKO Ranch Western street and Lone Pine supply the locations for this film. Tug's ranch house is the Anchor Ranch hacienda and the Lone Pine cabin is utilized as the outlaw hideout.

Chito gets a thrill out of carrying leading lady Elaine Riley on his horse, much to the amusement of Tim, in this scene from *RIDER FROM TUCSON*. Notice the third stirrup that was rigged on Chito's saddle for Elaine Riley. During production this film was entitled *GUN THUNDER*.

Tim and Chito daringly attack their captors in this lobby card scene. (Photo courtesy of Johnny Efird.)

DYNAMITE PASS   ***

61m. June 1950

Producer	Herman Schlom
Director	Lew Landers
Screenplay	Norman Houston
Photography	Nicholas Musuraca
Musical Director	C. Bakaleinikoff

CAST:

Tim Holt	Ross Taylor
Richard Martin	Chito
Lynne Roberts	Mary Madden
Regis Toomey	Dan Madden
Robert Shayne	J. Wingate
Don Harvey	Missouri
Cleo Moore	Lulu
John Dehner	Anson Thurber
Don Haggerty	Sheriff
Ross Elliott	Striker
Denver Pyle	Whip

PLOT: Dan Madden (Regis Toomey) is a road builder who has been hired by the good people of Clifton, New Mexico, to build a new road to the nearby town of Mesa City because unscrupulous toll road operator Anson Thurber (John Dehner) is charging outrageous rates for its use. Later it is discovered that Thurber has an underground cohort in Clifton businessman J. Wingate (Robert Shayne), who will no longer be able to charge high rates for shipped goods

John Dehner (left) and his three gunmen stop Tim, Lynne Roberts, and Chito as they attempt to enter a toll road. The scene is from *DYNAMITE PASS* (which was entitled *DYNAMITE TRAIL* during production). That majestic mountain in the background is Lone Pine Peak.

Tim is going to get the information he wants out of Ross Elliott or else! (Photo courtesy of Ed Shetterly.)

Tim and Chito shoot it out with John Dehner and his men. (Photo courtesy of Ed Shetterly.)

when the new road is completed. Thurber and Wingate plan to do whatever is necessary to scuttle the plans for the new road and are only foiled by the intervention of Tim and Chito, who go to work for the road builder and his feisty wife Mary (Lynne Roberts).

COMMENT: Lynne Roberts has always been one of my favorite Western film heroines. Going back to the late 1930s when she was billed as Mary Hart in the early Roy Rogers films, Lynne was extremely appealing as the traditional supportive "love interest" for the young cowboy in period Westerns (such as Rogers' *ROUGH RIDERS' ROUNDUP*), and she could winningly play the coolly professional "modern" young lady who becomes embroiled in conflict with the cowboy hero (as in Gene Autry's *SIOUX CITY SUE*). Unfortunately, Ms. Roberts is not well served by this Tim Holt episode. She appears too young to be the wife of the heavy drinking and middle-aged Regis Toomey. Her character would have worked better as the daughter of Regis Toomey, and this would have allowed a love interest for Tim in the film—not that he usually relished this. As it is, the writer inserted an awkward scene where Tim innocently dances with Lynne, and the villains try to make it seem like a romance to cause jealousy in husband Toomey. In addition, the actress is costumed in very unflattering attire which makes her appear dowdy and tends to camouflage her natural attractiveness.

Lynne Roberts is about to spring Tim and Chito from Sheriff Don Haggerty's jail in this scene from *DYNAMITE PASS*. See what I mean about the unflattering costumes worn by Ms. Roberts in the film! (Photo courtesy of Chuck Thornton.)

It's always a bit scary looking into the shadows for what or who might be lurking there. (From left to right) Robert Shayne, Lynne Roberts, Regis Toomey, and Don Haggerty. (Photo courtesy of Chuck Thornton.)

Lone Pine and the RKO Ranch serve as the locations for *DYNAMITE PASS*. The Anchor Ranch hacienda in Lone Pine is used as villain John Dehner's ranch house in the film.

As a sidebar to all of the above on Lynne Roberts, the reader might be interested in a letter I received in 1991 from Major Edmund W. Liddy of Ohio, who provides follow-up information on this popular actress who dropped from sight in the 1960s:

> My mother's best friend for some 20 years was Lynne Roberts. I'm sorry to say that these latter years of her life were not her happiest, but she would often reminisce about her days in the movies. I now regret that I was too young, or otherwise not inclined, to pay attention to what I see today as fascinating anecdotes of a vanished age. Lynne died in January or February 1978 following a fall a couple of months earlier which left her in a coma. She was married three times, divorced twice—first in the late forties or fifties to the father of her son Billy, second in the early or mid fifties to Hi Samuels, an executive in the lingerie business and father of her daughter Perri, and last in the early 1970s to a former pro wrestler named Don Sebastian. She should be remembered as a fine lady—you could not ask for a better friend.

(Photo courtesy of Johnny Efird.)

BORDER TREASURE **1/2

60m. August 1950

Producer	Herman Schlom
Director	George Archainbaud
Screenplay	Norman Houston
Photography	J. Roy Hunt
Musical Director	C. Bakaleinikoff

Tim and Chito come to the assistance of the wounded Julian Rivero in this lobby card scene from *BORDER TREASURE*. (Photo courtesy of Johnny Efird.)

CAST:
Tim Holt	Ed Porter
Richard Martin	Chito
Jane Nigh	Stella
John Doucette	Bat
House Peters, Jr.	Rod
Inez Cooper	Anita Castro
Julian Rivero	Felipe
Kenneth MacDonald	Sheriff Kerrigan
Vince Barnett	Pokey
Robert Peyton	Del
Dave Leonard	Padre
Tom Monroe	Dimmick

PLOT: Wealthy Anita Castro (Inez Cooper) has organized a relief effort for Mexican earthquake victims and is taking it to Mexico via pack train—much of it gold, silver, and jewelry that will be converted to food and supplies for the sufferers. Saloon owner Bat (John Doucette) and con man Rod (House Peters, Jr.) take a gang out to steal the valuables. Cowhands Tim and Chito become embroiled in the situation when they come to the aid of Senorita Castro and her pack train of mules.

COMMENT: The characters are rather sketchily drawn by screenwriter Norman Houston in this average episode of the series. Most main characters only have first names and their existence outside of the main plot (thieves robbing the pack train of valuables) is never clearly stated. For example, we see Tim and Chito mending a fence, so we assume they must be cowhands working on a ranch, but once they become involved in the main plot their real occupation is not mentioned again until the end when Tim says vaguely that he and Chito need to get back to "chasing cows." We see John Doucette acting

John Doucette is in big trouble with the law in this scene from *BORDER TREASURE*. (From left to right) Sheriff Kenneth MacDonald, Tim, Chito, John Doucette, Deputy Vince Barnett. (Photo courtesy of Bobby Copeland.)

authoritatively in a saloon and walking into an office as if he is the boss/owner, so we assume that he is, but the plot never clearly delineates this to us. But if the viewer is looking mainly for action rather than characterization, the film delivers in spades as the outlaws try repeatedly to get the loot, eventually do get it, and then are finally foiled by Tim, Chito, and the town sheriff and his men.

Tim's stunt double (not identified) is used rather obviously in a saloon fight with John Doucette early on in the film; it's a good fight though! The locations are the RKO Ranch and Lone Pine. The Anchor Ranch hacienda is used as the hacienda of Anita Castro. At one point in the film Tim and Chito stop near Gene Autry rock in the Alabama Hills of Lone Pine as they search for the pack train. The spot is one of the most spectacular location scenes in Western films.

SONGS: "When I'm Walking Arm in Arm with Jimmy" and "Up in a Balloon, Boys" are belted out vigorously by Jane Nigh as Stella, the thrush of the Silver Dollar Casino. There is no composer credit provided for the two songs.

RIO GRANDE PATROL **1/2

60m. November 1950

Producer	Herman Schlom
Director	Lesley Selander
Screenplay	Norman Houston
Photography	J. Roy Hunt
Musical Director	C. Bakaleinikoff

CAST:

Tim Holt	Kansas
Richard Martin	Chito
Jane Nigh	Sheree Blyss
Douglas Fowley	Brag Orchid
Cleo Moore	Pepe
Rick Vallin	Captain Trevino

John Holland	Fowler
Tom Tyler	Chet Yance
Larry Johns	Dr. Reynolds
Harry Harvey	Conductor

PLOT: Tim and Chito, officers in the Border Patrol, are in Laredo, Arizona (see comment below regarding state), attempting to break up a gang of gun smugglers led by a man named Fowler (John Holland), who runs the Music Hall Saloon. The evil plan is to secret a shipment of automatic machine guns to insurrectionists below the Mexican border. Tim and Chito, working in cooperation with Mexican officials, finally bring Fowler and his fellow gunrunners—chiefly Brag Orchid (Douglas Fowley) and Chet Yance (Tom Tyler)—to justice.

COMMENT: Writer Norman Houston has some trouble keeping his story focused in this film. For example, the person we interpret to be the main villain (Fowler), takes his dance hall girls and goes across the border to Monterey about forty minutes into the film and is never seen again! The secondary characters of Brag and Chet become the main targets for Tim as they try to smuggle the guns across the border. Tim does mention that he has to get Fowler and take him back to Texas, presumably to prison, just before the fade out at the end, but by that time we have almost forgotten all about him. The leading lady role of Sheree (Jane Nigh) is sketchily drawn too, and her love interest in the Mexican officer seems an unlikely plot contrivance. Sheree's main contribution is the singing of two songs in the Music Hall Saloon. The redeeming feature in the film is the mile-a-minute action, which helps to gloss over some of the weaknesses in Houston's script.

There apparently is a caption mistake near the beginning of the film. (Do we blame this on writer Houston?) When the camera comes up from black on a long shot of the town, the caption indicates that we are in "Laredo, Arizona." It seems clear that the caption should have read "Laredo, Texas," where the Rio Grande actually flows nearby and thus logically serves as the motivation for the title of the picture.

Several locations close to Hollywood are used in the film. Iverson's Garden of the Gods is used for a

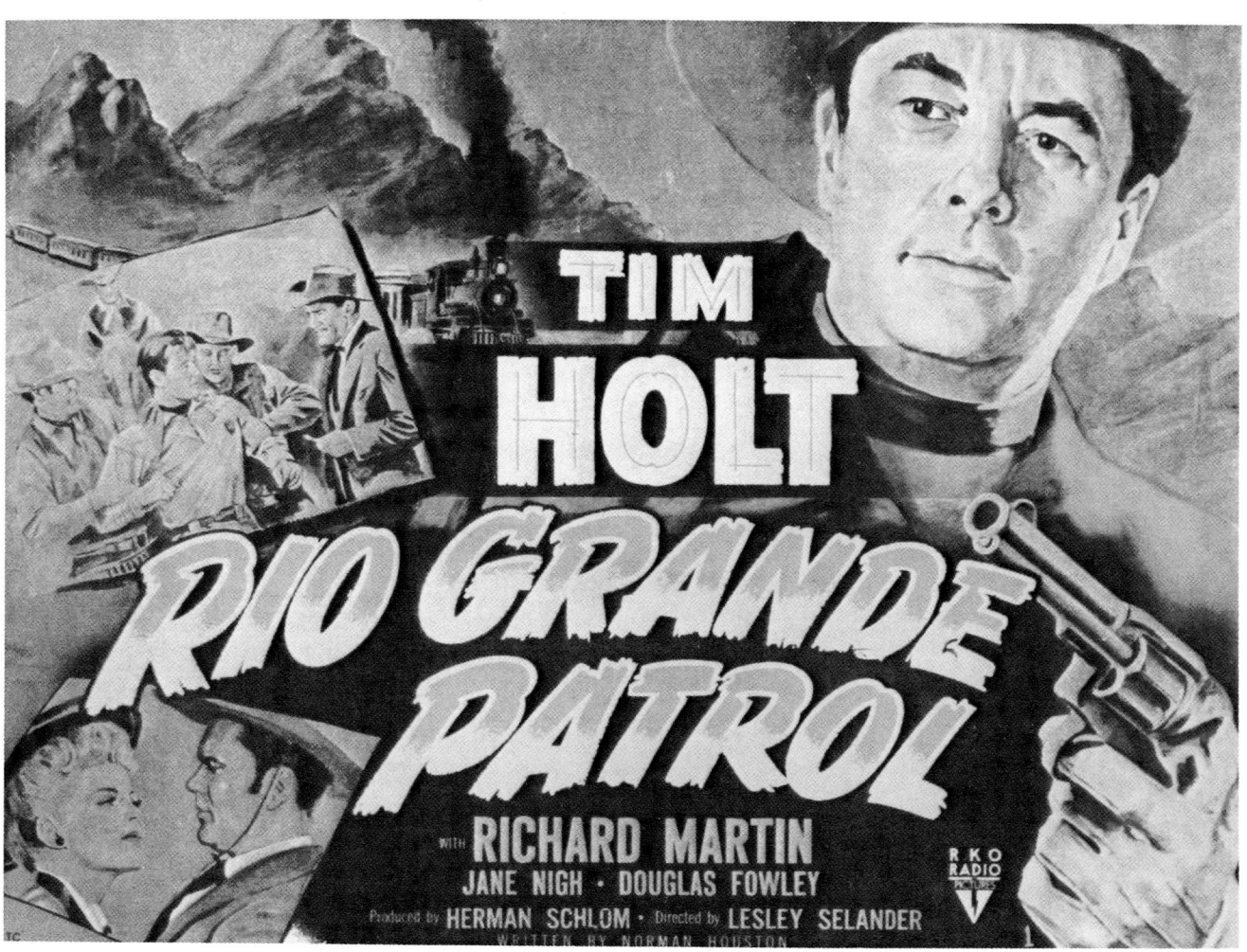

(Photo courtesy of Johnny Efird.)

Douglas Fowley (center) and his men have just been brought to justice by Tim and Rick Vallin (left). (Photo courtesy of Johnny Efird.)

shoot out scene. The sub-surface cabin at Corriganville is used for the outlaw hideout. This is the same cabin that is Grant Withers' trading post in *FORT APACHE* and the stage relay station in Randolph Scott's film, *HANGMAN'S KNOT*. Our old watering hole on the RKO Ranch Western street, the Stampede Saloon, is here named the Music Hall Saloon.

SONGS:
"You May Not Remember (All the Things I Can't Forget)" and "Camptown Races" are sung by Jane Nigh in the film.

LAW OF THE BADLANDS   **1/2

60m. February 1951

Producer	Herman Schlom
Director	Lesley Selander
Screenplay	Ed Earl Repp
Photography	George Diskant
Musical Director	C. Bakaleinikoff

CAST:
Tim Holt	Dave Saunders
Richard Martin	Chito
Joan Dixon	Velvet
Robert Livingston	Dierkin
Leonard Penn	Cash Carlton
Harry Woods	Bert Conroy
Larry Johns	Lafe Simms
Robert Bray	Benson
Kenneth MacDonald	Captain McVey
John Cliff	Madigan

PLOT: In this episode Tim and Chito are undercover Texas Rangers posing as outlaws (The Tioga Kid and Pancho Chompez) to nab some clever counterfeiters in the Texas badlands. They discover that saloon owner Cash Carlton (Leonard Penn) and his gang are behind the counterfeiting. Before they have all of the evidence they need to make an arrest, an old girlfriend of Chito's arrives (with some other new dancers at Cash's saloon) and unwittingly reveals to

Leading lady Joan Dixon comes between an angry Chito and bad guys Leonard Penn (left center) and Robert Livingston (left). (Photo courtesy of Bobby Copeland.)

Tim and Chito finally round up the clever counterfeiters (Robert Livingston and Leonard Penn) in this lobby card scene from *LAW OF THE BADLANDS*. (Photo courtesy of Ed Shetterly.)

Texas Rangers Tim and Chito go underground as outlaws in *LAW OF THE BADLANDS*. A disturbance in the distance has just distracted them as they were nailing up posters advertising their outlaw ways as the Tioga Kid and Pancho Chompez. (Photo courtesy of Chuck Thornton.)

Tim confides with lovely Joan Dixon in this lobby card scene from *LAW OF THE BADLANDS*. (Photo courtesy of Johnny Efird.)

Cash that Chito is a Texas Ranger—thus blowing their cover! The finale finds Tim and Chito saved through the delivery of a pigeon-carried message to the Texas Ranger station and the counterfeiters captured.

COMMENT: The overall plot is quite actionful and is developed well right up to the finale, but then the time line of events gets totally bollixed. This is the way it happens: Tim and Chito are trapped in a building with the outlaws across the street firing at them. A carrier pigeon is sent to the Texas Ranger headquarters at the somewhat distant town of Willcox. The pigeon gets to the Rangers with the message, the Rangers travel all the way to Badlands before the gunfight is over, and they save our trapped heroes. These concluding scenes are sharply edited to suggest that all of this action takes place in just a few minutes, though it is pretty obvious that in reality it would have taken at least a day—and most likely longer.

It has been reported that the cost of *LAW OF THE BADLANDS* was the lowest for a Tim Holt feature since he returned from World War II service—$98,000. The really shocking information is that it lost $20,000 at the box office, a testament to the severe encroachments of television on the movie industry by 1951.

Locations for the film are the RKO Ranch Western street and the Russell Ranch in Agura, California, which supplied the two-story ranch house, bunk house, and large barn. According to my best sources, the ranch house was only a movie set even though it looks very real. The whole area around Agura has been highly developed during the forty-some years since this film was made, and it is believed that the ranch buildings no longer exist. The scouting of this location continues even as I write this.

Tim would like to clean up on cattle rustler Mauritz Hugo (left center) as Mexican captain George Lewis gets an arm hold on him in this scene from *SADDLE LEGION*. **(Photo courtesy of Chuck Thornton.)**

SADDLE LEGION   ***1/2

61m. April 1951

Producer	Herman Schlom
Director	Lesley Selander
Screenplay	Ed Earl Repp
Photography	J. Roy Hunt
Musical Director	C. Bakaleinikoff

CAST:

Tim Holt	Dave Saunders
Richard Martin	Chito
Dorothy Malone	Doctor Ann Rawlins
Robert Livingston	Reagan
Mauritz Hugo	Ace Kelso
James Rush	Gabe
Movita Casteneda	Mercedes
Cliff Clark	Fred Warren
Stanley Andrews	John Layton
George Lewis	Capitan
Dick Foote	Player
Bob Wilke	Hooker
Reed Howes	Unbilled

PLOT: Saloon owner Ace Kelso (Maurice Hugo) devises a clever scheme to rustle cattle and move them below the border to his operation in San Lenore, Mexico. He and his gang kill the regional cattle inspector (who is not known by ranchers in the district) and replace him with their own man (Robert Livingston). Then a member of the gang makes a few decoy cattle appear diseased with blackleg; the phony inspector condemns the whole herd and orders it moved away by his men to be destroyed. The rustlers then sneak the herd across the border into Mexico and sell it. Tim and Chito, newly hired hands on Fred Warren's (Cliff Clark) ranch, become suspicious and ultimately discover the clever ruse and, with the assistance of the other ranchers in the area, bring the rustlers to justice.

COMMENT: *SADDLE LEGION* is a strong entry in the Holt series. The scripting is taut and populated with well-developed characters, and the action is plentiful. Young Dorothy Malone (who, of course, would go on to bigger films) makes a nice impression as the female "sawbones" who supports Tim in his suspicions regarding the validity of the cattle inspector's diagnosis. The final shoot out—Tim trapped in a box canyon as the outlaw gang fires at him from the ridge—is nicely staged by director Lesley Selander. The locations include the RKO Ranch and the Jack Garner Ranch in Idyllwild, California. Notice that the same ranch house that Marjorie Lord owned in MASKED RAIDERS (1949) is also used in this film.

Tim shoots it out with the gang that murdered his ranch boss. The sycamore tree that Tim is using for a shield is a pretty good clue that we are at the Walker Ranch film location—and we are. (Photo courtesy of Ed Shetterly.)

(Photo courtesy of Ed Shetterly.)

Tim locates Robert Clarke, long-lost brother of his fiancee, Joan Dixon, through their duplicate medallions. The scene (which does not actually appear in the film) is from PISTOL HARVEST (1951). (Photo courtesy of Robert Clarke.)

PISTOL HARVEST   **1/2

60m. July 1951

Producer	Herman Schlom
Director	Lesley Selander
Screenplay	Norman Houston
Photography	J. Roy Hunt
Musical Director	C. Bakaleinikoff

CAST:

Tim Holt	Tim Holt
Richard Martin	Chito
Joan Dixon	Felice
Robert Clarke	Jack Green
Mauritz Hugo	Elias Norton
Robert Wilke	Andy Baylor
William Griffith	Prouty
Guy Edward Hearn	Terry Moran
Harper Carter	Johnny
Joan Freeman	Felice as a girl
Herrick Herrick	Captain Rand

PLOT: Cowhand Tim Holt is in love with Felice (Joan Dixon), the boss's daughter, and plans to

Tim had to contend with the nefarious activities of slick villain Mauritz Hugo in four films during 1951 and 1952. In this scene from *PISTOL HARVEST*, Tim is trying to restrain himself from separating Hugo's head from his shoulders. (Photo courtesy of Bobby Copeland.)

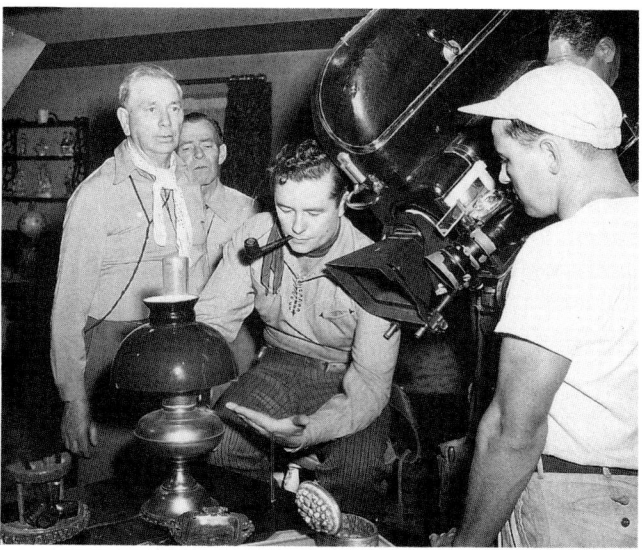

Cameraman J. Roy Hunt lines up an insert shot of Tim Holt holding a medallion, an important clue in the plot of *PISTOL HARVEST*.

Tim is about to capture the fleeing crook, Mauritz Hugo, in this windup scene from *PISTOL HARVEST*.

marry her. Her father, Terry Moran (Guy Edward Hearn), is killed and robbed by Elias Norton (Mauritze Hugo), a local shipping magnate, because he needs money for a big deal, and he has recently paid Moran a sizable amount for a herd of cattle. Tim seeks to discover the killer of his fiancee's father (with Chito's help) and gradually narrows in on Norton. The climax features a hellbent-for-leather chase—Tim on Lightning; Norton in a buckboard—that culminates in a fistfight on the ground after Tim has stopped the buckboard.

COMMENT: Although Tim is supposed to be in love with leading lady Joan Dixon, don't expect any smooching or lovey-dovey stuff. Chito tries to get them to kiss at one point but to no avail; Tim remains the taciturn, "no nonsense" cowboy we have come to know.

Locations used include the RKO Ranch, the

Walker Ranch, the Andy Jauregui Ranch, and Iverson's Ranch. The final pursuit of Norton was filmed on the Iverson Ranch chase road. The Jauregui Ranch was utilized as Terry Moran's ranch in the film. The budget for this picture was a low (by RKO B-Western standards) $93,000, but the skimping only shows in the close-to-Hollywood locations. For the balance of the series there would be no more journeys to far-off locations for filming.

Tim is having a little altercation with Marshall Reed as Joan Dixon and Richard "Chito" Martin look on in this lobby card scene from *GUNPLAY*. (Photo courtesy of Ed Shetterly.)

GUNPLAY **1/2

60m. August 1951

Producer	Herman Schlom
Director	Lesley Selander
Screenplay	Ed Earl Repp
Photography	J. Roy Hunt
Musical Director	C. Bakaleinikoff

CAST:

Tim Holt	Tim Holt
Richard Martin	Chito
Joan Dixon	Terry Blake
Harper Carter	Chip Martin
Mauritz Hugo	Curt Landry
Robert Bice	Sam Martin
Marshall Reed	Dobbs
Jack Hill	Sheriff
Robert Wilke	Winslow
Leo McMahon	Zeke

PLOT: Young Chip Martin's (Harper Carter) father (Robert Bice) has been hanged, and ranch hands Tim and Chito, along with their boss, Terry Blake (Joan Dixon), vow to find the murderer. In town Tim learns that wealthy businessman Curt Landry (Mauritz Hugo) claims to have been robbed by Chip's father. He states that it was his men (with the sanction of the weak town sheriff) who carried out the quick "justice" by hanging Martin and that it was not murder. Tim and his friends are still suspicious of Landry, especially when he moves to adopt the boy, now an orphan. Presently, Tim learns that Landry had snatched a fortune from Chip's dad years before under another name, and when Martin returned to claim the wealth, Landry had had him killed.

COMMENT: This is only an average effort in the series, and part of the problem lies in the somewhat overly involved and weakly motivated plot. There seem to be unnecessary plot situations that detract from the main story line (examples: a lengthy scene at the beginning where Tim and Chito are hired by Terry Blake; later, Landry being blackmailed by one of his own men). Regarding motivational problems, why does Landry adopt the boy? No reason is ever mentioned; we just find out that he's doing it. At the end of the film, after Landry has revealed his hand during a stage trip with Terry Blake, Tim captures him and tells Blake to continue her trip, that she shouldn't have any more interference now. Her whole reason for going on the trip was to get evidence on Landry, something that has considerably less importance now that he is caught. That she would continue on her journey seems unlikely. Despite my carping on plot weaknesses, the film has a nice pace and the action is well handled by director Lesley Selander—except for the wrap-up capture of Landry on the stage. For the climactic moment of the film, it was too easy and not very suspenseful. See what you think.

Iverson's Ranch is used for some of the chase scenes, and Joan Dixon's ranch in the film is in reality the Andy Jauregui Ranch.

Another indication of the encroachments of television during this time in the early 1950s is that *GUNPLAY* reportedly only grossed $145,000 in total film rentals. The handwriting was on the wall regarding the future of B Westerns.

HOT LEAD ***

60m. October 1951

Producer	Herman Schlom
Director	Stuart Gilmore
Screenplay	William Lively
Photography	Nicholas Musuraca
Musical Director	C. Bakaleinikoff

CAST:

Tim Holt	Tim Holt
Richard Martin	Chito
Joan Dixon	Gail Martin
Ross Elliott	Dave Collins
John Dehner	Turk Thorn
Robert Wilke	Stoney
Paul Marion	Dakota
Lee MacGregor	Bob Jackson
Kenneth MacDonald	Sheriff Lacy
Jack O'Shea	Unbilled extra in saloon
Stanley Andrews	Unbilled warden

PLOT: Slick train robber Turk Thorn (John Dehner) shrewdly gets convict/telegrapher Dave Collins (Ross

Chito is up to his usual romantic hijinks with an unidentified saloon/dance hall girl as Tim seeks his help to round up a clever train robber. The scene is from *HOT LEAD*. (Photo courtesy of Johnny Efird.)

Elliott) released from prison so that he can work in the telegraph office in Trail Head to learn of future gold shipments that he and his gang can steal. Tim becomes involved when his friend Bob Jackson (Lee MacGregor) is killed trying to stop a train robbery. Tim gets to know Dave and learns that he is an ex-con and wants to go straight. Dave tells Tim of Turk's scheme and promises to help catch the train robber and his gang.

COMMENT: Tim sports an uncharacteristically flashy Indian-design jacket in the first scene of the movie, but after that it vanishes. Surprisingly, the town signs from *GUNPLAY*, the previous film, are still advertising the establishments run by jailed villain Curt Landry. The RKO art department was a little lax in its work, it would seem. Another unusual occurrence for an RKO feature: cattle stampede footage from *SADDLE LEGION* is used intact in this film (including Tim and Chito). And on a personal note regarding Tim, he shows signs of the impending weight problem that would remain with him to some extent for the rest of his life.

Close-in Hollywood locations are again utilized. Iverson's Ranch and the Walker Ranch are used for most of the outdoor and chase scenes. The Andy Jauregui Ranch is once again owned by Joan Dixon, and it's called the Circle Bar Ranch.

OVERLAND TELEGRAPH ***

60m. December 1951

Producer	Herman Schlom
Director	Lesley Selander
Screenplay	Adele Buffington
Photography	J. Roy Hunt
Musical Director	C. Bakaleinikoff

CAST:

Tim Holt	Tim Holt
Richard Martin	Chito
Gail Davis	Terry Muldoon
Hugh Beaumont	Brad Roberts
Mari Blanchard	Stella Scott

(Photo courtesy of Chuck Thornton.)

George Nader	Paul Manning
Robert Wilke	Belue
Cliff Clark	Terrence Muldoon
Russell Hicks	Colonel Marvin
Robert Bray	Steve
Fred Graham	Joe
Jack O'Shea	Unbilled

PLOT: The telegraph is being installed outside Mesa City and the result is that Paul Manning's (George Nader) supply contract with the army is to be cancelled because the post is closing and going back to its headquarters upon the opening of the telegraph. Paul goes into cahoots with saloon owner Brad Roberts (Hugh Beaumont) to blow up the telegraph supply camp so that the army will stay. Little does Paul realize that Roberts is double-crossing him so that he will go to jail. It seems that Roberts is in love with Paul's girl Stella (Mari Blanchard). With Paul out of the way, Roberts can make his romantic move on Stella. Tim and Chito are working as trouble shooters for the telegraph installer and so become involved in solving the sabotage.

COMMENT: Tim is not riding Lightning in this film. His mount is a sorrel with a blaze face and four white socks. The horse looks very much like Gene Autry's Champion, especially with the similar silver tack and ringed saddle blanket. The film is helped by strong performances by all except callow George Nader, who is exceedingly whiny. Gail Davis (as the feisty daughter of the telegraph installer) is particularly effective, although she does not get a great deal of time on screen. A few years later she used some of the spunkiness in the *Annie Oakley* television series. Hugh Beaumont, known primarily as the father on TV's *Leave It to Beaver,* is surprisingly menacing and ruthless as the double-dealing saloon owner.

Location scenes were shot at Iverson's Ranch (including the familiar line shack), the Walker Ranch, and the Andy Jauregui Ranch—this time used as Hugh Beaumont's ranch.

TRAIL GUIDE **1/2

60m. February 1952

Producer	Herman Schlom
Director	Lesley Selander
Screenplay	Arthur E. Orloff
	(from a story by William Lively)
Photography	Nicholas Musuraca
Musical Director	C. Bakaleinikoff

Tim serves up "the old one-two" to John Pickard in this saloon fight from *TRAIL GUIDE*. (Photo courtesy of Ed Shetterly.)

I'll bet John Pickard won't try to mess with Tim again! (Photo courtesy of Ed Shetterly.)

CAST:

Tim Holt	Tim Holt
Richard Martin	Chito
Linda Douglas	Peg Masters
Frank Wilcox	Regan
Robert Sherwood	Kenny Masters
John Pickard	Dawson
Kenneth MacDonald	Wheeler
Wendy Waldron	Player
Patricia Wright	Player
Tom London	Old Man
John Merton	Dale

PLOT: Tim and Chito guide a wagon train to Silver Springs, where the homesteaders get a cold welcome from the area ranchers. When the wagon master is shot and the homestead claims and money are sto-

Tim and Chito give aid to wagon master Kenneth MacDonald after he has been shot and robbed of the homesteaders' money and claims. The scene is from *TRAIL GUIDE*.

Tim chats with leading lady Linda Douglas in one of the quieter scenes from *TRAIL GUIDE*.

Fleeing Robert Sherwood is about to confess his crooked activities to Tim, but it's too late. He's about to be murdered by Frank Wilcox and his men. The scene is from *TRAIL GUIDE*. (Photo courtesy of Chuck Thornton.)

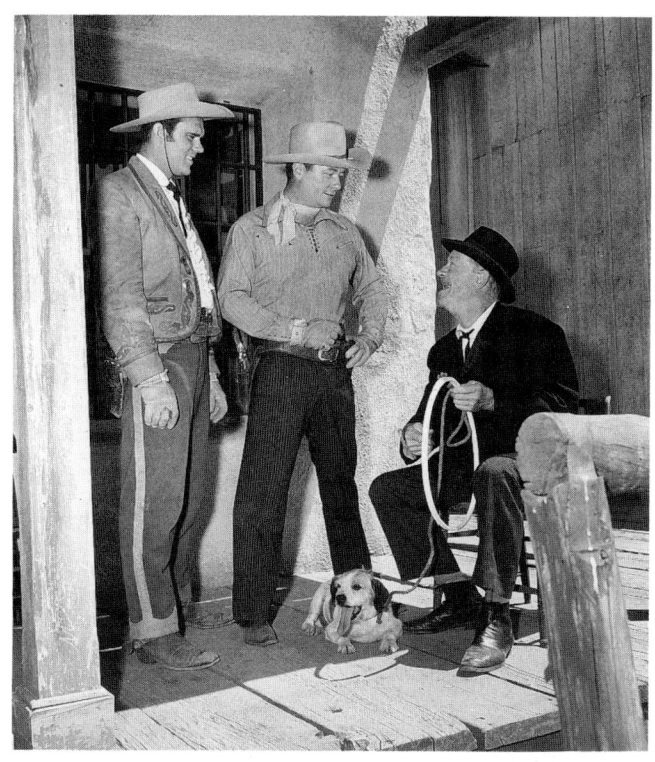

Toothless old Tom London tells Tim and Chito about the wondrous abilities of his "trained show dog, Genevieve" in this humorous scene from *TRAIL GUIDE*.

len, Tim and Chito remain on the job to catch the perpetrators. It soon becomes apparent that young Kenny Masters (Robert Sherwood) is behind the skulduggery because there is valuable oil on the land, and he wants to get control of it. Kenny seeks the assistance of saloon keeper Regan (Frank Wilcox) and his men to pull off the nefarious activities, but soon Kenny loses control of the scheme to the more powerful Regan. When Kenny tries to flee the territory, Regan and his men kill him. Tim finally sorts out the situation and brings Regan and his men to justice.

COMMENT: The opening shots of a wagon train are stock footage from John Ford's 1950 film

WAGONMASTER. Tim continues to ride the sorrel horse in this film, and Chito is riding a good-looking Appaloosa for the first time. Toothless old Tom London has a cute reoccurring bit with his "trained show dog, Genevieve." He keeps telling Tim that the dog has great talent, but the mutt never performs a lick throughout the entire film. The Andy Jauregui Ranch serves as the Rocking M Ranch owned by leading lady Linda Douglas in this picture. Iverson's

Ranch is also used for many of the location scenes. As always, the RKO Ranch is used for the Western street scenes.

ROAD AGENT **1/2

61m. March 1952

Producer	Herman Schlom
Director	Lesley Selander
Screenplay	Norman Houston
Photography	J. Roy Hunt
Musical Director	C. Bakaleinikoff

CAST:

Tim Holt	Tim Holt
Richard Martin	Chito
Noreen Nash	Clara Drew

Tim, in his *ROAD AGENT* cape and mask, menaces nervous bad guy Robert Wilke. (Photo courtesy of Chuck Thornton.)

Tim is trying to convince sheriff Guy Edward Hearn and villain Mauritz Hugo that he and Chito have not left their room because Chito has come down with something. Now, tell me, would you believe that those splotches on Chito's face are caused by measles—or smallpox? Supposedly, the sheriff and Hugo believe it! The scene is from *ROAD AGENT*.

Tim and Chito let Dorothy Patrick in on the fact that they are the ROAD AGENTs robbing from the villainous Mauritz Hugo and giving money to the needy ranchers.

Mauritz Hugo	Milo Brand
Dorothy Patrick	Sally Clayton
Bob Wilke	Slab Babcock
Tom Tyler	Larkin
Guy Edward Hearn	Sheriff
William Tannen	Bill Collins
Sam Flint	George Drew
Forbes Murray	Adams
Stanley Blystone	Barton

PLOT: When Tim and Chito are overcharged by Milo Brand's (Mauritz Hugo) men at a toll road, they become angry and force, at gunpoint, henchman Slab Babcock (Bob Wilke) to give them a rebate. Later they learn that area ranchers are being bankrupted by the exorbitant toll charges imposed by Brand to move their cattle to market. Tim and Chito decide to pose as masked Robin Hood-type bandits who rob from the unjust Brand and give to the needy ranchers who have been cheated.

COMMENT: The plot is surprising and not a little bizarre. No matter how you (or the scriptwriter) try to justify it, Tim and Chito *steal* the money that they give to the needy ranchers; they are illegal road agents The sheriff is exceedingly (and unrealistically) lenient when they tell him about their activities at the end of the film. And speaking of unrealistic scenes, the ruse of dabbing iodine on Chito's face to convince the sheriff that he has measles (or even small pox, as the villain suggests), is pretty farfetched even for the smallest smallfry in the audience to believe. Some stock footage from a previous Holt film is utilized and doesn't always match the current film—the tack on Lightning, for example, is different. These elements hurt an otherwise well-done B Western.

Tim is riding a palomino again in this film, but it is not Lightning; the markings do not match. Chito continues to ride the good-looking Appaloosa. And big surprise!! The usually taciturn Tim, much to Chito's amazement (and with very little motivation provided by the plot), gives leading lady Noreen Nash a big, no fooling-type kiss at the fadeout!

Many familiar locations are again used in the making of the film. The Andy Jauregui Ranch is Noreen Nash's ranch. The Walker Ranch cabin is the outlaws' hideout, and the Walker chase roads are used frequently. Iverson's chase roads are also utilized extensively throughout the film. The RKO Ranch is used for the town of Trail City, Arizona.

TARGET **1/2

60m. April 1952

Producer	Herman Schlom
Director	Stuart Gilmore
Screenplay	Norman Houston
Photography	J. Roy Hunt
Musical Director	C. Bakaleinikoff

CAST:
Tim Holt	Tim Holt
Richard Martin	Chito
Linda Douglas	Terry Moran
Walter Reed	Conroy
Harry Harvey	Carson
John Hamilton	Bailey
Lane Bradford	Garrett
Riley Hill	Foster
Mike Ragan	Higgins

PLOT: A man named Conroy (Walter Reed) is buying land for the incoming Texas and Gulf Railroad and is not making many friends in the process. Ranchers who refuse to sell at Conroy's low prices are "bullied, terrorized, and robbed," according to businessman Carson (Harry Harvey), the head of the town council in Pecos. Conroy's plan, it turns out, is to get the land at rock-bottom prices through coercion, then deliver the deeds to the railroad officials, claim the price was much higher, and pocket the difference. Because there's no law officer in Pecos, the town council (at Tim's urging) sends for famed marshal Terry Moran to clean up the situation—but there is a slip-up. The Terry Moran who arrives is the feisty daughter (Linda Douglas) of the famous lawman, and she wants to fill in for her father until he recovers from a gunshot wound he recently received. Despite the protests of the town council and the hoots of the outlaws about a "petticoat marshal," Terry insists that she be given a chance, and Tim and Chito agree to assist her as deputies in her efforts to clear up the crooked activities of Conroy.

COMMENT: The interesting plot device of the lady marshal never gets properly developed in TARGET. Despite Terry Moran's protestations that she wants a chance to prove herself as a competent law man (or law person), the script allows her to be the typical Western heroine who must be saved by the cowboy hero.

Tim and Chito are riding very nondescript horses in this film—certainly not "star" horses, and Tim looks and sounds as if he is fighting a cold during much of the film; he's also the most overweight we have seen him.

The locations include Iverson's; the Russell Ranch in Agura, California (with the two-story house, bunk house, and large barn), which John Hamilton supposedly owns; and the RKO Ranch Western street. The Stampede Saloon of previous Holt episodes is converted into a land office via use of large banners that only partially cover the saloon signs.

DESERT PASSAGE ***

60m. May 1952

Producer	Herman Schlom
Director	Lesley Selander
Screenplay	Norman Houston
Photography	J. Roy Hunt
Musical Director	C. Bakaleinikoff

CAST:
Tim Holt	Tim Holt
Richard Martin	Chito
Joan Dixon	Emily Brice
Walter Reed	John Carver
Dorothy Patrick	Roxie Von Zell
John Dehner	Bronson
Clayton Moore	Dave Warrick

Leading lady Linda Douglas wants to be taken seriously as the new marshal, but even with Tim and Chito's help, the townspeople do not cotton to this petticoat lawperson. (Photo courtesy of Bobby Copeland.)

Lane Bradford	Langdon
Michael Mark	Burley
Denver Pyle	Allen

PLOT: Tim and Chito are operators of a failing stage line near the Mexican border. Prison parolee and former bank clerk John Carver (Walter Reed) returns to the town of Lavic to recover $100,000 he embezzled and hid some years before. After he secures the loot, Carver hires Tim and Chito to take him to Mexico. At first they defend Carver when the stage is attacked; they don't realize the attackers are old pals of Carver who want a split of the money. Eventually, Tim and Chito get the real lowdown on Carver, confiscate the money, and return it to Emily Brice (Joan Dixon), the daughter of the bank president who was robbed by Carver years before.

COMMENT: In a fairly obvious attempt to save money, much of this final episode is spent indoors, there is a lot more talk and a lot less action, and the cast list is small. Clayton Moore, who had just left *The Lone Ranger* TV series in a dispute over money, has a small part as a nicely-dressed black hat. Popular radio actor John Dehner (he was practically a regular on the radio *Gunsmoke* and would become Paladin on radio's *Have Gun, Will Travel* in 1958) is appropriately shifty and wiley as the bank robber's lawyer. Locations include the RKO Ranch, the Walker Ranch, Iverson's Ranch, and the Russell Ranch—which again supplied the two-story ranch house and barn. *DESERT PASSAGE* is a very adequate (if not outstanding) windup to the overall excellent Tim Holt Western series.

* * *

(Photo courtesy of Chuck Thornton.)

Tim's first appearance upon returning from military service during World War II was as Virgil Earp in John Ford's memorable Western, *MY DARLING CLEMENTINE*. Aside from his post-war B-Western series, Tim appeared in six feature films between 1946 and 1971.

Chapter 6
Just a Sideline— The Other Films (1946-1971)

In addition to and beyond his post-war B-Western series for RKO, Tim was involved in the production of six movies from 1946 until 1971. They range from A-budget classics to Z-grade embarrassments. It is a bit dismaying (within the framework of one short chapter) to start with an examination of such top-of-the-line productions as *MY DARLING CLEMENTINE* and *THE TREASURE OF THE SIERRA MADRE* and then end with such dismal offerings as *THE YESTERDAY MACHINE* and *THIS STUFF'LL KILL YA!* (In between there are the middling productions of *HIS KIND OF WOMAN* (in which Tim plays in support of Robert Mitchum) and the science fiction thriller, *THE MONSTER THAT CHALLENGED THE WORLD*.)

For the uninitiated Tim Holt fan it might appear that Tim hit the professional skids after he left Hollywood in 1952 and was forced, years later, to end his film career in support of amateurs in embarrassingly inept productions that were financed with little more than pocket change. But what *appears* to be so is not always the reality of a situation. One has to examine very carefully the Tim Holt persona to fully understand his participation in those last two films, and that's really the main focus of this introduction to Chapter 6.

Tim appears to have been that most rare of successful actors—the complete professional who one day decides to retire from his chosen field and does so without a look back and without a concern for where the recorders of film history will place him. He enjoyed his film career while it lasted, but then it was time to turn to other things that interested him. (Randolph Scott was another of those rare persons who left the film business and never looked back and almost never talked about his previous career as an actor.) The record shows that Tim received film offers many times after he left Hollywood and moved to Oklahoma to his new life with Berdee and the three children. If he had felt the urge or had badly needed the money, he could have returned and found film work. All the evidence indicates that he really didn't want to do that. The film business had changed, he had changed, and he really didn't want to be a part of it any more.

Tim was the least self-conscious and the least pretentious of people; therefore, he saw participating in *THE YESTERDAY MACHINE* and *THIS STUFF'LL KILL YA!* as favors for friends that had no bearing on his film career because he perceived it as already over. In his eyes he wasn't a film actor any more; he was just helping out friends; it was something to do for kicks for a couple of days; it was nothing to be taken seriously, and, besides, the films obviously were not going to get much distribution. He undoubtedly felt they would be seen by a small audience for a few weeks and then would be forever gone from sight—the way most independently produced, low-budget films of that era disappeared and were soon pretty much forgotten.

On that point, of course, Tim was a bit shortsighted. He (and most of us) did not foresee the cable TV and home video revolution that was just a few years away—a revolution that would make virtually everything that had ever been put on film available to the general public. Tim could never have guessed that all of his old films would have a renewed life on cable TV channels such as American Movie Classics and Ted Turner's TNT. He could not foresee that his films would be available for rental or purchase at local video stores—or that these new outlets would spur renewed interest in "forgotten" stars of the past (such as Tim Holt) and make a film-buff public curious about these actors of an earlier time

If Tim could have known about the future influence of cable TV and home video, he very possibly might not have participated in those last two films. But what the heck, forget them! We are very fortunate; we have all of Tim's excellent B Westerns available for viewing. Then there are such varied classics as *STAGECOACH, THE MAGNIFICENT AMERSONS, MY DARLING CLEMENTINE,* and *THE TREASURE OF THE SIERRA MADRE* to savor at our leisure. Yes, there is an abundance of Tim Holt treasures available to us, so sit back and enjoy!

MY DARLING CLEMENTINE ****

97m. November 1946 Twentieth Century-Fox

Producer .... Samuel G. Engel
Director .... John Ford
Screenplay .. Samuel G. Engel and Winston Miller
(Based on a story by Sam Hellman from the novel *Wyatt Earp, Frontier Marshal* by Stuart N. Lake)
Photography .... Joseph P. MacDonald
Musical Director .... Alfred Newman

CAST:
Henry Fonda	Wyatt Earp
Linda Darnell	Chihuahua
Victor Mature	Doc Holliday
Walter Brennan	Old Man Clanton
Tim Holt	Virgil Earp
Cathy Downs	Clementine
Ward Bond	Morgan Earp
Alan Mowbray	Granville Thorndyke
John Ireland	Billy Clanton
Roy Roberts	Mayor
Jane Darwell	Kate
Grant Withers	Ike Clanton
J. Farrell MacDonald	Mac the Bartender
Russell Simpson	John Simpson
Don Garner	James Earp
Francis Ford	Town Drunk
Ben Hall	Barber
Arthur Walsh	Hotel Clerk
Louis Mercier	Francois
Mickey Simpson	Sam Clanton
Fred Libby	Phin Clanton
William B. Davidson	Owner of Oriental Saloon
Earle Foxe	Gambler
Aleth "Speed" Hansen	Guitar Player/Townsman
Dan Borzage	Accordion Player/Townsman
Charles Anderson	Townsman
Duke Lee	Townsman
Don Barclay	Opera House Owner
Margaret Martin	Townswoman
Mae Marsh	Townswoman
Frances Rey	Stagecoach Driver
Robert Adler	Stagecoach Driver
Jack Pennick	Stagecoach Driver
Frank Conlan	Piano Player
Charles Stevens	Indian Charlie
Harry Woods	Marshal

PLOT: On their way from Texas with a herd of cattle, Wyatt Earp (Henry Fonda) and his three brothers (Holt, Bond, and Garner) pause near the wide-open town of Tombstone to get a haircut and a drink, leaving youngest brother James to guard the cattle. During their sojourn in town—where Wyatt tames a drunken Indian for the town marshal—old Man Clanton (Walter Brennan) and his boys rustle their cattle and murder James. Wyatt takes over as town marshal in order to have the legal power to bring the rustlers to justice. During the time it takes to identify the Clantons as the culprits, Wyatt develops an uneasy relationship with saloon owner Doc Holliday (Victor Mature) and meets Doc's former nurse/lady friend (Cathy Downs) who arrives from back East, Miss Clementine Carter. Eventually, Wyatt pins the rustling on the Clantons, but it costs the life of Virgil (Tim) who is shot in the back by old man Clanton. This sets the stage for the climactic shoot out at the OK Corral where the Clantons are killed by the two remaining Earp boys and Doc Holliday, who has joined them. Holliday also loses his life in the gunfight. The fade-out scene finds Wyatt saying a reluctant good-bye to the new schoolmarm, Clementine, and promising to return after he has taken his brothers' bodies back home. "Ma'am, I sure like that name, Clementine," he says as he spurs his horse and rides off down the long trail back home.

COMMENT: Just one of the greatest Westerns of all time, *MY DARLING CLEMENTINE* (as mentioned in the previous chapter) marked Tim's return to films after serving in the Air Corps during World War II. Although his role as Virgil Earp was not very large, Tim handled the part with quiet professionalism and garnered good reviews. Tim looked upon his two films with John Ford as highlights of his career even though neither role was especially showy. It was just the fun of working with the Old Man, cantankerous as he could be, that delighted Tim.

THE TREASURE OF THE SIERRA MADRE ****

126m. January 1948 Warner Brothers

Producer .... Henry Blanke
Director .... John Huston
Screenplay .... John Huston
(Based on the novel by B. Traven)
Photography .... Ted McCord
Musical Director .... Max Steiner

CAST:
Humphrey Bogart	Fred C. Dobbs
Walter Huston	Howard
Tim Holt	Curtin
Bruce Bennett	Cody
Barton MacLane	McCormick
Alfonso Bedoya	Gold Hat

In *THE TREASURE OF THE SIERRA MADRE* Humphrey Bogart and Tim play a couple of down-on-their-luck drifters who meet up in Tampico, Mexico, and have a drink together. From this point on their lives are inextricably entwined. The bartender is Harry Vejar.

In a Tampico flophouse Walter Huston spins yarns about gold prospecting and proclaims that greed is usually the undoing of prospectors—especially when they work in partnerships. Bogart avers, "It wouldn't happen to me; all I'd want is my fair share."

A. Soto Rangel	Presidente
Manuel Donde	El Jefe
Jose Torvay	Pablo
Margarito Luna	Pancho
Jacqueline Dalya	Flashy Girl
Bobby Blake	Mexican Boy
Spencer Chan	Proprietor
Julian Rivero	Barber
John Huston	White Suit
Harry Vejar	Bartender
Pat Flaherty	Customer
Clifton Young	Flophouse Man
Ralph Dunn	Flophouse Man
Jack Holt	Flophouse Man

During a break in the filming of *THE TREASURE OF THE SIERRA MADRE*, the leading cast members chat with director John Huston. (From left to right) Humphrey Bogart, Walter Huston, Bruce Bennett, Tim Holt, and John Huston. Notice paintbrush strokes on Bogart's shirt and the strange appearance of his hands and arms. I'm not even sure that Bogey was in the original picture (or all of the others, for that matter). (Photo courtesy of Chuck Thornton.)

PLOT: Three men (Bogart, Holt, and Huston) accidentally meet in Tampico, Mexico, and form an uneasy alliance to go prospecting for gold in the rugged Sierra Mountains. Eventually they actually find gold and begin to work the mine, each man separating his share each day. Soon mistrust and greed begin to surface, especially on the part of Fred C. Dobbs (Bogart), who gradually becomes paranoid, irrational, and, finally, homicidal—attempting to kill Curtin (Tim) when Howard (Huston) is away. In the conclusion Dobbs, now in possession of all the gold, is killed by a gang of Mexican outlaws who take his burros and animal hides, while discarding on the ground the bags of (they think) worthless dust and nuggets. Howard and Curtin, in hot pursuit of Dobbs, encounter a dust storm which scatters their gold dust and nuggets to the four winds. Howard breaks into uncontrollable laughter and says, "Laugh, Curtin, old boy! It's a great joke played on us by the Lord or fate or by nature...whichever you prefer, but whoever or whatever played it, certainly has a sense of humor! The gold has gone back to where we got it! Laugh, my boy, laugh! It's worth ten months of labor and suffering...this joke is!"

COMMENT: Originally, Ronald Reagan was announced to play the Curtin role, but he had a last-minute change of mind, and Tim was selected for the part—and a great part it was. Tim and his father Jack got to work together briefly in the film. During the flophouse scene early in the picture, Jack can be spotted as one of the flophouse men. The cameo came about when Jack visited the set to see his son and was invited to take part in the scene just for kicks. Almost the entire film was shot in the rugged country in and around Jungapeo, Mexico.

HIS KIND OF WOMAN ***

120m. August 1951 RKO

Producer	Robert Sparks
Director	John Farrow
Screenplay	Frank Fenton and Jack Leonard
	(Based on the story "Star Sapphire"
	by Gerald Drayson Adams)
Photography	Harry J. Wild
Musical Director	C. Bakaleinikoff

CAST:

Robert Mitchum	Dan Milner
Jane Russell	Lenore Brent
Vincent Price	Mark Cardigan
Tim Holt	Bill Lusk
Charles McGraw	Thompson
Marjorie Reynolds	Helen Cardigan
Raymond Burr	Nick Ferraro
Leslye Banning	Jennie Stone
Jim Backus	Myron Winton
Philip Van Zandt	Jose Morro
John Mylong	Martin Krafft
Carlton G. Young	Hobson
Erno Verebes	Estaban
Dan White	Tex Kearns
Richard Berggren	Milton Stone
Stacy Harris	Harry
Robert Cornthwaite	Hernandez
Paul Frees	Corle
Anthony Caruso	Tony

PLOT: Gambler Dan Milner (Robert Mitchum) is anonymously and mysteriously offered $50,000 to go to a Mexican resort town and wait for instructions. There he meets buxom Lenore Brent (Jane Russell), a singer in a local night spot who has had a crush on film actor Mark Cardigan (Vincent Price), but with astonishing speed learns to love the laconic Milner. It is soon apparent to Milner that it was exiled gangster Nick Ferraro (Raymond Burr) who gave him the $50,000 and who now intends to use him to expedite his return to the United States. Ferraro's plan is to have a plastic surgeon transform his face into that of Milner, and Milner is then to be disposed of by Ferraro's coterie of thugs once the operation has taken place. Before Ferraro can carry out his devilish scheme, Milner is warned by Bill Lusk (Tim Holt), an immigration agent who is after Ferraro but who is soon murdered by Ferraro's henchmen. Milner, with the aid of the hammy Cardigan and some adventurers he is able to round up, finally fights his way out of the perilous situation.

COMMENT: This melodrama has become something of a cult classic because of its potboiler steaminess (between Mitchum and Russell) and somewhat overwrought performances (especially by Vincent Price, who chews up the scenery and spits it out with reckless abandon). Some viewers have found that the sleaziness of the characters and the quirky situations exude a sort of macabre campiness (i.e., a nutso one-time Nazi surgeon who is eager to take knife to face to see if he can really pull off the transformation). Tim (fortunately or unfortunately, depending on your perception of the film) has little on-camera time before he is dispatched by a hitman. One critic stated that "Holt handles himself well in a comparatively brief spot."

SONGS:
"Kiss and Tell" and "Five Little Miles from San Berdoo" by Ben S. Coslow. "You'll Know" by Jimmy McHugh and Harold Adamson.

THE MONSTER THAT CHALLENGED THE WORLD **1/2

83m. June 1957 United Artists

Producer	Arthur Gardner and Jules Levy
Director	Arnold Laven
Screenplay	Pat Fielder
	(Based on a story by David Duncan)

The plot thickens in the melodramatic *HIS KIND OF WOMAN* as Philip Van Zandt (left) and Jim Backus (right) chat with immigration agent Tim Holt, while a nonchalant Robert Mitchum looks on.

This is a lobby card for the Mexican release of *THE MONSTER THAT CHALLENGED THE WORLD*.

Tim discusses the potential danger of the monster with scientist Hans Conried in this scene from *THE MONSTER THAT CHALLENGED THE WORLD*.

Photography .... Lester White
Musical Director .... Heinz Roemheld

CAST:
Tim Holt Lieutenant Commander John Twillinger
Audrey Dalton .... Gail MacKenzie
Hans Conried .... Doctor Jess Rogers
Harland Warde .... Lieutenant Bob Clemens
Casey Adams .... Tad Johns
Mimi Gibson .... Sandy MacKenzie
Gordon Jones .... Josh Peters
Marjorie Stapp .... Connie Blake
Dennis McCarthy .... George Blake
Barbara Darrow .... Jody Sims
Bob Beneveds .... Mort Beatty
Michael Dugan .... Clarke
Mack Williams .... Captain Masters
Eileen Harley .... Sally
Jody McCrea .... Seaman Fred Johnson
William Swan .... Seaman Howard Sanders
Charles Tannen .... Wyatt
Byron Kane .... Coroner
Hal Taggert .... Mr. Davis
Gil Frye .... Deputy Scott
Don Gachman .... Deputy Brewer
Milton Parsons .... Lewis Clark Doggs
Ralph Moody .... Old Gatekeeper

PLOT: The setting is an isolated naval research center in the California desert. An earthquake resurrects some pre-historic eggs that are in a saltwater desert sea near the center; the eggs soon hatch into giant caterpillar-like monsters that go in search of food. Unfortunately, the delicacy they prefer is human flesh. Naval personnel and the local police work together under the direction of intelligence officer John Twillinger (Tim) to quell the amphibious monsters.

COMMENT: Tim returned to film making after a five-year hiatus for *THE MONSTER THAT CHALLENGED THE WORLD,* an average-quality, science-fiction thriller possessing a rather hyperbolic title. In general, the film's special effects were praised by critics and audiences, but the plot was considered rather shopworn and one critic, pretty much reflecting the general feeling, stated that there were "a number of ludicrous and cliche moments" in the film. Tim's performance was considered appropriately heroic and well suited to the demands of the picture.

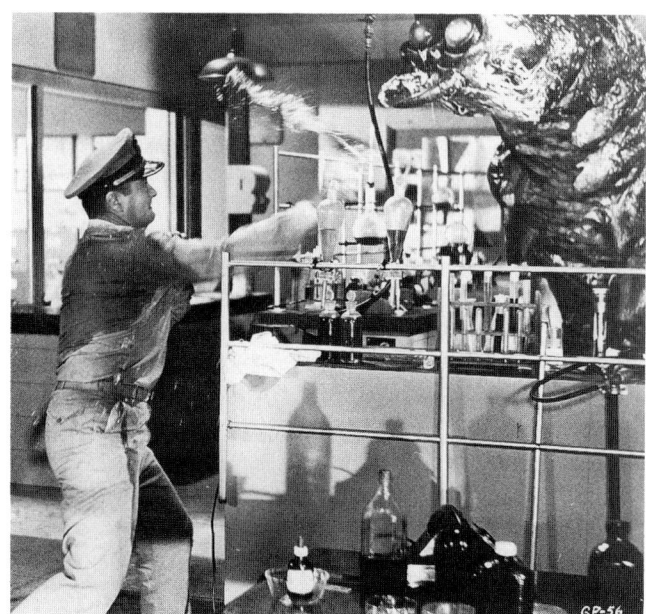

The monster certainly seems to be challenging Tim (if not the whole world) in this exciting confrontation scene.

THE YESTERDAY MACHINE 1/2

85m. 1962 Carter Film Productions

Producer and director	Russ Marker
Screenplay	Russ Marker
Photography	Ralph K. Johnson
Musical Director	Don Zimmers

CAST:
Tim Holt	Lieutenant Partano
James Britton	Jim Crandal
Jack Herman	Professor Von Hauser

Ann Pellegrino
Linda Jenkins
Jay Ramsey
Robert Kelly
Bob Brown
Charles Young
Carol Gilley
Bill Thurman
Olga Powell
Marvin Seabright
Lee Arthur
Charles McLine
Carolyn Adams
Frank Cole
Jerry Brown
Joseph (Pat) Cranshaw
Robert Peel
James L. Howe
David Beckham
Ramon Lence Legar

PLOT: A Nazi-sympathizing mad scientist/professor (Jack Herman) invents a "way back" machine that transports people back and forth in time. After a college student is wounded by a time-traveling Civil War soldier and his cheerleader girlfriend vanishes, a nosy newspaper reporter (James Britton) and the police get involved. (The reporter and the mad scientist/professor are the main characters in the plot.) Lieutenant Partano (Tim) of the police department is assigned to the case and ultimately comes to the rescue of the buttinsky reporter and thwarts the plan of the crazy Professor Von Hauser to bring Adolph Hitler back to life.

In this very rare still from *THIS STUFF'LL KILL YA!* Tim and another Secret Service agent are forced into a compromising situation as they attempt to arrest a bootlegging preacher. (Photo courtesy of Nick Nicholls.)

COMMENT: This extremely low-budget independent production is the first of two Tim Holt "mystery" films. (The other is *THIS STUFF'LL KILL YA!*) One can only speculate on why Tim would lend his good name, reputation, and person to this amateurish film. (See the Berdee Holt interview for her comments on this.) If he did it as a favor for a friend, it was a GREAT favor! Tim appears to be embarrassed as he plays out his few scenes in the silly script. He is only on screen for about fifteen minutes of the film, but it seems a lifetime for devoted Tim Holt fans.

SONG:
"Leave Me Alone" was composed by Russ Marker and sung by Ann Pellegrino.

THIS STUFF'LL KILL YA!

100m. 1971 Ultima

Producer, director, screenwriter .... Herschell Gordon Lewis
Photography .... Alex Ameripoor, Daniel P. Krogh
Musical Director .... Sheldon Seymour

CAST:
Jeffrey Allen .... Roscoe Boone
Tim Holt .... Clark
Gloria King .... Elsie
Ray Sager .... Grady
Eric Bradly .... Sam
Terence McCarthy .... Carter
Ronna Riddle .... Lynn
Larry Drake .... Bubba
John Garner .... Turnip
Bill Mays .... Policeman
Lee Danser .... Zeke
Pamela Polsgrove .... Maryellen
Doffy Candler .... Beau
Skip Nicholson .... Lawyer Grimes
Carol Merrell .... Bubba's Nurse
Pamela Bloomfield .... Marcia
Debbie Gardiner .... Janet

PLOT: A moonshining preacher named Roscoe Boone (Jeffrey Allen) runs into trouble with Secret Service agents and the townspeople of a Southern backwoods community when a series of ritualistic, gory murders plague the area and appear to have some connection with his illegal bootlegging activities. Eventually the blame is accurately placed on a crazy religious fanatic by the name of Grady (Ray Sager), who has been assisting the preacher. In the gross climactic scene Grady gets his head blown off by his own shotgun.

COMMENT: The less said about this film the better. This picture makes *THE YESTERDAY MACHINE* look good. Interestingly, the distributor of the home video version refers to *THIS STUFF'LL KILL YA!* as a "cult classic" because producer/director/writer Herschell Gordon Lewis has been able to foist a few other weird films onto a minuscule segment of the film-going public without them catching on that they are just metaphors for trash.

* * *

The Holt clan gathered in October of 1992 for the Lone Pine Sierra Film Festival, which honored Tim for the many films he made in Lone Pine. Pictured from left to right are Tim's son Jack, sister Jennifer, son Jay (in back), Jay's son Shaeffer, Jay's daughter Kennedy (holding the painting), daughter Bryanna (in sunglasses), and Tim's wife, Berdee Holt. (Photo by Ken Taylor.)

Chapter 7
You Can Know A Man By His Family—Reminiscences

Jennifer Holt and author David Rothel posed for this picture prior to the guest star panel session at the 1989 Raleigh Western Film Fair. (Photo by Ken Taylor.)

Jennifer Holt Interview
August 2, 1993

Jennifer and I have gotten to know each other in recent years through the Western film festivals we have both attended. She has been a frequent guest star at these affairs, and I have had the pleasure of hosting several guest star panels in which she has been an intelligent and delightful participant. I have come to know the deep love she has for her brother as she has responded to my occasional questions and the numerous questions she has received from Tim's many fans at the festivals.

Ever the gracious and charming lady, Jennifer greeted me warmly when I phoned her at her home in Cuernavaca, Mexico, and asked if I could talk with her about Tim. She had known for some time that I was working on this book and had probably guessed that I would soon be asking her to reminisce about her big brother. She was ready for my questions and spoke to me with candor about the brother that she has loved so much and still misses today. She began by talking about their parents and grandparents.

Margaret Wood Holt, wife of Jack Holt and mother of Tim and Jennifer. "Mother had a delightful sense of humor, kind of a sense of whimsey, I would call it, but she was generally serious, quite a serious person." (Photo courtesy of Jennifer Holt.)

Jennifer Holt: Mother's father (Henry Morton Stanley-Wood) was an industrial tycoon, first generation out of England. He migrated from England, and he started a company in St. Paul, Minnesota, called American Hoist & Derrick; they made steam shovels, among other things. When Mother (Margaret) was a little girl, she traveled all over the Orient with him while he was selling his big machines. She went to the Philippines, she stayed in the Hawaiian Islands, she was in Djakarta. That was her girlhood. Her mother had died very young. Mother had a delightful sense of humor, kind of a sense of whimsey, I would call it, but she was generally serious, quite a serious person. Theologically, she was all over the place. She was, at one time or another, everything except a Roman Catholic.

She had had a prior marriage, which my grandfather had arranged for her and which she didn't want at all, but in those days, in her generation, girls didn't go to school; they were taught at home, and marriages were arranged. My grandfather was quite a martinet, a handsome man and strong, but a martinet nevertheless. He decided she was going to marry this man whom she hated. Anyway, she went through with the marriage and got pregnant with my half-sister Imogene and left the marriage immediately. So Mother ended up a divorcee when it really wasn't the thing to do, but she was strong-willed, and she wasn't going to stay in a marriage that she didn't like.

My aunt brought Jack Holt to tea when my mother was living in Alhambra. Later, my mother said that she took one look at the back of Jack's head and remarked, "That's for me!" She said that the back of his head was so beautiful; she'd never seen a head shaped so beautifully, but she discovered that he was dressed that day in tattersal from head to foot. From then on she devoted herself to changing his image.

Jack had just come down from Alaska. (Some years before, a prank had caused him to be asked to leave the Virginia Military Institute prior to his graduation. After knocking about for a time, a flip of a coin sent him to Alaska for nearly six years to seek his fortune in such varied occupations as miner, surveyor, prospector, and trapper.) Jack's version of it was that having just been up in Alaska with all of those "ladies of the dancehall," so to speak, Mother and my aunt were the first "ladies" he'd seen in quite some time. At that time he had just entered pictures; he may still have been doubling actors or maybe just getting started in small roles.

DR: What was your mother's attitude toward the movie industry?

Jennifer: Oh, absolutely zero. Back in those days it wasn't considered a gentleman's profession, really. And, of course, my grandfather was absolutely horrified that Mother would marry an actor, so she was disinherited.

Mother was inclined to melancholia. Not real deep, deep melancholia, but a sort of thoughtful one, if you know what I mean. When she was fun, she was fun; when she was quiet, she was quiet. She was

A Holt family portrait. Tim (looking quite the self-assured young man), Jennifer on mother Margaret's lap, half-sister Imogene, and father Jack. (Photo courtesy of Jennifer Holt.)

Tim, Jennifer, and half-sister Imogene. (Photo courtesy of Jennifer Holt.)

prone to hypochondria. Tim couldn't stand illness; I think because Mother was always ill. I'm inclined to the same reaction except I tend to panic when people are ill. We both wanted to run away from an illness situation.

DR: Your mother seems to have had a disdain for Hollywood, but yet she was taken with your father.

Jennifer: Well, she didn't have a disdain; she just didn't want any part of it. As a result, the social group in our house was what we called the "ladies and gentlemen" of the movie colony then. It included Ronald Coleman, Clive Brook, Bill Powell, Herbert Marshall, and Ernest Torrence—whom she adored. It was the aristocratic class of Hollywood—very much the British colony. They were ladies and gentlemen, so she enjoyed these people very much. But she didn't have much use for the trappings of Hollywood. The thought of publicity to her was abhorrent. Her feeling was that you only had your name in the paper twice: when you got married and when you died.

DR: Tell me now about your father, the dashing leading man of motion pictures.

Jennifer: He had the sense of humor and the sense of fun which, I assume, is what brought them together. Father was a ladies' man—no, I take that back. Father was a man's man, but ladies were crazy about him—and were usually on the make. This, of course, didn't suit Mother at all. I'm not saying that he was fooling around, but I'm sure the temptations were there. Anyway, I would say that's why the marriage didn't really work out. I think probably that other women did creep into the picture.

DR: Where did he fit into the Hollywood social circle? Was he very comfortable with the type of people, the aristocratic English, you just mentioned?

Jennifer: Yes. You have to remember that Dad came from an Episcopal family. Dad's father was an Episcopal minister and very highly thought of in Virginia, and my grandmother was the great granddaughter of John Marshall (Chief Justice of the United States from 1801-1835)—and she never let anybody forget that. So Father was Virginia proud. This meant horses, pastures, polo, the sport of kings—the gentleman's thing. Dad was not a cowboy. He was not called "Sir Charles" for nothing—that was his nickname. Everybody liked him; he was terribly popular with the men as well as the women. He had an absolutely delightful sense of humor. He was very quick, very witty. I thought he was hysterically funny. With a few drinks in him, he became even funnier. Nobody could ever drink Jack under the table. As he drank he just got ramrod straight while others fell down sick drunk; Jack would still be cold sober.

Dad always told the story of the funny incident that occurred after the marriage of Rod LaRocque and Velma Banky, at which he and three of his film colony friends had been ushers. I guess they had had a few drinks, and they were coming back up Hollywood Boulevard—our house was on Hollywood Boulevard, which was then just two lanes. It was quite late at night and, of course, they were loaded, all of them—Bill Powell, Ronnie Coleman, Clive Brook, and my father. As they drove along, they got behind a house that was being moved by a truck. They honked their horn, trying to pass, but they couldn't get by this moving building. So, finally, they parked the car, got out, and climbed inside the moving house. They found a couple of orange crates and a candle; they lighted it and sat there, in their formal wear from the wedding, playing cards—or pretended they were playing cards, because they had no actual cards with them. They were just clowning around, having fun. The driver eventually saw the flickering light in the house he was moving, stopped the truck, got out, and went around to the door of the house to see what was going on. There he came upon four of the top movie stars of the day playing poker with no cards! They were pranksters! (laugh)

DR: What were Tim's interests when he was a child?

Jennifer: Well, he went to the Carl Curtis School for Boys, which was where all the celebrity children went, so that meant swimming and other athletics. He was a good student and a good athlete. I remember him playing tennis and horseback riding, of course, because he was always with Dad, who loved riding. When Tim was a youngster, he was *always* around the stable with Dad. I remember once when we were very little that Mother and Dad were eating in the dining room, and Tim and I were playing on the landing of the staircase, which was not very far from the dining room. Tim had me by the hair, and he was screaming something like, "You do as I tell you, you little son-of-a-bitch." I was saying, "Oh, stop pulling my hair." Mother looked at Dad, and Dad's jaw went out. He came to the stairway and said, "What did I hear you call your sister?" I, of course, always being protective of Tim, said, "Oh, that's all right, Daddy. He always calls me that!" (laugh) I can remember hearing Mother say, "See! You always have him around the stable. That's where he picks up that language." Tim was *really* punished—sent to bed where he cried all night with me stealing food from the kitchen for him and sob-

Jennifer and Tim occasionally got to play dress-up for family photos. Here they are seen as Pilgrims.

And here as Indian scouts. (Photos courtesy of Jennifer Holt.)

bing at the foot of his bed. He wept and wept. I'll never forget it!

DR: Was Tim closer to his father than his mother?

Jennifer: I think yes. Certainly that was the case after their separation because Tim decided to stay with Dad. I wasn't given a choice; I think Tim was given a choice. I went with my mother, but I probably would have anyway.

DR: You went to Belgium for almost three years with your governess when you were only seven years old. Was that a result of the breakup of the marriage?

Jennifer: I think it probably was. Things were getting a bit out of hand. Dad was not handling his drinking problem very well, doing quite a bit of it. The drinking was abhorrent to Mother. I was having a fit because Mademoiselle, my governess, was going on her sabbatical, and I couldn't bear to be parted from her. So Mother said, "It's a good thing; take her with you." It was supposedly for a year, but as it turned out, it was about two and a half years. By the time I came back, the marriage was over. I then went to South America with Mother for several years.

DR: I know you and Tim missed a lot of time together when you were kids, but when you were together, how did you get along?

Jennifer: Well, I guess I was sort of "the brat" to Tim. I don't think I really was a brat, but I was so adoring of Tim that I probably drove him crazy. He would have friends over to play tennis, I would hang around, and it would become an "oh, get lost, get out from under foot" kind of thing. They'd deliberately hit the balls way over the fence and tell me to go fetch them—and I would, just like a well-behaved dog. Of course I was taken advantage of. You know, they'd tease me. But I always felt that as long as Tim teased me, he loved me—because at least he was paying attention to me. Both Tim and Dad were great teasers. That was their way of showing affection. It could and did hurt sometimes, but if you couldn't take it, that was a bad mark against you. I learned this at an early age. It became "our" sense of humor,

"Tim had an imaginary playmate named Casey. The doll in the picture was named Casey too, also his first dog. Who knows why the name Casey? Of course, if Tim had an imaginary friend, I had to have one too. Her name was Margorie. Kids!!" (Photo courtesy of Jennifer Holt.)

"Tim was a knockout-looking young man. I think he was just a natural: he was athletic, he was gorgeous, he had beautiful manners, he was a well-brought-up young man. Walter Wanger saw him and signed him to a contract." (Photo courtesy of Jennifer Holt.)

Jennifer Holt is seen here in a "glamour" pose from the 1940s, when she was a very popular Western film heroine.

you might say. I never felt they loved me unless they were teasing me unmercifully at times.

We spent our formative years apart; we didn't have the opportunity to be close. When I came back from South America, he was at Culver (Military Institute) and was a complete stranger to me, although a delightful one. Soon, however, we picked up pretty much where we had left off.

Tim became very protective of me when I came back from South America and entered The Bishop School in La Jolla. His letters from Culver to me were almost like those of a parent. They were awfully sweet. He'd write, "Now you've got to learn to play tennis, and you've got to learn to play bridge. You have to learn how to dance. And please be sure to write Dad because he's so lonely. A letter from you would make him so happy." It went on and on like that. He wrote me every week while I was at Bishop—loving, sweet letters. I gave them all to Sandra, his son Jay's wife; she's putting together a scrapbook.

During Tim's junior year, I went to the Culver dance. My date was Hal Roach, Jr., Tim's roommate. I've often teased him since then. I've said, "What did you do, lose a bet and have to take me to the dance?" Poor Hal, stuck with me. (laugh) And having been brought up abroad, I was very much less sophisticated than the girls of my age in the United States. I felt I was an infant, and Tim sort of looked at me like that. I think Hal Roach did too—"My god, I've got this baby that I have to take to the dance!"

A few years later, when Tim was on weekend leave from the army, we used to go out together to Victor's Steak House, a place where we all went during the first years of the war. All of us kids were actors—or trying to be—and that was our hangout. Tim and I used to tell people we were twins—don't ask me why. He had an eagle eye as to whom I became friendly with. I lived way out in the Valley then, and he *made sure* I went home alone!

DR: Do you think it was your father who served as an inspiration for Tim to become a film actor?

Jennifer: I think Tim fell into it more or less as I did. We weren't trained to do anything else. (laugh) We weren't trained to do a darned thing, you know. Tim was playing polo, and he was playing with people like Walter Wanger (the film producer), Walt Disney, and Spencer Tracy. And, you know, Tim was a knockout-looking young man. I think he was just a natural: he was athletic; he was gorgeous; he had beautiful manners; he was a well-brought-up young man. Walter Wanger saw him and signed him to a contract.

When I got out of school, I was very interested in music and wanted to be a singer. I was given singing lessons, but I didn't have that good of a voice, so I suppose Mother probably decided I might as well go and study (acting) with Maria Ouspensjaya my first year out of high school—in other words, get out from under foot. I did get to study with Ouspensjaya and later with the Peterborough Players in New Hampshire.

During this time Tim was working in films pretty much; I won't say steadily, but quite a bit—*STELLA DALLAS, I MET MY LOVE AGAIN, GOLD IS WHERE YOU FIND IT*, things like that. Tim married Virginia around this time; I guess he and Dad were having a rough time. Dad was drinking pretty heavily then, and it was difficult. Dad with a few drinks would be pretty abusive in words. I remember once when this happened—we were probably about eighteen or nineteen years old—we both tried to get up and go. We were told to "sit down!" He hadn't finished with us. A bit later was when Tim ran off and got married to Virginia.

I know I wanted to go see Dad on weekends, but if he was drinking, I didn't stay very long—and Tim didn't either. I think that Tim probably married in haste to establish his own independence, maybe to get out of the house; I don't know, but he finally had some money of his own and could afford to do it.

DR: How did your parents' breakup affect Tim's relationship with his mother?

Jennifer: Very badly. They never really made up. I think Mother never forgave Tim for choosing to stay with Dad, and I think Mother made a terrible mistake every time Tim came, quite dutifully, to see her. She would say, practically before he was in the door, "Did you bring your father's check?"—referring to her alimony check, which was sometimes a little late in coming. Now this is something you just don't do with children, and you certainly don't do it with Tim, because he was a deeply loyal person. Well, the rift was really never healed, it never really was. He tried hard. In a way, she couldn't forgive him for choosing Dad instead of her. She didn't understand that he was just a child, just a little boy about nine years old—so she was lacking in understanding. I blame Mother much more than I blame Tim on that one.

DR: When did your mother die?

Tim's wife Berdee, son Jack, and sister Jennifer at the 1992 Lone Pine Sierra Film Festival. (Photo courtesy of Tom Wyatt.)

Jennifer: It was ten years to the day after Dad. Dad died in 1951, so Mother died in 1961. She was living in Ojai at the time. The tragic thing is that I had it all set up, after all the years of pleading with Tim, that he was going to come out and see Mother, and they were going to finally try to make up. We had long conversations about "let's put this behind us because she's the only parent we have left, and she's not too well." Mother died before he could get there. He still came out to be with me, but she died before that could ever happen. Tim couldn't go and look at her (in death). Years later when he was dying, he begged me to forgive him for that. He said he just couldn't.

DR: Was your father pleased when Tim became a film actor?

Jennifer: I suppose Dad was; yes, I think so. Oddly enough, I think there was a little jealousy there and a sense of competition. The minute that Dad died, Tim no longer was interested in films. I think when a father or dominating figure dies, within the sadness and sense of loss there can also sometimes be a small corner of relief. I observed this in Tim's hyper reaction at the time of our father's death, a kind of "elation"—that may not be the right word—as if he, Tim, had become a full-grown man in his own right, a completed individual in his own right. The umbilical cord cut was complete. It was almost as if he was established now as his own person, and he didn't have to compete anymore. I don't know if that makes any sense.

DR: I think so. Quite often children feel almost as if they are in competition with their fathers, especially if their fathers are strong individuals and have been very successful.

Jennifer: I think he did feel that he was in competition. He seemed to lose all interest in films after Father died.

DR: It was the very next year, 1952, that Tim pretty much ended his film career.

Jennifer: There was no need to compete anymore.

DR: How did your mother respond to Tim's career in films?

Jennifer: Well, she just thought the whole thing was utter nonsense, I think. I did make her go to see Tim in *TREASURE OF SIERRA MADRE*. I made her; I dragged her. But as far as I know, she never saw either Tim or me on screen outside of that. She didn't go to movies. I made her see two movies: *TREASURE OF SIERRA MADRE* and *BRIEF ENCOUNTER*. (laugh) Those are the only two pictures I know that Mother saw, because I took her.

DR: So she wasn't terribly impressed with your movie careers.

Jennifer: No, but she had watched Dad in Dad's younger days. Dad had a ring on his little finger that mother had given him, a gold ring with an amethyst in it. You can notice in pictures like *DIRIGIBLE* or *FLIGHT* that every once in a while he twists the ring, and that was his signal to her—a sort of affectionate message to Mother.

DR: Sort of like Carol Burnett tugging on her ear.

Jennifer: That's it exactly.

DR: Well, here comes the old stock question about Tim that gets asked so often—and maybe you just answered it partially. Tim was in Orson Welles' production of *THE MAGNIFICENT AMBERSONS*, he was in John Ford's *MY DARLING CLEMENTINE*, and he was one of the stars of *THE TREASURE OF THE SIERRA MADRE*. It certainly appeared that he had opportunities to move into the big-budget A pictures and to leave the B Westerns if he had wanted to, and yet he never did. Why?

Jennifer: I'd love to know myself. Of course, the war interfered after he made *AMBERSONS*. I don't suppose that the powers at RKO understood what in the world Orson Welles saw in Tim to choose him for *AMBERSONS*. I remember it shocked the studio. Orson Welles just said, "I don't know, I saw that one shot in *STAGECOACH* with Tim, and there was something about that shot of him saluting as he turned to go off with his cavalry unit that was so gallant that it just broke my heart." Welles said, "I just knew I wanted that boy for *AMBERSONS*."

DR: Tim, of course, always said—and I know you have also said at some of the film festivals—that he just loved making the Westerns.

Jennifer: Well, I think he was more in control of production with the Westerns. If he had hung around Hollywood, he might have ended up producing and directing his own films, because he was interested in every aspect of making pictures. I think when he was making the smaller budget Westerns there wasn't as much pressure, and he was more in control, he was the star—as opposed to working with Orson Welles, John Ford, or John Huston. And this would have been necessary for his ego. Tim's ego was frail. That's one thing that people don't really know about Tim. His ego had a hard time growing because Dad and Mother were so strict. It was a period of "no nonsense" in bringing up children. We weren't loved and cuddled. We weren't touched an awful lot or kissed. We just didn't have that kind of upbringing. If we started to get a big head or conceited, boy, we didn't show it around Dad because we knew he would cut us down to size. Our self-esteem was knocked down plenty of times. As a matter of fact, the minute we started to get any, it seemed as if it was kicked out from underneath us.

DR: You seem to be saying that Tim's lack of self-esteem and ego might have inhibited him from

Jennifer and Tim's son Jack rode together in the 1992 Sierra Film Festival Parade down the main street in Lone Pine. (Photo courtesy of Tom Wyatt.)

"I poured all of my love and affection into him, and Tim was very protective of me in many ways and very caring." (Photo courtesy of Jennifer Holt.)

leaving the B Westerns, where he had control, to go off and be in the hands of other people.

Jennifer: It's possible. It's just my guess. You also have to remember that Howard Hughes was dumping that series with Dick Martin and Tim. The B Westerns were dying at about that time. I don't know that Tim had ever had to hang around looking for a job. Maybe his ego couldn't take it, so he left town. I think maybe all of it combined, and there was the fact that Dad was gone. There was no more need to excel or compete, and there was nothing, really, left to hold him in Hollywood. Even the breach with Mother couldn't be healed at that time.

You know, Tim was never quite at ease with his social equals. He had perfect manners, of course, but he was not a "social animal" by any stretch of the imagination. Home and hearth were what he wanted, certainly not the Hollywood scene. My opinion only, Tim was always searching for his mother in other women. Berdee was perfect for him in this respect. She really is a superb woman in all respects, including a mother figure.

I have to tell you one more thing about Tim. As we grew older, even though Tim and I didn't see each other very much, he trusted me completely. He would tell me things that nobody else knew and that I certainly wouldn't divulge. We might not see each other for five or six years, but when we got together, it was like finishing a sentence. We'd pick up right where we had left off the last time we'd seen each other. He came to Chicago once to be on my television show, and, oh god, we had a wonderful visit. By this time we were both grown up, and we'd stopped the horsing around and teasing. We became each other's confidant. I knew all about him, and he knew all about me. It didn't make any difference; we adored each other.

DR: And we all need someone like that.

Jennifer: I remember when I was a little girl I used to wake up at night crying because I wondered what I would ever do if Tim died before I did. That was part of my childhood nightmare, that Tim would be the first to go, and I wondered what in the world I would do without him. And, you know, I still feel that way. It used to terrify me as a child. I don't know why it hung over me. Maybe it was because we weren't that close to Mother and Father. I was closer to my governess than I was to my mother and father, so Tim was my idol. I poured all of my love and affection into him, and Tim was very protective of me in many ways and very caring. When he was so ill about two weeks before he died, I went to Oklahoma to be with him, and he couldn't stop telling me how much he loved me. He was just the best brother in the whole world, and I'll always miss him.

* * *

I first met Tim Holt's family in October of 1992 at the third annual Lone Pine Film Festival, which was honoring Tim for his many Westerns shot at Lone Pine. I had talked with Mrs. Holt on the phone several weeks before the festival about the fact that I was beginning a book dealing with Tim's life, and she had promised her cooperation on the endeavor—and an interview while we were all in Lone Pine. During a later phone conversation, she affirmed that the children—Jack, Bryanna, and Jay—would also be available for an interview about their father.

The opening bash of the festival was a cocktail party in the lobby of the Dow Villa Motel—the historic diggs for the casts and crews of film companies since the 1920s. (In fact, my wife and I and our friends Ken and Judy Taylor were sharing the John Wayne suite during the festival. It wasn't quite as glamorous as that sounds since the suite was two tiny rooms with a shared bath tucked in between. I had the distinct feeling that Wayne hadn't shared this abode with three other people when he was at the Dow for *TYCOON* or any of the other films he shot in Lone Pine.)

Anyway, during the noisy, elbow-to-elbow cocktail party, I was suddenly stopped short by the appearance of a young man in Western-cut suit and big black stetson who bore a striking resemblance to the young Tim Holt. It was hard to cast my eyes away from this youthful apparition from the past, and it was readily apparent that I was not the only one to recognize and be fascinated by the likeness.

A few minutes later I came upon a charming acquaintance of mine, Tim's sister, actress and lovely lady, Jennifer Holt. After exchanging loud greetings amid the cheery din, she took me over and introduced me to the young man, her nephew Jack Holt—Tim's oldest child from his marriage to Berdee Holt. Jack's firm handshake and ready smile greeted me warmly, and we chatted for a few moments, tentatively scheduling an interview session for the next morning, before the crush of the crowd separated us.

Everybody wanted to meet and talk with Jack; his charismatic smile and Tim-like looks made him a human magnet in the Dow lobby, which more and more resembled a variation on the old how-many-people-can-we-pack-into-a-telephone-booth routine as the cocktail party partied on.

As I continued to mingle through the crowd, I came upon Jennifer again, who was now with Tim's widow and other two children. She introduced me to Berdee Holt, an attractive silver-haired lady whose dark-rimmed glasses gave her a friendly wise-old-owl look. I immediately recognized her honey-modulated Oklahoma accent when she spoke her greeting to me. She was very much as I had imagined her from our two phone conversations—warm, friendly, but cautious with a yet-to-be-fathomed writer, and writers, of course, should always be suspect.

But I had no such preconceived notions about Tim's only daughter and younger son. Bryanna, who appeared to be somewhat shy and perhaps a bit uncomfortable in the midst of the happy-hour crowd, looked like a fifty-fifty blend of her parents, taking the best from both, and she was certainly beautiful enough to be one of those fresh-scrubbed Hollywood starlets we used to see in the fan magazines from the golden era of films. Jay, the jolly giant of the family, seemed to favor his mother in appearance, and his husky build, I discovered later, had allowed him to pursue his great interest in sports, especially football, while in school. I came to realize during the next couple of days that Jay didn't seem to enjoy the limelight as much, say, as his older brother Jack, but once in it he was comfortable and very articulate.

So, I had now met the four Holts of Tim's family and had had a chance to also chat again briefly with Jennifer, as fine a Western film heroine as ever there was and a gracious lady whom I had had the pleasure of interviewing several times at Western film festivals. I walked out into the chill Lone Pine evening, a cacophony of happy voices trailing behind me, and gazed up at the distant Sierra Mountains silhouetted against the deepening purple sky. I thought about the fun it must have been for Tim and Chito—coming up from Los Angeles, staying at the Dow Villa, and spending their days chasing outlaws in the Alabama Hills nestled down below those Sierra Mountains, the mountains which now were gradually fading into indecipherable shadows. Lone Pine—what a great place to shoot Western films!

* * *

Jack Holt Interview
October 20, 1992

Son Jack had not yet visited the Alabama Hills where his father had shot so many Westerns, so Ken Taylor and I met him after breakfast the next morning and headed out that way. It seemed like a good place to talk with thirty-four-year-old Jack about his

What more appropriate place to conduct an interview with Jack Holt about his father than the Alabama Hills of Lone Pine. "He [Tim] was just a regular guy. The character you saw on the screen was the man himself. He did the work because he loved the work, and he loved people." (Photo by Ken Taylor.)

dad—whom he frequently referred to as "Daddy" in the respectful manner that Southern or Western-raised sons often do. With the tape rolling, we showed him some of the locations where Tim had ridden Lightning at breakneck speed through the rocky terrain. And while Jack, of course, had no recollections of his dad in that setting, he could imagine him there—and it jogged memories of his father.

David Rothel (DR): Did you ever perceive your dad as a star of movies or as a cowboy star?

Jack Holt: Not really. He was always just Dad, just like anybody else's dad, I guess. It didn't sink in until later on just who he was, because he never really dwelled on it much around the house. For a while on Saturday mornings he used to have a TV show in Oklahoma City where they'd show some of his films. We were sitting around the house one morning watching TV, and I was flipping through the channels and passed his TV show. He said, "Aren't you going to watch that?" I said, "Oh, Daddy, it's just *you!*" That tickled him a lot. He thought that was hilarious and used to tell that on me all the time. He never came across as a movie star and so we never perceived him that way.

DR: Well, I never met your dad but everything I've heard about him suggests that he seldom acted like the stereotype of the "movie star."

Jack: Yeah, he was just a regular guy. The character you saw on the screen was the man himself. He did the work because he loved the work, and he loved people.

DR: It has always been a mystery to those who have followed his career that sometime in 1952 he packed in his movie career and went off to Oklahoma and never came back to films except for a couple of brief excursions. I've heard that he had many offers over the years to return to a film career. Why did he just walk away from it?

Jack: He did have a lot of offers, but he just didn't like the way Hollywood was going and the people who were beginning to run the business. He had grown up in the business and knew well all of the people he had worked for and with; he had been raised with them. He knew them and they knew him and his father, and Hollywood wasn't all that big of a deal to him. But after World War II so much changed out there (Hollywood) that he just didn't really like it anymore. Most of the people that he'd worked for were not in the same positions anymore, and he just didn't like what it was becoming.

DR: Just about every film actor whoever walked away from the business eventually returned and tried for a big comeback, but your dad seems to have walked away from the business with hardly a backward glance.

Jack: Daddy and Grandpa and, I guess, I'm the same way, we set our mind to do something, and we just do it and that's it. When he walked out, when he left, it wasn't in his nature to go back and ask somebody for a job. He just wouldn't do that; he wouldn't allow that to happen. And those things that he did do, he wanted to do.

DR: Did he ever have friends from the Hollywood years show up in Oklahoma City?

Jack: Well, I was really too young to know most of his movie friends. Most of the people who were friends with Daddy were very much like him—like Ben Johnson. He's just Ben Johnson, a down-to-earth kind of guy. Daddy was the same way; he was Tim Holt. Like it or not, this was who he was and most people liked it—liked being around him. He didn't see a whole lot of the movie people, but John Wayne was a good friend of his. They worked together in *STAGECOACH*. He had been around and worked with John Ford, and John Wayne was kind of a pet project for John Ford. He was working on Wayne to make him a big star and *STAGECOACH* was the vehicle that did it.

Long before I was born, my dad had a beach house at Malibu, and he and Wayne would go there. My dad had one of those carbines with an oxbow ring, and they would go out and work with their rifles, getting the feel of them and making them work, just getting used to them.

He said they used to practice with different holster riggings too. When you see gunslingers in the movies, they always wear their pistols low. Daddy and John Wayne talked about that and practiced carrying their guns in different positions. You don't want it in your way getting up and down off a horse. You don't want it hanging so low that it keeps falling out all the time, but you want it someplace where it's handy, where you can get to it, draw it easily. If you notice—especially in John Wayne's later films—it was real noticeable that his pistol was back, cocked forward, and up high on his hip. And it was while they were fooling with their pistols out at my dad's Malibu home that they worked out that gun and holster business.

DR: Your dad wore his guns a couple of ways over the years.

Jack: He started out wanting to wear the butts forward like Wild Bill Elliott, but Daddy was a very practical person, and he came to the conclusion that wearing them that way was not such a hot idea and tried other ways. Most of the time, of course, he wore them the standard way, butts back, but for a while he wore one forward and one regular, which made it easy to draw the left gun with the right hand.

DR: Your dad made some A pictures during his career, but it's the low-budget B Westerns that most people seem especially drawn to.

Jack: Yes, those Westerns were the ones that meant more to people, and they meant a whole lot to him too. He was a versatile actor, and he could play a variety of roles. He was a Nazi in *HITLER'S CHILDREN*, for instance, and he was the lead in *THE MAGNIFICENT AMBERSONS*, a very different role. Then there was *THE TREASURE OF SIERRA MADRE*—again a very different-type role. He could play very different parts. One of his early roles was in *STELLA DALLAS*, a movie soap opera with Barbara Stanwyck. He had the talent, the ability, and the range to play a variety of characters, but the Westerns were what he loved.

DR: He received a lot of acclaim for *TREASURE OF SIERRA MADRE*. It would seem that that was the time for him to get out of B Westerns—much as Wayne did after *STAGECOACH*—and go into big-budget pictures. Tim was certainly right there where he could have made that move if he had wanted to.

Tim flashes his well-known smile as he takes a break during the filming of *GUN SMUGGLERS* (1948) in the Alabama Hills of Lone Pine, California. Tim's son Jack went to the Alabama Hills for the first time when he did his interview with author David Rothel.

Jack: Most actors would want to do that for money reasons, I suppose, but Daddy wasn't in it just for the money. He was in it because he enjoyed the work, especially in the B Westerns. Sure it paid well, but that wasn't his main concern. His concern was making good films for people to go and see.

DR: Working in *TREASURE* with Humphrey Bogart

and John and Walter Huston must have been quite an experience. I've read one story about your dad and Bogart going off together when Bogart got a little bit fed up with how long Huston was taking with the filming.

Jack: From what I understand, Bogart was upset because there was a big yacht race somewhere in Mexico, and he wanted to go enter it—or he was entered in it already; I'm not sure which. Huston said, "No, you're not going. We're making this film." They were apparently having delays on the set. One thing led to another and finally Bogart said, "I'm leaving," and he walked off the set and went to Mexico City. I think Daddy went along just to try to keep him out of jail. (laugh) I think that is what he was there for. Huston wasn't very happy with them, but eventually the film got made.

DR: Bogart was a notorious drinker, of course. Was your dad a drinker?

Jack: He was, but he wouldn't go out drinking just to get drunk. He would go out and have a drink with them. I'm sure in the story about Bogart going off to Mexico City, that Dad knew that's why Bogart was going off, so he decided that somebody was going to have to watch him, and he went along for that purpose.

DR: Is *TREASURE* your favorite of your dad's films?

Jack: That's a tough question because I see something different in all of them. I like them all, of course. As far as favorites go, I'd probably say *TREASURE OF SIERRA MADRE*. I guess because I really get to see Dad work.

DR: You mentioned John Ford a few minutes ago. Can you recall any comments from your dad about him?

Jack: He was a master at what he did, and I think my father was intrigued with how unorthodox Ford frequently was. Daddy once said that during the filming of *STAGECOACH* they sat around and watched John Wayne wash his face so many times that they thought they never would get the picture made. John Ford just made him do it over and over again. My dad finally blurted out, "Oh, give him a break, will ya!" You didn't talk to John Ford that way.

DR: From what I've heard, if you stood up to Ford and got away with it, it meant that he liked and respected you—but he could make life hell for you if he wanted to.

Jack: And he was doing that to John Wayne in the washing scene. As I said before, John Wayne was one of Ford's pet projects—to make Wayne into the actor that Ford thought he could be. In the process of making that happen, he could just tear an actor apart, and he did that with Wayne day after day, according to my dad. If you survived it and you got to the point where you could stand up to him, then I guess Ford felt as if he had done his job. If you could take it, you got his admiration.

I was told about one scene—I don't remember which film this was in—where they were supposed to be keeping their heads down because the bad guys were shooting at them. They had special effects set up which would pop little shots and the dust would fly where supposedly a bullet had struck. These actors were not keeping their heads down the way Ford had told them to, so he went to his car and got a rifle with a scope on it. Then he sat up on a ladder and every time they stuck their heads up when they shouldn't, he'd fire off a round. He said that got 'em to keep their heads down! But, as I said, Dad didn't talk a lot about his film-making years. He was more into what we, the children and our mother, had been doing than what he had done in the past. Unless we sat down and specifically asked him about something, he just didn't speak much about those years.

I do know that he admired and respected Agnes Moorehead greatly. He co-starred with her, of course, in *THE MAGNIFICENT AMBERSONS*. He thought she was a magnificent actress and a magnificent lady. She helped my dad a whole lot through that film. Evidently in between scenes she was always with him, helping him and coaching him. He really admired and respected her for taking the time with him.

DR: How about Orson Welles, the director of *AMBERSONS*? Did he say anything about him?

Jack: Dad thought he was a genius as a director. Orson Welles had seen my dad in *STAGECOACH* and admired the way in which he had played the cavalry lieutenant. There was one particular scene where Daddy saluted and rode off. Welles commented that in that one scene there was such gallantry and such an essence about him when he did that salute, turned, and rode off, that he immediately turned to his assistant and said, "He's the man I need for *MAGNIFICENT AMBERSONS*."

DR: Casting a man known primarily for B Westerns was really an unexpected thing for Welles to do—

Tim and co-star Agnes Moorehead are seen here in a tense scene from the Orson Welles production of *THE MAGNIFICENT AMBERSONS* (1942). According to son Jack, Tim had a deep respect for Agnes Moorehead who encouraged and helped him throughout the film as he developed his characterization.

and it was such a departure for your dad. You know, that movie was considered a flop when it came out and is now admired by critics all over the world as one of the ten best movies ever made. Do you remember your dad talking about his movie sidekick, Richard Martin?

Jack: Oh, they were good friends, and from what I understand, they kept in contact over the years through letters and phone calls. Dad loved him. They would just have so much fun together. He just loved being around Richard, and I've found him fun to be around too—like here at the Lone Pine Film Festival.

DR: Which leads me into my next question very nicely. How do you react to the attention you get when you come to a film festival such as this one?

Jack: Oh, I just hope I can be what they expect me to be and serve my father well.

DR: And that's a tricky business too—being what people expect you to be. Has that been a problem any time during your life, being the son of Tim Holt?

Jack: No, it really hasn't. I think my dad prepared me pretty well. He would always consider what the fans, what the people, would think of whatever he did. He kind of instilled that in us. He would say, "There's more to life than you. You've got to interact with people; you've got to be in this society, and if you're going to put yourself out there to be something for them, then you've got to take them into consideration whenever you do something.

Ben Johnson, when he was asked if he minded when people came up to him and asked for autographs, said, "No, it bothers me when they don't." (laugh) It's a sort of customer/businessman relationship, and you've got to give the customer what he wants. In this kind of business, show business, you've got to do it all the time, no matter where you are. You've got to live that way, and that's the way Dad always was.

DR: You know how show business kids often seem to turn out to be hellions—or worse. Have Tim Holt's kids pretty much avoided that?

Jack: Yeah, I think pretty much. One thing I guess

Tim (right) and the sheriff's posse round up the bad guys and gal (Veda Ann Borg) in this scene from *RIDER FROM TUCSON* (1950), staged in the Alabama Hills of Lone Pine, California.

we do have a problem with is that we speak our minds. That's one of the things that Daddy taught us. We try not to be overbearing about it, but we tell people what we think.

DR: Let's go back to when you were a little kid. What kind of a father was Tim Holt? Was he a disciplinarian?

Jack: (Laugh) I went through basic training at thirty-one, and it was a piece of cake because of what I'd grown up with. (laugh)

DR: You've got to explain that remark!

Jack: In basic training they teach you to work as a team and forget your individual self. But, at the same time, you've got to see your own assets and liabilities and work within the scope of the team. You've got to be able to think independently and work for yourself to work for the team. And that was always what Daddy taught us to do. He taught us that we aren't in this life by ourselves; nobody said it was going to be easy, and nobody said it was going to be fair—but *you* have to be. That's just the way we were brought up. It has served us well.

DR: Was he the one to discipline you?

Jack: Yes. He was strict but fair, always fair. There's a line in a song by Dan Fogleberg entitled "The Leader of the Band" which I feel a lot of kinship to because he's speaking of his father. There's a line that goes, "His thundering velvet hand." And that's exactly the way my dad was; it fits perfectly.

DR: He did spank you then.

Jack: Not if he could resolve the problem without spanking. He had this look about him. When he

Jack Holt examines the rugged terrain of the Alabama Hills of Lone Pine where his father Tim and sidekick Richard "Chito" Martin used to catch outlaws for RKO Pictures. "Dad loved him. They would just have so much fun together — he just loved being around Richard, and I've found him fun to be around too — like here at the Lone Pine Film Festival." (Photo by Ken Taylor.)

looked at you, he looked straight into your eyes right through to your soul, and you knew that there was to be no more of that bad behavior. You knew you were wrong, and you fixed it right then. He spanked us a time or two, and that was about all it took. (laugh) But when you got "the look," you froze in your tracks and straightened up.

This'll give you a better idea of what kind of dad he was. The first job where I actually got a check was for KLPR radio in Oklahoma City, where my dad worked. I guess I must have been eight or nine years old at most. Dad would go out on remote broadcasts for advertisers, and, as part of it, the station had a popcorn machine, and they would give away popcorn during the remote. My job was to make the popcorn. I got five dollars a day, and Dad made me learn how to deal with the money I made. Instead of handing me a five-dollar bill, I was given a check. I had to deal with it. ."What do I do with this?" I asked him. He told me I'd have to take it to a bank and cash it. Then the question came up regarding what I would do with the money after that. Well, I really didn't need to spend it on anything right then that I could think of, so he suggested that I start a savings account. Then anytime I wanted something like a bicycle, he'd ask, "How much have you got in that savings account?" He'd send me down to the bank to get the money and then we'd go looking for a bike. When I found one that I wanted, I'd check to see that I had enough money. When I went to pay for it, he'd say, "Put your money back in the bank." And he'd buy it for me. But he would go through the whole procedure with me. He wanted me to learn about money and how to deal with it—but then, usually, his fatherly generosity would help me out at the close of the lesson.

Not too long after my popcorn business, Dad got me involved with announcing. He was doing the announcing for my little league ball games at the time. When I wasn't playing, I'd be over with him, hanging around—getting him something to drink or popcorn, whatever. He'd often take some time to teach me what to watch for in announcing a game. "You've got to keep your head in the ballgame here in the announce booth just as much as when you're on the field," he'd say, "because it's just as important when you're doing the announcing as it is when you're out there playing."

So one day I was sitting there with him, watching it all, when he suddenly said, "I'm going to go get something to drink." He tossed me the mike and told me to take over—and he didn't come back to save me. At first I was tongue-tied. Then a couple of people said, "Are you going to announce or are you just going to sit there?" Suddenly I realized I really had to do it—and I did okay.

Pretty soon I wanted to get my own PA system, so he found one for sale and told me it would cost $100. He said, "How are you going to pay for it?" I told him I really didn't want to take it out of my little savings account, so he said, "Okay, we'll go down to the bank and get a loan." So my first real bank transaction was a loan for a hundred dollars that he co-signed for—and I must not have been over ten or eleven years old.

I would get paid a little something for announcing the ball games, and I would take that money and go to the bank and make the payment on the PA system. He taught me about business and how things work. It wasn't just sitting and listening to him tell me about it; I was out there doing it.

DR: What was his job at the radio station?

Jack: He was in sales at KLPR, and was, I guess, something like an assistant manager. At that time it was a small organization, but it was a large radio station, and they just kind of worked together on everything they did. He and the station owner were great friends.

DR: I heard about a company named JAMCO that he worked for. What was that all about?

Jack: Well, they were a parts manufacturer. They made front-end parts for cars. He went to school and became a front-end alignment specialist for cars. As

Tim and Richard "Chito" Martin are "having fun" as they follow a rugged trail in Lone Pine to locate claim jumpers in this scene from *RIDER FROM TUCSON*.

a result of that, he taught me a lot about automobiles and being a mechanic. He was very mechanically minded, and he liked that stuff.

DR: It seems a bit surprising that a former actor from Hollywood would take an interest in that and would work in that field later on.

Jack: Well, he did what he wanted to do. If something caught his interest, he'd go for it, see what it was about. It was the same way with me. When I got the chance to go back to school at thirty-three years of age, I jumped at it. I started out in aviation because that interested me. I want sometime to get into engineering, but right now I'm in the middle of getting a business degree, and that has got my attention for the time being. But at the same time, I enjoy acting; I love doing that. I just wish I had more opportunity to do it.

DR: There are a lot of actors who wish they had that. Do you have any interest in getting into the film business?

Jack: Yes. I've done some film work around Oklahoma. I haven't done anything major, just some commercials, and I've done an "Unsolved Mysteries," which was a lot of fun. I've also done some industrial films too. Right now, as I said, I'm in school, a business major. I'm also a commercial pilot, instrument rated. I work at the Will Rogers Airport in Oklahoma City in operations and field service.

You know, there are so many interesting things to do in the world. That was something else that Dad taught us. "Don't limit yourself; you can do whatever you feel you want to do. Whatever you're big enough to do, go do it. Just do it right and be fair with those around you."

I'm a member of the Oklahoma Army National Guard. The regular army wouldn't take me because I've got pins in my ankles. The National Guard gave me a waiver on it. I guess I got my interest in the military from my dad. He got most of his schooling at the Culver Military Academy. When he joined the Army Air Corps, he rose to the rank of major during his years in the service. He knew the military system suited him well, and it suits me too. And my Aunt Jennifer told me that my granddad almost became a career man at the Virginia Military Institute, so I guess it has run in the family.

DR: What is your job in the Guard?

Jack: I'm assistant tower supervisor for the 145th Air Traffic Control Platoon of the Oklahoma Army National Guard. I'm mainly in charge of the training in the tower and in the workings of the tower.

DR: Are you married?

Jack: No, I'm divorced. I've got one son and his name is Tim. He's probably one of the neatest guys I've ever met. He's four.

DR: You've mentioned your grandfather and namesake, Jack Holt several times.

Jack: Yes. My grandfather and John Wayne are two people I wish that at some point in time I could have met.

DR: I've got to ask you about the difficult time when your dad died. I understand he had a cancerous brain tumor.

Jack: Yes. I was about thirteen at the time. I used to go with him when he would go get his treatments at the hospital. He got to the point where he could almost not walk. He had a cane, but if he saw a lot of people in the waiting room—and most of them recognized him—he would take the cane and curl it in his arm and walk in. Where he got the strength I'll never know. He would not let them see him down. He was always on his own two feet, and he stayed that way until he just couldn't get up anymore. He would not allow other people to see him that way, nor would he allow anyone to have pity for him. That was not going to happen. I would see him at times when it was all he could do to stand up and then from somewhere he would find this strength and march right into the hospital, right into the treatment room as if there wasn't a thing wrong with him.

I know that he told his doctors that they could do to him whatever they felt they needed to do as far as the insurance would pay. They suggested that he go to Houston where they had better facilities for cancer patients. He said, "I'm not spending the money. I didn't work my entire life and put together what I have now just to spend it on myself. I'm fifty-four years old, and I'm not going to do that. I'll either live through this or I won't, but I'll do it within the scope of what is available here."

And he did not take morphine; he did not take any kind of painkillers whatsoever. He also insisted that they should never put him on life support just to keep him alive. He was a man of faith in a way that a lot of people don't understand.

DR: Would you call him religious?

Jack: Well, that's where a lot of people get confused. There is a big difference between being a religious

Jack Holt enjoys meeting and talking with fans of his late father, Tim. "I just hope I can be what they [the fans] expect me to be and serve my father well." (Photo by Ken Taylor.)

Jack Holt: "[Dad] taught us that we aren't in this life by ourselves; nobody said it was going to be easy, and nobody said it was going to be fair—but *you* have to be. That's just the way we were brought up. It has served us well." (Photo by Ken Taylor.)

man and being a faith man. My father had faith in the word of God and a faith in God on a personal basis. He didn't necessarily need a church, and he didn't really see eye-to-eye with what a lot of churches were teaching. He had his own relationship with God, and he knew what it was, and God knew what it was, and they got along well together.

There was a preacher that came into the hospital room when Dad was asleep towards the end. He told me later that he sort of felt the presence of the preacher, looked up and saw this man standing over him with a Bible in his hand. The preacher said, "Have you made your peace with God?" Dad looked him straight in the eye and said, "I didn't know we were fighting." The man just turned around and walked out. There wasn't much he could say to that.

DR: How did your family get along after your dad passed on?

Jack: Well, it was tough, some rough spots. But Daddy taught me early on to think for myself and to take care of myself—if for no other reason than to take a load off everybody else. Mom looked after all of us, and eventually we made it through that awful time in our lives.

DR: Do you have any memorabilia from your dad's film career?

Jack: Not much. We have the pistol holster set, a pair of spurs, and a shirt and his hat. And that's all he had left. Basically, they were just movie props to him. To him there was no history behind them; they were just things. However, to other people there is a history behind them. We're going to donate these things to the Gene Autry Western Heritage Museum. They have my granddad's alligator gun belt, and I understand that my Aunt Jennifer is giving them a few things too. She didn't keep much of her

Author David Rothel and Jack Holt. "My grandfather [Jack Holt] and John Wayne are two people I wish that at some point in time I could have met." (Photo by Ken Taylor.)

Tim on Lightning canters through the Alabama Hills of Lone Pine, California, in search of bad guy Stuart Randall in this scene from *RIDER FROM TUCSON* (1950).

Jack and his son Tim. "I just hope I can turn out to be as good a father as he was. When I look at my four-year-old son Tim running around, I ask myself, 'What am I going to do for him!' He's the main focus; he's what counts." (Photo courtesy of Berdee Holt.)

memorabilia either. I understand that the museum would like to do a Holt family display, and that suits us fine.

DR: Standing out here in the Alabama Hills where your father made so many films, do you have any final thoughts about him before we wrap this up and head back to Lone Pine?

Jack: Yes, I do. Daddy often said that his measure of a man was not so much what a man did, but what he left behind. He felt that the most important thing he could leave behind was the children. He said, "It's not what you know or what you do, it's what your children know." I just hope I can turn out to be as good a father as he was. When I look at my four-year-old son Tim running around, I ask myself, "What am I going to do for him?" He's the main focus; he's what counts.

*   *   *

Bryanna and Jay Holt Interview October 20, 1992

After lunch, I got together with Bryanna and Jay in the Dow Villa Motel and talked with them about their father. Since all three children were born within a three-year period, it was not surprising that their memories covered approximately the same period of time in their father's life and dove-tailed nicely with Jack's reminiscences to provide an intimate portrait of Tim Holt, the father.

David Rothel (DR): Bryanna, how did you come by your name? It's very unusual.

Bryanna Holt: I think I was supposed to be a boy. Jack was named after Dad's dad. When I came along, I was going to be named after Mom's dad, William Bryan Stephens. Since I wasn't a boy, and they had already decided what they were going to name me, Daddy said, "We'll just call her Bryanna." I'm real proud of it.

Jay Holt: My father and mother had a good friend who was in the aviation business back in Oklahoma by the name of David Jay Perry. When I came along, I guess they had run out of fathers and others in the family to name me for, so they called me Jay Perry, and my godfather is David Jay Perry.

DR: Okay, just start anywhere and tell me about your father. Just ramble on, if you want to.

Jay: Oh, he was the friendliest person. It doesn't matter who you talk with who knew him. He is always described as the friendliest, nicest guy. Everything that's ever been written about him has said the same thing, and that's exactly the way he was.

Bryanna: "Kind" probably describes him the best. A little old man came up to me a while back and said, "I knew your father. I was at a rodeo and got hurt on a horse, and your daddy gave me this liniment to take away the pain. I'll never forget him for that." And that's just how it was with Dad. If he had something that you needed or wanted, it was yours.

Jay: He didn't really worry about life or anything. Mom always said he was like a little kid. He would walk out the door and wouldn't have a nickel in his pocket. She'd say, "At least take a dime for a phone call." (laugh)

What I especially remember is the grab bags he'd bring home. They would contain a variety of toys—nothing special, no big toys. Just a little something he'd pick up and put in a bag. He'd come home and say, "Okay, here it is. Everybody reach in and grab, and what you get is yours."

Bryanna: "Girl first," he would always add.

Jay Holt: "It doesn't matter who you talk with who knew him. He is always described as the friendliest, nicest guy." (Photo courtesy of Chuck Thornton.)

Bryanna Holt, Tim's only daughter, is shown here in the Dow Villa lobby during the 1992 Lone Pine Sierra Western Film Festival, which honored her father. (Photo by Ken Taylor.)

handy for his Westerns and rodeo appearances.

Jay: My interests were always sports—football, baseball. My brother Jack loved automobiles. You could go outside and find my dad working on a car with my brother, showing him how to set the timing or why you set the timing—anything. And, of course, he'd always furnish me with a football or whatever I needed to play in sports. When I was playing football in grade school, I was wearing glasses and having difficulty with them, so he got me what was probably one of the first pair of sport glasses—of course, they were ugly things (laugh) that had a big rubber nose, frames that were black horn-rims, and hinges that folded out—sort of break-aways. But whatever we needed in our special interest, he had an insight into it and would try to help us in some way. He introduced me to Don Meredith, the quarterback of the Cowboys, one time; it was one of the greatest thrills of my life.

Bryanna: He was a pretty strict father. I don't remember ever being spanked, but he would give you that look, and you just froze. (laugh) He was strict, but mama said people always commented on

Jay: Yeah, that was a problem.

Bryanna: He taught my brothers that it was "ladies first." When he wasn't there, I reminded them. (laugh)

Jay: There were some times when he would try to steer certain toys toward Bryanna because they were just meant for a girl. When you would pull out something obviously meant for her, you'd know you got the wrong thing. I wasn't into horses, for instance, so I'd look at a toy horse and know I got the wrong toy—it was meant for Bryanna who loves horses. Well, if it turned out that each of us got the wrong toy, he'd say, "Well, you can trade." The surprise was what was fun. You didn't know when he was going to have the grab bag, but he'd come in every once in a while with a bag and say, "Go for it."

Bryanna: My interest has always been horses, and, of course, with all of Daddy's knowledge of horses, we would spend hours together around my horse. He'd teach me all the basic things and spend a lot of time with me because he knew I was interested. Well, I showed cutting horses for a while, and that's really my first love right now. Daddy had played a lot of polo when he lived in California, but he was never involved with any of the show part of horses. He appeared in a lot of rodeos but as a star and not as a contestant. His skill with horses, of course, came in

Jay Holt poses next to the street sign in Lone Pine, California, which honors his father for the many films he made there. (Photo by Ken Taylor.)

how well-behaved we were—and that was his doing. It sounds corny, but he was very much a "right is right, wrong is wrong" kind of person. I keep a lot of those same feelings. If I see something that is not right, I want to do something about it. He really taught us that.

DR: What sort of thing would upset him?

Bryanna: (long pause) Injustice, I think.

Jay: Yeah. I remember one incident that would illustrate that trait in him. Our school had a dress code, and, of course, that was the time in the 1960s when long hair was coming in for boys. My dad was very open-minded about it. It didn't really matter to him what a person looked like; it was the person inside that counted to him. He didn't care for long hair or the hippie movement of that time, but he wasn't disparaging of it or them. As a matter of fact, he enjoyed talking with them.

Now, my hair wasn't that much out of the ordinary, but it didn't quite match the dress code of the school, so Dad took me to the barber shop for a haircut. Of course, I didn't want to abide by the dress code; I didn't think it was right—even though I was only in about the sixth grade at the time and didn't have much of a say-so in the matter. Surprisingly, Dad felt the same as I. He said, "Well, you ought to be able to wear your hair the way you want to."

So we went down to the barber shop, I got up into the chair, and Dad said, "This is what we want done." The barber said, "Okay, that's fine." Dad went next door to the coffee shop and waited about twenty minutes, came back, and discovered that it was all cropped off—exactly the opposite of what he had told the barber. And he got upset! He said, "I thought I told you how I wanted my boy's hair cut." The barber said, "Well, the school has got a dress code, and I have to follow that."

Dad didn't shout; he didn't scream; he just took me by the hand and we started walking out the door. The barber said, "That'll be $2.50." My dad turned and said to him, "Let the school pay for it," and we walked out. (laugh)

Bryanna: He couldn't stand anything that he felt was unfair. If somebody got a raw deal, it really, really bothered him. But I don't remember him ever being moody. He'd get up early in the morning, and the minute he woke up, he was happy. He was not one of those people who dragged around for an hour sullen until he got his coffee. He would be in the bathroom singing. He'd come into my room and wake me up and say, "Don't I look good today? Doesn't this suit look good?" And I'd be lying there barely able to open my eyes, much less talk.

Jay: More often than not, it was his singing in the shower which woke us up in the morning. He couldn't sing, but that didn't stop him! (laugh)

Bryanna: Not at all! (laugh)

Jay: You could hear him humming as he got dressed, and you just knew he was out to have a good day. I remember one day when it was just rank, just a downpour outside. About the only thing he said was, "Oh, I don't want to get out in that today." I said, "Why don't you just call in wet, just tell them you're not coming in?" "No, I can't do that," he said, "I've got a family to provide for." Nothing could really get him upset enough to depress him for any length of time. He might get mad for a couple of seconds, but then it was over—even during the times when we were disciplined. After the discipline was over, it was back to normal—just that quickly.

Bryanna: Most of the time he disciplined us with that look.

Jay: Yep, he did have a look. It was a look that was frightening. You knew that you had done wrong or were about to do wrong—something that was not approved. (laugh) And if you didn't know what it was, you were going to quickly find out what it was. The best thing was to stop and ask, "What?" After that, he would steer you in the right direction and life would go on. It was just that simple.

DR: Did you ever have visits from any famous persons at your home near Oklahoma City?

Jay: Well, the one that I only remember vaguely is Nick Adams, who was in *The Rebel* TV series. We have an amusement park in Oklahoma City at which he was appearing, and he came into town and looked Daddy up—wanted to see him. No phone call, no nothing, just a knock on the door and, according to Mom, we opened the door and yelled, "Mom, it's the Rebel!" (laugh) And then went running and screaming through the house. I do remember going out to Frontier City—that was the amusement park where he was appearing—and seeing him sitting in the caboose of a train and signing autographs. That does stick in my mind. That was the only famous person I recall coming to the house, but then, we didn't usually recognize famous people because they weren't famous to us.

DR: Your brother Jack told me about going with

your dad on remote radio broadcasts. Did you ever do that with him?

Jay: Oh, yes. As we'd be going to the remotes, he'd be talking to the station on his two-way radio.

Bryanna: He'd ask us, "What song do you want to hear?" He'd then call the disc jockey and have him play it on the radio as we were going to the remote.

Jay: It was KLPR Radio, and he drove a 1964 station wagon. It was white and he carried the popcorn machine in it. He'd do remotes for all sorts of places—carpet places, furniture stores, car dealerships. The radio station would offer free popcorn, balloons, and free soft drinks during the remote broadcasts.

Bryanna: It was all free. Jack would pop it, and I would sack it up and hand it out.

Jay: Jack and Bryanna had jobs to do. I was the youngest and didn't have a job at first. When I complained, he put me in charge of Cokes. It started out real good; everything was fine. There were several different soft drinks you could order, and pretty soon I was getting orders like one Coke on ice, Seven-up with ice, large Tab with ice, small Coke without ice. Wait a minute! One order at a time was okay, but I looked out and there was a huge, never-ending line there. I said, "That's it! I want out of here." It was the shortest enterprise in history.

DR: Would a whole program be done at the remote spot or would the remote just be used for commercials?

Jay: They would patch in for the commercials. You see, my dad wasn't an on-air personality. He was the sales manager. That was unusual in itself. Most of the people on remotes were air personalities; that's who the people usually wanted to see, air personalities. But at KLPR they wanted Dad to go out for the remotes—and he drew a crowd. There are a lot of people in Oklahoma City today who still talk about the remotes that Dad did at their places of business back in those times.

KLPR went to "Golden Country" and Dad had a gold Volkswagon that he drove called the "Golden Bug." I remember that he also drove a Corvair; you know, one of those rear-engine cars that were popular for a time. That was his favorite; it was his work car. We had a big car for the family.

DR: Jack told me about the period of time after your father was diagnosed with cancer. What are your recollections of that time?

Jay: If you hadn't known that he had cancer, you wouldn't have known. He did, later, go on television and do an interview about his cancer, but that was it. I have never seen that interview, but I remember him making it. I remember going into the city with him for the interview. He was walking with a cane at the time. He was wanting to tell people about cancer and to let them know that he wasn't afraid and that they shouldn't be afraid if they got cancer too.

I remember it was close to Christmas time and, of course, he died in February. He wasn't really able to work, but he had Mom drive him up to the radio station, and he gave Ralph Tyler, the manager there (this time it was KEBC Radio in Oklahoma City), a silver and turquoise belt buckle, and I think there were a couple of other things too, but that's all I remember. My dad used to wear the buckle, and Ralph always commented on it. I think Dad knew that he didn't have much longer, and he just wanted to do this in person—see that Ralph got it.

DR: At that time you'd think that he would be obsessed with his own problems.

Bryanna: Never, never. He was mostly worried about what was going to happen to us.

Jay: He went to my aunt, my mom's sister, and asked her to help take care of us.

DR: Was your dad a religious person in the sense of church?

Bryanna: No.

Jay: In fact, it wasn't until really later on in life that I realized that he was a Christian Scientist. I don't know their beliefs all that well, but I know that he believed in a creator. He mentioned it to somebody one day when he was standing out in the yard talking about religion. He said that he was a Christian Scientist, but not a practicing one. He said he followed the Ten Commandments and had never hurt anyone knowingly, and so he felt he was in good standing with God.

DR: Obviously, it was devastating when your father died. You were at an awkward age to suddenly be without a father.

Bryanna: I remember coming out of the church after the funeral and seeing all of the people with cameras and the TV cameras—and I know they had to cover it, I know—but I felt that it should have been

Jay is seen here with wife Sandra, son Shaeffer (in back), daughter Katheryn (front), and daughter Kennedy. The photo was taken the evening Tim was inducted into the Cowboy Hall of Fame. (Photo courtesy of Berdee Holt.)

a more private moment for us. I also remember the first day back at school after the funeral. We had taken Aunt Jennifer to the airport, and I think I went to school later that day. I remember kids coming up and asking, "Was so and so at your dad's funeral? Was John Wayne at your dad's funeral?" It really made me angry.

Jay: Mom and the family did all they could to keep the funeral as dignified as possible. When he died, I didn't go to the funeral home even though it was a closed casket. I just said I couldn't deal with it. I just wanted to remember him as he had been. It was difficult, of course. We all dealt with it in our own certain ways. I guess we rebelled a little bit. I think I was pretty much in a daze for a couple of years even. I'd see my friends at sporting events and other things with their fathers. I missed him.

DR: The years have passed, and you have grown up.

Jay: I've got a wife and three wonderful kids. We live in Norman, Oklahoma. Kennedy is eleven; Shaeffer is seven, and Katheryn is five—we call her "Spotty." She assumed that nickname for herself. I guess in lieu of having a dog we just have her pet name. (laugh) I work for a carpet company; I'm a carpet cleaner. I work for one of the Southwest's largest carpet distributors, Carpet World. I've been a carpet cleaner for about ten years, and I've worked for them for about a year and a half.

Bryanna: I'm divorced. I've got an eleven-year-old daughter named Jennifer—named after her aunt. She is crazy about horses and does very well at school. I'm very proud of her. I work in Guthrie, Oklahoma, at the Lazy E Arena. It's the world's largest privately-owned arena. We have mostly horse-related events there. I'm involved with the ticketing department, but eventually I'd like to get back into the horse part of it, whether there or someplace else.

DR: What's your reaction when you see your dad on the screen in movies?

Bryanna and daughter Jennifer (named for her aunt) pose for their picture at the 1991 Cowboy Hall of Fame ceremony in Oklahoma City. (Photo courtesy of Berdee Holt.)

Jay Holt: "Dad never really got into the flamboyant type of cowboy outfit that so many of the B-Western stars did. He and Richard played their roles pretty straight as working cowboys." Richard "Chito" Martin and Tim Holt are pictured here in a scene from THE STAGECOACH KID (1949).

Jay: First of all, I didn't believe that he was a movie star when I was a little kid. I had heard these stories about my dad, but I didn't really believe them. Then Mom told me, "Your father used to be in the movies." I still couldn't quite believe it. I remember the first time ever seeing him on the screen. I was sitting in our living room watching TV, and he was sitting across the room in the recliner. I believe it was either MY DARLING CLEMENTINE or TREASURE OF SIERRA MADRE. I remember seeing his name in the credits at the beginning. That was the first indication that they hadn't been kidding me, that he had really been in the movies. The first time I saw him I looked at the screen, looked back at him, looked at the screen. "Hey, that's my dad!" I blurted out.

Bryanna: Something funny happened to me at the mall in Mid West City not long ago. There is an art gallery there that has Jesse's (artist, Ivan Jesse Curtis) print of "All My Heroes Are Cowboys." We had just met Jesse and his wife at the Golden Boot Awards a week or so before. Well, I was standing there looking at the print when the man behind the cash register said, "Young lady, if you don't know who those cowboys are in the print, I can tell you." (laugh) I told him I could not only name them, but one of them was my father.

DR: What is your favorite movie of the ones your dad made?

Bryanna: I like TREASURE OF SIERRA MADRE probably the most.

Jay: Yes, TREASURE, as far as the big-budget movies. I didn't like CLEMENTINE so much because he got killed in it. It's really hard for me to choose because each one has something about him that just comes through to me personally. For example, I like the very end of TREASURE when they are riding off, laughing. That was really his laugh. I especially liked MAGNIFICENT AMBERSONS where he did a little bit of singing about the bank of Monte Carlo. It was so off key and awful, but it was just him. (laugh) I guess in most of the B Westerns that I've seen he's always the happy-go-lucky cowboy, and I like that quality in him.

Bryanna: That's what I like too, especially in the Westerns with Richard Martin. The rapport between Dad and Richard was so great. Knowing Daddy and meeting and talking with Richard, I can see the fun they were having as they made that series. It makes it so much fun for me to watch the films, knowing them both.

Jay: Dad never really got into the flamboyant type of cowboy outfit that so many of the B-Western stars did. He and Richard played their roles pretty straight as working cowboys.

Bryanna: Dad was that way in real life too. I remember him wearing the Wranglers. That was his favorite way to dress, the Wranglers.

Jay: He would wear them until they were threadbare. And he didn't own a pair of shoes that I know of. He was buried in his cowboy boots.

Bryanna: When he worked for the radio station, he wore suits, but they were Western suits.

Jay: Just a fine Western-cut suit—no fringe or anything.

Bryanna: There was nothing gaudy or flamboyant about him.

Jay: The actor Walter Reed pointed out to me one time that Dad almost always wore gloves in his Westerns. He said that was a smart thing for Dad to do because all that rugged work was hard on the hands—the fight scenes, the roping, riding, crawling over rocks. Walter pointed out too that Dad was always tugging at them. He kidded Dad one time by saying to him, "If you didn't have gloves on, you'd be pulling your wrists up." (laugh)

Richard Martin has said that he and my father were afraid that the studio was going to find out how much fun they were having and cut their salaries. And that's the way my father was. Whatever he did, he enjoyed doing it. He built houses for a while, and he enjoyed it. He worked for a front-end company in Denver called JAMCO, and he enjoyed that—although he didn't like being away from the family. He got into radio and enjoyed that.

DR: But apparently he never wanted to go back out to Hollywood to make films.

Jay: It probably wouldn't have been too difficult for him to move back out to California and start his film career again. He probably would have been welcomed, but, I guess, he just decided that Hollywood wasn't for him anymore; it wasn't fun anymore. The lifestyles had changed in Hollywood, and, especially after having children, he felt he didn't want us exposed to that kind of life. So he raised us in a little bitty hometown atmosphere in Oklahoma.

* * *

Berdee Holt Interview
October 20, 1992

The hubbub of the Lone Pine Sierra Film Festival had spilled over from the streets into the lobby of the Dow Villa Motel where we had planned to get together to talk about Tim, so Berdee Holt and I found privacy in a deserted office in the back of the motel. There, as the late afternoon sun filtered through the window, giving the room a pre-twilight reddish-gold radiance, she reminisced about her years with Tim Holt.

Berdee Holt: We met back in the 1940s. Tim was in Oklahoma to do a rodeo—he had some stock in a rodeo—and we met through some friends in Oklahoma City. It was probably two or three years after that we decided to get married. He had come back to Oklahoma City at Christmas in 1950, and we got engaged and then got married in 1952.

He had a good personality and people just liked to be with him. But they'd have to seek him out. He wasn't one to impose himself on somebody else. I think he sort of had a feeling that if he made the first

Berdee Holt poses for Ken Taylor's camera in the lobby of the Dow Villa Motel in Lone Pine, California.

move people might think he was trying to impose himself upon them. He didn't want to seem to be the Hollywood actor taking charge of the party or meeting. But if you approached him, you found him very charming, very down to earth, very modest. I would say there was a bit of shyness there.

David Rothel (DR): What attracted you to him?

Berdee: All of those qualities I just mentioned, and we just seemed to have a lot in common. I was somewhat involved in politics, and he loved politics. He sort of got into politics when we first went back to Oklahoma. A friend of ours, Bill Atkinson, was running for governor. He and Tim had known each other while Tim was still in Hollywood. Mr. Atkinson needed some help during his campaign, so he got me to work in his office and Tim to go out on the road with him.

DR: I heard that Tim made appearances during that campaign with some Shetland ponies.

Berdee: Yes, he did. Mr. Atkinson had built Mid West City as a builder/developer. It is across from Tinker Air Force Base, and it has become one of the largest cities in Oklahoma. He was giving away Shetland ponies with each home that was purchased. He had a Shetland pony farm; it was a lovely place, and he had a club where kids could come out on week-ends and ride. Also, the ponies would make appearances at many affairs in the area—pulling a little wagon and later a calliope when they appeared in parades. Well, Tim went with these ponies to different parades and appearances for Mr. Atkinson's campaign.

He didn't win the election, by the way, but Tim kept his interest in politics after that and especially after he got into radio. He would deal with politicians about their broadcast time and commercials. Some of them got to visiting with him and found out that he knew quite a bit about Oklahoma politics. At one point they asked him to run for lieutenant governor. They thought he'd make a good one to help promote the state, but during the times he was urged to run there always seemed to be a good friend of his already in the race, so he would decline to run.

Berdee Holt (followed by daughter Bryanna) is being escorted to the Lone Pine Sierra Film Festival tribute to her husband Tim Holt. "He didn't want to seem to be the Hollywood actor taking charge of the party or meeting. But if you approached him, you found him very charming, very down to earth, very modest. I would say there was a bit of shyness there." (Photo by Ken Taylor.)

DR: Jack told me that he thought his dad partly backed away from running because he felt maybe they wanted to use his name because he had been a famous Hollywood star.

Berdee: Well, they tried that even in Mr. Atkinson's campaign. Some remarks were made about him having a Hollywood actor at the campaign stops, and what did that have to do with Oklahoma? What they didn't realize was that Tim was living there and was very much a part of Oklahoma, loved Oklahoma, and had adopted it as his home state. Well, sort of; he always knew where his roots were. Some thought that he was just a "flash in the pan," so to speak, for Atkinson's campaign. When they talked with him and realized that he knew quite a bit about Oklahoma and Oklahoma politics and that he was living there, then it was different.

DR: During the twenty-some years that Tim lived after leaving his Hollywood career, he worked at quite a number of different jobs—all kinds of jobs—but he apparently never thought seriously of returning full time to acting in films. Why not?

Berdee: I don't know for sure, but when he first came out from under contract to RKO, he said to me—he was probably thirty-two or three at the time, "Do you realize that this is the first time in my life that I can make my own decisions and do what I want to do?" And, you know, that was true. He said, "First it was my parents who told me what to do, then RKO told me what to do, then I went into the service and Uncle Sam told me what to do. I came back out and RKO still told me what to do. This is the first time I have not been under somebody's thumb in my life."

DR: Didn't he go out on several personal appearance tours after completing his Western film series in 1952?

Berdee: Yes. Tim did a little bit of touring with Ray Whitley, Richard Martin, and Jack O'Shea, just a few weeks, in Ohio, Indiana, and up through New York. At that time Ken Murray was doing a popular live television show from New York, and he had Tim on the program.

Well, Tim thought it wasn't all that bad, so when

At the time this photograph was taken (circa 1959), Tim was managing a 1400-acre dude ranch and hosting a Saturday morning *Tim Holt Western Theatre* television show on KOCO-TV, Oklahoma City. During each program Tim showed one of his Western films and promoted the ranch. (Photo courtesy of Nick Nicholls.)

his agent in Charlotte, North Carolina, got in touch with him later, asking him to go out on the road again for a tour of the South, he said he would. Tim had ranked very highly with movie exhibitors, and they were after him to make personal appearances. So the agent lined up an itinerary for the tour that looked pretty good, and I went every speck of the way with him. It was just the two of us then, and we thought, "Why not?"

It was a little country/Western show. Tim had a comedian in the act, and they would bounce jokes back and forth to each other for part of the show. There were four musicians that played some Western music, and then Tim would display his guns—firing them and doing tricks with them. There were a lot of performers who were doing that sort of show in those days in the early 1950s.

Tim was told all during that tour that he and his group put on one of the better stage shows. And Tim demanded a good show from the men in his show. He told them, "You be nice to people; you be on time. These people don't pay their money to see an empty stage or a drunk up there." And there were a lot of touring shows that had that problem.

DR: Wasn't it shortly after the tour that you moved to Marshalltown, Iowa, where Tim decided to enter college?

Berdee: Yes, he studied animal nutrition with a professor at Ames, Iowa, who had developed a special mineral for animals and a company called the So-Rite Mineral Company. This was through a friend of ours named Henry Wolfe. He and Tim had met when Tim went to Marshalltown to make an appearance for some celebration. Henry asked if he would come to Iowa to help him if he started a mineral company. He prevailed upon us to move to

Tim is seen here in uniform (and with ever-present pipe) for his role in the science-fiction thriller, *THE MONSTER THAT CHALLENGED THE WORLD* (1957). The producer of the film, Arnold Laven, had once been the "script boy" (as Berdee Holt remembered it) on Tim's film *THE ARIZONA RANGER*. Laven later went on to produce *The Rifleman* and *The Big Valley* television series.

Marshalltown and give it a try, and we did. We stayed there for a year or two and then Tim went down to Oklahoma to promote the So-Rite Mineral Company there. At that time the company was only in about three or four states. Well, it didn't go too well in Oklahoma. The company had some problems, and, during that time, Bill Atkinson came to Tim and wanted him to help him in his political ambitions, so Tim left the company.

Later he got into home building through Atkinson, and he had his own building company. Some of the people Tim built homes for told me that he built a fine home, but, unfortunately, he went into it at a bad time in Oklahoma economics in the 1960s—home building had taken a slump. They said that Tim put too much into his homes to make a good profit. Tim said, "If a man gives half of his life to pay for a home, I feel that it should be the best I can build for him." That was just the way he was. I'm sure he reaps his reward in heaven because he just would not take advantage of somebody to line his own pockets.

DR: And wasn't there a period when Tim ran a dude ranch for a man named Ike Hall?

Berdee: Yes. Ike was an Oklahoma real estate developer that we had gotten to know. Ike had some property east of Norman, and it was called Hall Ranch. He wanted to get it going again, revive it, so we moved down there and Tim ran it for him for a while. He had horseback riding, fishing, hunting.

DR: Basically, a dude ranch.

Berdee: Right. Tim loved it, and it went pretty well for a while. Ike owned the Oklahoma Club, a men's club in Oklahoma City. If you belonged to the club, it gave you the use of all the facilities at the club—banquet rooms, sauna, gym, that sort of thing. It was a pretty elaborate and exclusive club, and Ike was trying to hook up the ranch with the club. In particular, he thought it would give his club members more of an outlet to fish and hunt. He was sort of experimenting with it, and it just didn't go—again because the economic conditions were not good at the time. Tim did a Saturday morning television show during that time to promote the ranch. It was called the *Tim Holt Western Theatre*.

DR: It seems that Tim was interested in all kinds of things.

Berdee: Yes, and once he set his mind to do something, he was always successful at it. It wasn't always successful, but he fulfilled his part of the agreement successfully. After that period of time at the dude ranch, he went into radio at KLPR in Oklahoma City, which was owned by his friend Jack Beasley. He loved radio, but some years later when Jack sold the station, Tim wasn't too happy with the new setup, so that was when he worked for a period of time in Denver for JAMCO, an automobile parts manufacturer. Then he went back into radio when Ralph Tyler got a hold of him. When Ralph found out that Tim had left KLPR, he said, "I wish I'd known he was going to leave; I would have liked him to come work for my station." As I said, Tim really loved radio; that was his true love, so he went with Ralph at KEBC. It was while he was with KEBC that he became ill.

DR: Did Tim have a Hollywood agent after he moved to Oklahoma?

Berdee: Yes, Jerry Cloutman. Jerry was always after Tim to make a picture, but Tim didn't like making that trip to Hollywood. If he was into something else, he didn't want to take the time away.

Tim is seen here in a candid (circa 1972) photo that was taken of him while he was account executive with radio station KEBC-FM in Oklahoma City. (Photo courtesy of Valery Anne Zurn.)

DR: He did a few times though. Once for *MONSTER THAT CHALLENGED THE WORLD.* How did that picture come about?

Berdee: We were living in Marshalltown at the time. Jerry sent Tim the contract, and then Tim discussed it with Dr. Wolfe. Henry was interested in the movies, so when Tim got this script and offer to do the film, I think Dr. Wolfe talked him into it, urged him to go ahead and do it.

Usually when Tim did some film project it was at the urging of a friend. That's why he agreed to do *The Virginian* television show in 1969. That was at the urging of Jack Beasley who owned the station KLPR, the radio station where Tim was working. He said, "Tim, I just think it's time you got back to doing some film work." Between Ralph Winters (also at the station) and Jack Beasley urging him, he finally agreed to do the program; he really wasn't very interested in it. But he thought, well, why not? And then he was surprised at how much they paid him. He thought they must have made a mistake, and he wanted me to send it back. (His contract called for $1,500 in payment for the three-day assignment; he received $2,300 because of overtime.)

DR: He made two other films: *THE YESTERDAY MACHINE* in 1962 and *THIS STUFF'LL KILL YA!* in 1971. What can you tell me about those two films?

Berdee: I don't know much about either one of them. I don't know if they were ever actually released. My remembrance is that *THE YESTERDAY MACHINE* was shot in Texas, but I don't know who is in it or even what it is about. I've never seen it.

THIS STUFF'LL KILL YA! was done by a group of people in Oklahoma; it was shot there. Again, I think Tim did it at the urging of Jack Beasley, but I'm not positive. All I knew at the time was that Tim was doing it, and he only spent a couple of days on it. When Bob Anthony, who is one of the Oklahoma State Corporation Commissioners, was elected to office, his aide was a young man by the name of Skip Nicholson. When I met him, he told me that he had been in this picture with Tim, but he said, "I don't tell that to many people; I don't even tell people I know anything about that picture—it's so horrible!" He said, "The only one I know who came out of that picture was Larry Drake, who went on to have a major role in "L.A. Law." That was the first I knew that Larry Drake was in it.

DR: Tim's willingness to help out a friend or do a favor, as in his appearances in these later films, certainly demonstrates what an easy touch he could be—sometimes even when it was not beneficial to

Tim was working for KEBC radio in Oklahoma City when this photo was taken in May of 1972, three months before his reoccurring illness was diagnosed as cancer. (Photo courtesy of Nick Nicholls.)

him personally.

Berdee: I remember years ago when Tim was touring and a couple of fellows hit him up for a loan that left us temporarily without any money. This was at a drive-in theatre in the Tampa, Florida, area. In those days people didn't have credit cards; you had to go to a bank and cash a check to get money. If I'm not mistaken, it was getting stormy and there was a concern about the show getting rained out. We hadn't picked up any cash, and we had to go on to the town where Tim's next appearance took place. Well, two fellows came to Tim and told him that they needed to get back to a sick relative and needed some money. I didn't hear the story; Tim told me about it later. He gave them the last dollars he had on him and then came and told me. "Well, it makes no difference," he said. "We're not as bad off as they are." Tim didn't have to have a thousand bucks in his pocket to make him feel comfortable or to be assured that he would make it through the next day. He just knew that he was taken care of, that he'd make it.

DR: You said earlier that it was while he was at KEBC that he first became ill.

Berdee: Yes. Tim had had some problems of blacking out. He did once at home, and we put him in the hospital for a couple of weeks. They ran every test they could think of, including a brain scan, but they found nothing. They did say that his heart had an irregular beat, and they seemed to feel that that might be causing his problems.

Then one day he collapsed while at a luncheon, and one of his friends there discovered that Tim had left his car running when he arrived for lunch—just left the car without turning it off. So he went back into the hospital again for more tests. They monitored him around the clock and found nothing, and in a few days he was released.

It wasn't until the next year in August—when I was scheduled for some tests in the hospital—that I urged Tim to go back for another physical examination. He had been losing weight and hadn't been looking too well. I had been telling him he must go and see the doctor, but it was one of those situations where I would nag and nag him, and he would keep putting it off. "I will, I will, but I can't right now because I've got this appointment to keep and that to do." So, finally, when I had to go into the hospital for

Berdee Holt (discussing the children and Tim with David Rothel): "They just adored him, and they had such a great rapport with him. We have always had good communication and good respect for one another, and that is so important in a family." (Photo by Ken Taylor.)

some tests, I said, "Tim, you're going to be there visiting me, so we're just going to make an appointment, and, while you're there at the hospital, you can have your doctor give you a checkup. He agreed that that would be fine.

It was during the checkup that the cancer was revealed. They removed a node on his neck at his lymph gland. When the doctor removed it, he said that it was so close to the nerve to the brain that it was most likely causing the blackouts, that they didn't have anything to do with his heart. I couldn't believe that he'd been to three different hospitals in Oklahoma City and they hadn't been able to detect this earlier, but they hadn't. Of course, back in the late '60s and early '70s they didn't have the equipment they have today to detect such things. Well, the doctor removed the node and said that it was malignant but that it had not gotten to any of his vital organs.

The doctor sent Tim to a specialist so that they could find out where the cancer was originating from. The tests revealed that it was in his sinus, so they gave him chemotherapy and pretty soon thought that they had it licked. Then, all of a sudden, he began to look pale again, and they did more tests which resulted in them telling him that he had brain cancer and probably just six months to live.

It was shortly after Thanksgiving of 1972 that he came in one night, packed his clothes, and said, "I'm going into the hospital because I feel so bad, and pretty soon I'm going to feel so bad that you won't be able to handle me." He went into the Shawnee Medical Center, which was not too far from our home in Harrah, and stayed there until he died in February of 1973.

During this time he told his doctor to run any tests or try any experimental-type medicines on him that might further the cause of cancer research. He also went to a friend at the local TV station and did a fifteen minute interview for the American Cancer Society on what he was experiencing, how he felt, and what he believed.

DR: I understand that John Wayne came to the hospital to visit Tim at the time he was near death.

Berdee: I didn't see him there personally, but others told me about it. Usually I would make a trip into my office to see that everything was going along okay and then I would leave and go to the hospital. When I got to the hospital in the afternoon that day, they said that John Wayne had flown into town and had come into the hospital through the back door, so only the nurses and doctors saw him. They took him to Tim's room, he walked in alone and stood there for a while. Tim was unconscious during the time he was there. They weren't able to talk. He just made the visit to pay his respects. He had earlier sent Tim a note saying that he'd heard Tim had the big C and hoped that he would be on the mend soon. He told Tim to talk to the man upstairs because He'd helped him through his cancer.

Tim told me during his last days, "I've had a good life, and I'm not afraid to die." He said, "I have just one regret—that I will not be here to see these children grow up." When he passed away, they were eleven, twelve, and thirteen. They were just entering into their teen years, a bad time for kids to be without their father. But they were great; they were wonderful; they gave me no problems and never have given me any problems.

DR: Do you have any idea whatever happened to Tim's son Lance from his first marriage? I know he visited you and Tim at least once over the years.

Berdee: I don't have any idea what happened to him. In Buck's book (*The Fabulous Holts* by Buck Rainey) he quoted somebody saying that they got in contact with Lance when Tim died and that he didn't want to come to his father's funeral. I just can't believe that. Of course, I was having a difficult time then, and they were trying to make all of the arrangements for the funeral for me, so I don't really know for sure if they got in touch with Lance or not.

I find it hard to believe because Lance had a good relationship with his father. When he was sixteen, he spent the summer with Tim and me, and they got along fine. He wanted to stay and go to school, but his mother wouldn't stand for it. She lived with her parents—they were quite wealthy—and they just laid the law down to Lance. "You come home or you're disinherited." Tim didn't want any problems, so he talked with Lance and told him, "Do what your mother asks; after all, she is your legal guardian.'" But he wanted to stay with his father.

When Lance became eighteen, he wanted to enlist in the Air Force. He wrote and said that his mother wouldn't agree to it but wanted to know if Tim would. Tim said that he thought that would be good for Lance, so he signed some papers for him to go into the Air Force. We heard from him when he got down to Randolph Field.

We received a letter later from his fiancee saying that she and Lance were getting married. After that there was no contact. I have no idea if he had a change of heart, but it wasn't Tim's fault because he didn't see Lance more. Lance's mother had a court order saying that when Tim came to see the child it upset him, and she didn't want anymore visitations unless it went through the courts. Tim would go very long periods of time without seeing Lance because of that.

But I can't verify Buck's story that Lance refused or didn't want to come to his father's funeral. I can't understand why it would be so, because their relationship had been good. I can't see why he would have had a change of heart. I asked Jennifer a couple of years ago if she had heard from Lance, and she said that she had not. We don't know where he is.

DR: From what Jack, Jay, and Bryanna have told me, it is pretty obvious they feel that Tim was about as good a father as there could be.

Berdee: They just adored him, and they had such a great rapport with him. We have always had good communication and good respect for one another, and that is so important in a family.

DR: In Western films it seems the cowboy always ends up marrying the schoolmarm. Weren't you a schoolmarm when Tim met you?

Berdee: Well, I wasn't teaching school, but I was employed by the state department of education in Oklahoma. In addition to being kidded about the cowboy marrying the schoolmarm, our friends also kidded us that Tim was the cowboy who married the Indian. You see, my great grandmother was a Cherokee. Later I went to work for the Oklahoma State Corporation Commission, and after being there for several years, they had a position they needed to fill called a marshal. They offered it to me—marshal of the court. When I became a marshal, that really gave the kids and our friends something to talk about. "My daddy's a cowboy, but my mother's the marshal!"

Eventually they appointed me secretary of the commission, and I loved it very much. I was there for about twenty-two years. It was fortunate that I had the position when Tim passed away. It gave me an outlet, something to work on, because his death was a great loss to all of us. I retired at the first of the year, 1992.

*   *   *

Chapter 8
You Can Know A Man By The Company He Keeps—More Reminiscences

Richard Martin Interview
January 5, 1993

Richard "Chito" Martin, who has no accent at all in real life, was born in Spokane, Washington, on December 12, 1917. When he was just a youngster, his family moved to Los Angeles. After high school he attended California University, where he nurtured his growing desire to become an actor. By the early 1940s his knocking on studio doors had paid off with a contract at RKO Pictures.

Richard's Chito character, surprisingly, did not originate in a Western picture. As Richard recalled in an interview some years back, "The part of Chito started out in a picture called *BOMBARDIER* (1943) with Pat O'Brien and Randolph Scott. It was a war picture designed to recruit bombardiers for World War Two. There was a character called Chito in the picture that Jack Wagner wrote as he went along; Jack was a friend of mine. I was under contract as a stock player at that time, as were Bob Ryan, Walter Reed, and Eddie Albert. We were all in the picture and all trying to get ahead in pictures. Barton MacLane was supposed to be the comic of the film, but Jack kept writing some pretty funny things for Chito to say. The result was that I kept saying them and the part kept getting better as the picture went along. Everyone liked the character of Chito so much that they put him into the Zane Grey films with Bob Mitchum for two pictures and one with Jim Warren. Then when I asked for a twenty-five-dollar-a-week raise, they fired me."

Bounced from RKO, Richard opened a restaurant just around the corner from the studio, which soon became a hangout for RKO actors, technical people, and directors. Richard was constantly pressed by actor friends and casting directors to return to pictures, but he countered that he could make more money at the cash register than from casting offices. For close to two years Richard resisted most urgings to forsake the role of restaurateur for that of actor again—although he did appear in two forgettable films during this time: the serial *THE MYSTERIOUS MR. M* (Universal, 1946) and *THE ADVENTURES OF DON COYOTE* (Comet/United Artists, 1947).

Richard played Chito in Zane Grey's *WANDERER OF THE WASTELAND* in 1945 with "tall, lean, 'n handsome James Warren" (as the publicity release stated). Two years later he revived the role for twenty-nine films in the Tim Holt Western series.

When Tim was mustered out of the Army Air Corps after World War Two and returned to RKO to resume his series of Westerns, it was decided (as mentioned elsewhere) that he would complete the Zane Grey titles that were still available to the

Richard Martin portrayed sidekick Chito Jose Gonzales Bustamonte Rafferty in Tim Holt's post-war Western series.

Richard "Chito" Martin poses for the author's camera at the 1981 Charlotte Western Film Fair.

studio. Since the Chito Jose Gonzales Bustamonte Rafferty character had been used in the previous Grey films, Richard was invited back to resurrect the character in the three films that Tim was to make using the Zane Grey titles. The pairing of Tim Holt and Richard Martin was so successful in those three films that the studio, Tim, and Richard thought that it would be a good idea to continue him in the role for Tim's regular series.

The refreshing thing about Richard's playing of Chito was that he never once fell into a horse trough—an avoidance few of the comic saddle pards could lay claim to in the B Westerns. Richard's portrayal was among the most subdued of the comic sidekicks but certainly one of the most engaging and enjoyable. Most of his comedy evolved out of his malapropos Spanish/English and his extraordinary zeal to dally with beautiful senoritas who usually sang and danced in the cantinas. But when they broached the inevitable subject of marriage to Chito, he beat a hasty *hasta la vista* down the trail—romance was one thing; marriage was something else entirely!

Unlike the physical comedy of most comic sidekicks, Chito's humor was usually verbal. In *ROAD AGENTS* (1952), Chito's difficulties with the language were well represented.

Chito: (Speaking to an outlaw who recently had the drop on him and Tim) How do you like it, senor, when the foot is on the other shoe?

Chito: (Remarking that he and Tim are a team) With every one of us there is always two.

Chito: (When Tim suggests they become Western Robin Hoods) Oh, with the left hand we rob Brant (the outlaw), with the right hand we give the cattlemen the money they need, and with the third hand they give it back to the banditos who stole it. Magnifico! That makes everybody honest—even me!

Chito: (On his frustration with women) If I ever get married, it will never be with women. They're always blaming somebody else for something they didn't do.

It was Tim's job, of course, to figure out how to capture the outlaws; Chito was supposed to be fun-loving, a rascal with the ladies, and in a constant tangle with the English language. Unlike most sidekicks, however, Chito could be counted on to hold his own in a shoot out or a fight. Chito explained his varied abilities in *THE ARIZONA RANGER* (1948).

Cowhand: Say, Chito, you were pretty good with your dukes in that fight today.

Chito: Oh, that was easy; that's the Irish in me.

Tim Holt: Don't let him fool you. He's pretty good with the girls, too.

Chito: Oh, that's easy too. That's the Spanish in me.

Cowhand: Hey, now wait a minute. Are you an Irishman or a Mexican?

Chito: I'm both—Chito Jose Gonzales Bustamonte Rafferty.

Richard Martin has been a frequent guest at Western film festivals for many years. Always popular with the fans, he is frequently accompanied by his wife, actress Elaine Riley, whom he met and fell in love with while making *RIDER FROM TUCSON* in 1950. Richard's manner is quiet and unassuming. He has warm remembrances of those years when he rode the range with Tim, but it's apparent from his answers to questions that he hasn't dwelt upon the past. Frequently, he will remind the questioner of how many years ago it was that all those events took place and acknowledge his forgetfulness. After all, it's been over forty years since he left the film business to discover a very different type of success in the insurance business. He tells fans, "I've enjoyed two careers: films and insurance. I have a lot of people in show business as my clients. I went back and got all of my old friends."

Richard was a guest at the 1992 Lone Pine Sierra Film Festival which honored Tim, and I had planned to talk with him there about the Western

Tim and Chito feign shoot-'em-up action for this in-studio publicity photo for *WILD HORSE MESA* (1947).

Actress Elaine Riley appeared with Tim and Richard in only one film, *RIDER FROM TUCSON* (1950). During the making of the picture, she and Richard fell in love and were later married. (Photo courtesy of Chuck Thornton.)

series they did together. (I had previously interviewed him for my book on sidekicks.) Unfortunately, in the hurly-burly of the festival we only had time to chat for a few minutes, so it was decided that I would call him at home later when we could talk more comfortably about those times.

David Rothel (DR): Tell me about Tim. What kind of person was he?

Richard Martin: I think he was one of the most giving guys that you could find. He was always going out of his way to help people. To give you an idea of what kind of guy he was, here he was the star of a series of Westerns, making excellent money, and I'm his sidekick. As far as I was concerned, it was like pennies from heaven to have this job as his sidekick, only it was dollar bills from heaven. He would skip his raise on his (contract) option every other year if they would give me the raise that year. How many leading men or actors or *people* do you know who would say, "Hey, I won't take a raise this year; you give it to my friend over here and then I'll take it next year and then he'll get another one the following year. We did that back and forth for six years. We had a great friendship over the years; it was just a true friendship between two guys. He was a very pleasant guy to work with too; I just had a great rapport with him. I really missed him when we broke up the deal, because we had so much fun doing the film series, and we got paid for it at the same time!

DR: Tim always played his Western hero character in a very serious and taciturn manner. Did he have much of a sense of humor off camera?

Richard: He enjoyed a good joke—and pranks. I remember one particular time when he played a practical joke on a new leading lady. As you probably know, we had trailers for dressing rooms while we were filming on location. Well, we were up in Lone Pine, and Tim and a couple of other fellows found a burro and put it in her trailer while she was at lunch. It scared the hell out of her when she opened the door to go in and found this long-eared little desert burro sharing her accommodations. When she recovered from the shock, she laughed and swore that she'd get even with him for this initiation to Western pictures.

We were always pulling gags on each other. Tim was great at loosening my horse's cinch at the wrong time so that the saddle would come down on top of me when I tried to mount for a quick getaway. He was just fun, and he had a great sense of humor. I don't ever remember him grouchy or ever yelling at anybody.

DR: The series Tim and you made for RKO was certainly one of the best B-Western series ever produced in Hollywood. Let's talk a bit about the making of the series. The first eight films—from *THUNDER MOUNTAIN* through *GUN SMUGGLERS*—were shot at Lone Pine, California.

Richard Martin was a guest at the 1992 Lone Pine Sierra Film Festival. In the big parade through town, Richard and character actor Walter Reed rode in a surrey with the fringe on top. (Photo by Ken Taylor.)

Richard: What a great location for making Western films, but it could be a rough place to shoot a film if it was the wrong time of the year. I remember once when we were up there in December and it was bitter cold and there was a hard wind blowing off Mount Whitney that cut right through you. Myrna Dell was in the picture (*GUNS OF HATE*); we were filming out near a little cabin we used quite often. I remember that she said, "What am I doing up here freezing to death!" She left where we were shooting, got into the car and said, "I am not going to get out there and perform any (blankety-blank) more." And she could use pretty colorful language when she felt the need. I said, "Myrna, we've got to get the scene done; the poor crew is freezing to death out there." It was damned near below zero, I would guess. Of course, the wind really rips through there in December. We had heaters and everything else in an attempt to keep warm. Well, we finally got Myrna out of the car to complete the scene, but it was rugged. I remember that little cabin only because of the weather that one time when we were shooting there.

DR: That cabin is still standing; I visited it when I was at the festival. I was allowed to go inside, and it looked as if it might have been used for interior shots. In the films when the door of the cabin was opened, the exterior matched perfectly—and didn't look like rear projection.

Richard: I don't remember that we ever shot in the cabin. I would say no, because acoustically the sound is so poor when you try to pick it up in those kinds of buildings, and we had a budget that warranted a little more quality than just trying to get it on film. No, I would say that the interiors were done down on the RKO lot. As you indicated, we shot quite a number of films up in Lone Pine, and it was one of the best locations for shooting Westerns—except occasionally when the weather would turn on you.

DR: Another location that you used for several films was the Garner Ranch. [The films included *BROTHERS IN THE SADDLE* (1949), *RUSTLERS* (1949), *MASKED RAIDERS* (1949), *RIDERS OF THE RANGE* (1950), and *SADDLE LEGION* (1951).]

Richard: The Jack Garner Ranch is up in Idyllwild, California, which is above Palm Springs in the San Jacinto Mountains. Those are the mountains you look at if you're lying in the sun in Palm Springs, the range of mountains adjoining Palm Springs. Idyllwild is somewhat of a resort area. USC has a music conservatory up there in the summertime and noted musicians come up to play. When we were there years ago, there was a lodge and individual cabins that you could rent. Snow was frequently on the ground in the wintertime; in summertime it was very pleasant.

The Garner Ranch is a cattle ranch; he runs around a thousand to fifteen hundred head of cattle up there. We used to use Jack's cattle in the pictures. The Garner Valley and the Garner Ranch itself have been used many times in Hopalong and Roy Rogers films, among others. As a matter of fact, I had dinner with Jack Garner just the other night, and he was talking about when he was young and remembering Hopalong when he first started coming up there to film.

DR: It looks a lot like Big Bear, California, in the films.

Richard: Well, it does have the similar trees, pine trees.

DR: The buildings you used in the films for the ranch houses....

Richard: One of them was the original Garner ranch house. Jack's grandfather built it; his father lived in it. Jack restored it, and his daughter has lived in it. Jack now has a rather modern house that he built near where the bunkhouse is for the ranch hands. The old ranch house was restored to the way it was in the late 1800s. There was also another ranch building that we used a couple of times for a cabin or ranch house.

DR: In *STORM OVER WYOMING* (1950) you and Tim were seen riding through a huge flock of sheep. Where was that filmed?

Richard: That was in Agura, which was a daily

The Lone Pine cabin as it appears today. The actors and crew thought that they were going to freeze to death here while filming *GUNS OF HATE* (1948) in a biting cold wind and near-zero December weather.

The background pine trees reveal the location to be the Jack Garner Ranch in Idyllwild, California. Tim shot five films there between 1949 and 1951. In this scene Tim is on Lightning and Chito is riding Taco. Taco can be identified by the small white star on his forehead.

location for us. We got up early in the morning and returned late at night. At that time they had cattle and sheep ranches out there that are now all home developments. The sheep were tended by Basque shepherds that had been brought here from Spain. They used to stay out there with those sheep until they were ready for market. They had their own covered wagons that they lived in.

DR: Tell me about the RKO Ranch in Encino where the Western street was located.

Richard: At the time the ranch was built, Encino might have been referred to as the west end of the San Fernando Valley. People were buying little ranchettes, as they referred to them, one to two acres. The Warner Ranch out there had racing horses. Barbara Stanwyck had her stable out there; Bing Crosby had his there. The RKO Ranch was about a mile off the main street, which was Ventura Boulevard in Encino. You'd go down Encino Avenue, down this street which had all the ranchettes, and at the end of the street was a gate. You'd go in the gate, turn the corner, and you were on the Western street—and that's all that was there, the Western street. It was a well-developed street; it even had a train which you could pull in and out of town on six- or seven-hundred feet of track.

DR: There were a couple of films where you had a train depot and used a train. I always assumed that it was shot elsewhere, but it must have been shot at the ranch.

Richard: Yes. They had to go get an engineer from the Southern-Pacific to run the steam engine. They had the train right there.

DR: Let's talk about the horses. Tim had his horse Lightning, of course. Did he have several double

Tim and Lightning pose for a publicity shot at the gate of the RKO Ranch in Encino, California.

horses for Lightning?

Richard: He had one double horse that was supplied by Fat Jones, who provided all of the horses for Tim's films. Tim owned Lightning, who was a stallion when we started the films, but, finally, Tim had to have him gelded to quiet him down. Lightning was all over the place.

DR: He *was* spirited! You could tell in some of the films.

Richard: It got to the point where it was taking too much time to get him quieted down to film, and that's when Tim had him gelded.

I had one horse that I especially liked, a bay horse named Taco. He was part thoroughbred and had very good conformation. Whoever had the horse before me had trained him for a roping horse. He was what was referred to as a lead horse because he would stand still in scenes, look alert, and had a nice stature when he was standing there. He didn't drop his head and fall asleep, and yet he wasn't spirited enough to move around so that you couldn't get your positions and get your lines out. I would say I used that horse in at least half of the films.

DR: There was one film (*RIDERS OF THE RANGE*, 1950) in which you referred to him as Taco, and that's the only time in the entire series that you mentioned his name. Was that his real name?

Richard: Yes, it really was—a perfect name for Chito's horse. He was a great horse. He would follow me around—not because of my smashing personality but because I used to carry sugar and carrots around with me. He would push and nudge me, trying to get me to give him a treat. I remember Herman (Schlom, producer) used to get upset because Taco would slobber on the back of my leather jacket, and it cost a few bucks to get it cleaned every

Tim and Chito fend off the badmen in this scene shot at the RKO Ranch train depot.

once in a while.

DR: Tim never wore flashy Western clothes in the series, but you had an interesting costume as Chito.

Richard: The jacket was the Spanish-type bolero jacket that the designer in the wardrobe department took as a basic motif and made into a sort of half Western/half Spanish-type leather jacket. Then he took a pair of twill pants and put a stripe of leather down the side and cuffed them with leather to dress them up a little bit. The original shirts I had were a Spanish-type shirt with the black tie, a rather full tie. The shirts were pleated in front, but we got rid of them later in the series. We had brown twill pants that the doubles used to wear because the leather-trimmed pants were expensive and the doubles would rip and tear them up in stunt scenes.

DR: Speaking of doubles, who doubled Tim and you in the pictures?

Richard: Well, Davey Sharpe doubled Tim much of the time. When I started, Dick Farnsworth doubled me a couple of times. He was much thinner than I, and I was quite thin, but nobody seemed to notice. Ben Johnson doubled me also. These guys were cowboys at the time, of course; they were unknown. Henry Wills doubled me in a scene in Lone Pine where he had to fall off the horse and go into the lake. He reminded me of it recently. I told him I didn't remember him doubling me, but I sure as hell would have remembered falling into that lake. A fellow named Carol Henry finally got the job of doubling me full time. I would say that he was in the last ten or fifteen pictures.

DR: Let me ask you about a couple of the leading ladies. Joan Dixon was in a number of them.

Richard: Yes, she was a contract player at RKO. She was part of the group of girls that were brought in after Hughes bought the studio. Joan Dixon liked to make Westerns. She enjoyed the horses and the outdoors, and she was a very nice young lady; she was really very pleasant to work with.

In the Tim Holt film series Chito (seen here in two unusually serious poses) wore a bolero-style leather jacket, the two pictured being the most frequently-used designs. The costume designer wanted the jackets to look half Western and half Spanish.

DR: I have the impression watching her that she probably didn't have very much experience at the time.

Richard: No, she didn't. Tim used to try to teach her film acting skills, and the three of us would go off to one side and rehearse. She was very open to suggestions regarding acting, because she was really very inexperienced.

DR: Were many of the leading ladies girls that Howard Hughes had romantic eyes for?

Richard: I don't know for sure. We used to hear all kinds of wild stories, but we could never get anybody to verify them. (In a previous interview Richard had commented, "Howard Hughes rarely came on the studio lot, but he did select our leading ladies in the latter group of Westerns we made. This was always pretty interesting because we never knew who we were going to meet, and the leading lady wasn't quite sure what she was doing there. Most of these gals had gone directly to dramatic school and from there they came over to the studio to get some experience in the Westerns.")

DR: Nan Leslie was Tim's most-frequent leading lady.

Richard: Nan was a contract player at RKO for years. She's now living in San Juan Capistrano, which is about thirty miles from me on the coast. I talked to her four or five months ago—a lovely lady. I really enjoyed working with her.

DR: How much input on the films did Tim have with the producer?

Richard: We'd always get together when the script was finished—the producer, director, writer, Tim and me. We'd sit down and go over the whole script, take a couple of days. Tim was pretty good on adding and suggesting things. They'd always listen to me if I found my dialogue difficult because of the dialect. They'd generally rewrite it. The writer was very open to making changes if we came up with something that was funnier for me to do or say. The whole idea was that everybody was trying to come up with something that would make the picture better.

DR: Norman Houston's credit as writer of the scripts comes up on the majority of the films. Was he under contract to the studio to supply the scripts?

Joan Dixon was Tim's leading lady in five films between 1950 and 1952. She is seen here with Tim and Chito in PISTOL HARVEST (1951).

Richard: I don't think he was under contract, but everyone liked his work, and I guess his price was right. Norman used to get out practically all of the scripts. He knew the characters, and he knew what the producer and director were after, so they got along pretty well.

DR: Tell me about the producer, Herman Scholm.

Richard: Herman was one of RKO's best B producers. He could get a lot of quality into a picture for very few dollars. He lived with the pictures he was producing twenty-four hours a day, trying to refine them, make them better. He fought for excellent music backgrounds and outstanding photography. Bakaleinikoff used to score the pictures, and you couldn't find anyone better than Constantine Bakaleinikoff. Paul Sawtell wrote the music and arranged it; then Bakaleinikoff would conduct as many as a sixty-piece orchestra on some of the pictures. Sometimes Herman managed to get Nick Musuraca, a contract cameraman at RKO, when he wasn't working on other pictures; he'd talk Nick into doing our pictures. Nick could paint pictures with his camera! It was quality work!

DR: Of the directors that Tim and you worked with, who were particular favorites?

Richard: There were two that we really enjoyed. There was Lew Landers; he was a fun guy, and he moved very fast and got the work out. Les Selander was the other one we especially liked to work with. We called him "the jumping gazelle" because he would run from one rock to another up at Lone Pine setting up shots. The cameraman would come huffing and puffing behind him with the camera. Another director that we used a few times was George Archinbaud; he used to do a lot of Hoppys too. He was much more "the gentleman" than Lew or Les and a rather quiet person.

DR: Selander also directed a lot of Tim's films before the war. Tim and Herman Schlom apparently liked his work very much.

Richard: Oh, yes. He directed most of the big cowboy stars at one time or another. He was a close friend of Buck Jones and directed him in many of his pictures. As a matter of fact, he was with Buck Jones in the fire in Boston. He was looking for Buck and couldn't find him. Les was one of the best of the Western directors. And he wasn't just worried about printing something, getting it on film. He'd take time with the actors and actresses who were having problems with lines or whatever. He'd work with them.

I really enjoyed making the pictures, whoever the director was. When you're out working on a Western, you're with a lot of folks; it's a big family. There are about seventy-five or eighty people connected with the picture in one way or another. Everybody knows everybody and it's a fun operation. Tim really enjoyed making the films too. He also enjoyed rodeos; they were one of his favorite pastimes. In fact, he owned a rodeo.

DR: Didn't you go out with him on a few rodeo tours?

Richard: Not with the rodeo; just for personal appearance tours on stage. The show was booked by an agent out of Philadelphia. It was a series of one-nighters. In the show we did a couple of little skits, and we had a heavy with us by the name of Jack O'Shea. Black Jack was always about to shoot Tim in one of the skits; I was always chasing a girl around the set. We also had Ray Whitley and his musicians with us for some Western songs. So there was some music, a couple of skits, and then Tim would sit with some kids and they would ask him questions. He'd show them his guns and do some tricks with them. It was probably about a forty-minute show. This was always in connection with the showing of one of our films. It was a lot of work, but it was fun. We did this in the early '50s while the series was still in production. We made the tour when we weren't filming. It was pretty close to the time when the series ended, I guess, because we were working on a television deal at the time. While we were on the road, the agent was supposed to be putting the deal together, and he screwed it all up. By the time we got back, all the TV slots were filled with other Western shows—Rogers and Autry, Guy Madison, Bill Williams, you name 'em. There seemed to be more cowboys than anything else in those days.

Tim and Chito handily thwarted film outlaws from 1947 until 1952 but, unfortunately, were unable to do likewise to RKO studio chief Howard Hughes when he decided to cancel their Western series. (Photo courtesy of Chuck Thornton.)

DR: It's a shame. You two would have been great in a television series.

Richard: We had a good package going. We had the cameraman who did many of the series Westerns, Roy Hunt. Les Selander was going to direct, and the writer was to be Norm Houston, who wrote our series. We had the whole package, and the idea was to sell the package. CBS was very interested, but by the time we got back it was too late.

DR: When did you learn the series was going to be cancelled?

Richard: Tim and I found out about it when we came off the road from the personal appearance tour. We had sort of sensed that Hughes didn't want to make anymore B pictures. We figured that we'd be next—and we were.

* * *

Tim comes to the defense of heroine Nan Leslie. Nan appeared with Tim in six consecutive films beginning with *UNDER THE TONTO RIM* (1947) and continuing through *INDIAN AGENT* (1948).

Nan Leslie Interview
August 6, 1993

Nan Leslie was Tim's most-frequent leading lady, appearing with the cowboy star in six consecutive films in 1947 and 1948. In addition to the Tim Holt films, Nan also appeared with such Western stars as Gene Autry (*RIM OF THE CANYON*, 1949), Monte Hale (*PIONEER MARSHAL*, 1949), Don Barry (*TRAIN TO TOMBSTONE*, 1950), and Rex Allen (*IRON MOUNTAIN TRAIL*, 1953). Nan also

Richard Martin is seen here with author David Rothel at the 1993 Charlotte Western Film Fair.

was prominent in TV Westerns, providing feminine support in such series as *The Cisco Kid, The Roy Rogers Show, The Gene Autry Show, Range Rider, Buffalo Bill, Jr.* and *Annie Oakley.* Gail "Annie Oakley" Davis and Nan have been best friends ever since they appeared together in Autry's Flying A Productions of the 1950s. Nan's first marriage in the early 1950s ended in divorce. In the late 1960s she remarried and had a long and happy marriage until her husband's death in 1990. It was during this second marriage that she pretty much retired from the motion picture and television business.

I wrote to Nan at her home in San Juan Capistrano, California, and requested an interview with her regarding Tim. I was delighted when she immediately responded by phone and said that she would enjoy reminiscing with me about Tim and the films they made together. Before we got specifically to Tim, however, I asked her about how she broke into films and about some of her experiences while making Western films.

David Rothel (DR): You were under contract to RKO for a number of years. How did that come about?

Nan Leslie: My family and I used to spend our summers at Newport Beach and Balboa when I was a kid. During the summer before I turned fourteen, a commercial photographer was also vacationing there. He and his wife and children lived over on the next street from us on the little island at Balboa. For some reason he decided that I might make a good model for magazine covers, so we went out every now and again and took some color photos—with my mom or my aunt always in the background someplace. There was one picture he took of me at the wheel of a sailboat that later got on the cover of *Liberty* magazine. It was wonderful because the photo was of my favorite vacation place, and *Liberty* was a major magazine then. I still have a couple of the old covers, a little bit tattered around the edges. Anyway, that was how it began.

One of the talent scouts at RKO, Ben Piazza, saw the *Liberty* picture and called me to ask if I would come in to meet him. I think I was about sixteen at the time. My mother and I went in to see him, and he proposed that they put me under contract because contract players were very much the thing then. Although I was a very shy and timid teenager at the time, I said to him, "Well, that'll be fine, but I have to finish school first." I guess this took him aback quite a bit. After all, he was quite a well-known figure in Hollywood. My mother heartily agreed with me. So he said, "Well, when you get out of high school, please contact me and let me know." We assured him we would.

In the meantime I worked during vacation time on a couple of movies. One of them was Michael Curtiz's *JANIE* (1944) with Joyce Reynolds. I had a very small part in the picture. After I graduated from high school, I made the call to Mr. Piazza and told him, "I guess I'd like to try it now." I was about eighteen at the time.

DR: You did it so easily. There are thousands of talented young people who spend years waiting on tables and hoping for a break that never comes.

Nan: Maybe it was a little too easy. I was born in Hollywood Presbyterian Hospital, and I had lived in Los Angeles all my life. Being under contract at that time was very wonderful and a little awing. It was a great experience because they gave you excellent training with a drama coach, a singing coach, a dancing instructor—the whole thing. It was a whole other education. I was at RKO for four or five years.

DR: How did you happen to be cast in the Tim Holt pictures?

Nan: As I recall it, first I did a few bit parts in things like *GEORGE WHITE'S SCANDALS* (1945). Also, they had short subjects then, and I played the part of a vocalist with Gene Krupa's band in one of those shorts. I had small parts in *THE DEVIL THUMBS A RIDE* (1946) with Lawrence Tierney and *WOMAN ON THE BEACH* (1947) with Robert Ryan and Joan Bennett. Jean Renoir was the director on that one, and I played the second lead. I didn't even realize what a wonderful opportunity that was, to appear in a big-budget picture with a top director. Actually, my first leading role in a Western was the year before *WOMAN ON THE BEACH*, when I made *SUNSET PASS* (1946) with James Warren. Of course, you have to go to auditions, readings, and they look at your work in other films before you are cast. They thought I was an outdoor-looking type, and after they had sorted out among the contract players they had at that time, I guess they decided that I was a pretty good bet for them. Apparently I managed well enough in the first one, so I was continued in some of the others.

DR: Yes, you were Tim's leading lady in six straight films. Did you enjoy making the Westerns?

Nan: I loved it. I was a horseback rider, and I loved the locations and being out-of-doors. In between scenes I could ride the horses, and the wranglers and the stuntmen on the set were so great to work with.

Honestly, we had so much fun, and the fact that I could ride seemed to appeal to all of the stunt men and wranglers. That I would take a horse and ride out onto the location between scenes, I think, appealed to them. "As long as you can stay out of the shot, go ahead," they would say. I truly believe that they (producers and directors) selected me a lot of times because I could ride. Although we always had doubles and standins, it's always much more credible if the leading lady can ride, get off and get on a horse, and looks as if she knows what she's doing.

DR: How did you happen to be a good horsewoman?

Nan: I rode when I was a little girl, and I had been taking riding lessons, all English flat saddle. Of course, these were Westerns, and you're not supposed to post in the Western saddle. It took a lot of learning to just sit the saddle instead of posting. I took a lot of razzing for that. Yes, the Westerns were pure pleasure, and some of those other things (A-budget pictures) were just plain hard work; you were shut into sound stages all day long. (laugh) I really had no business sense whatsoever, I guess.

DR: I've had a number of Western performers comment that the cast and crews that made the Westerns became a sort of family in the process of making the films.

Nan: There was a kind of camaraderie about the Westerns—although I didn't realize it until much later—that you don't find too many times. We went to beautiful places like Lone Pine and Apple Valley. When we were on location, there were always practical jokes being played on everybody. It was just a wonderful opportunity to have fun while you were working. I suppose that's not the most professional attitude one could have. (laugh) I remember them all with such fondness.

You know, Richard Farnsworth and Ben Johnson were both stunt men on those early pictures. I was so thrilled later on when they got their chance, because they were both so nice to be around. Dick Farnsworth was the wildest stunt man you can ever imagine and the most fun. Stunt men in those days were crazy, the Evel Knievels of the horse set.

Tim was a natural for the Westerns because he was a good horseman. Dick Martin was also a natural for the comedy relief, and he was such a darling man. He was genuinely funny and perfect for the part he played. Dick always gave the impression while acting that he was relaxed and at ease, and that's always reassuring to an actor playing opposite him. We didn't have all that many scenes

Tim and Nan play the big farewell scene at the end of *UNDER THE TONTO RIM* (1947). "Because I was usually playing the typical Western heroine, we didn't have very many personal or romantic scenes. But I had the feeling that if Tim and I had had occasion to play a more personal relationship on screen, rather than just the superficial romance thing, we probably would have done very well together." (Photo courtesy of Chuck Thornton.)

together, but Dick's presence there loosened us up. I think it did for Tim too. Tim was also very good to work with. Because I was usually playing the typical Western heroine, we didn't have very many personal or romantic scenes. But I had the feeling that if Tim and I had had occasion to play a more personal relationship on screen, rather than just the superficial romance thing, we probably would have done very well together.

Dick was just a wild, crazy kid. And, you know, they played so many practical jokes while we were making the films. They put a burro in my dressing room once. (laugh)

DR: *You're* the one who got the burro! (laugh) Richard Martin told me about the burro, but he didn't identify the leading lady.

Nan: It was so funny. They used to bring trailers for dressing rooms and make-up. It was a terribly hot day, and we were at Lone Pine. You know the costumes we wore—black cotton stockings and hoop skirts, all of that sort of paraphernalia. After about half-a-day's work—and it was really hot and steamy—I thought, "Oh, just to get back into the trailer is going to be so wonderful!" I noticed a lot of people were ringed around the trailer area and thought that it was funny because they were still supposed to be shooting. I opened the door of the trailer and inside there was a little burro standing, looking back at me. (laugh) I thought, "What are you doing in here?" He seemed to be thinking, "Why am I in here?" (laugh) I finally got my wits together, turned around, and said, "Well, it isn't the first time that a jackass has been in this dressing room!" (laugh) Everybody broke up! You see, this was the type of fun things that happened then. I think it adds to the whole show when you have that kind of fun.

DR: Lone Pine was the location for all six of your Tim Holt films. I've visited the area several times and just love it.

Nan: Do they still have the Dow Villa in Lone Pine?

DR: Oh, yes. That's were I stayed when I was last there.

Nan: Oh, I tell you, that hotel creaked from top to bottom. If anybody came in late, everybody who was already asleep or just about asleep knew that they were coming up the stairs and down the hall. (laugh) We did our make-up down in the lobby every morning at five or five-thirty—I don't know how I did it. I can remember the sun coming up over the Death Valley side of the Lone Pine area. I would tell myself, "Now this alone is worth being awake for, isn't it?" By the time the make-up was done, the day looked wonderful. I especially remember the sunrises and the sunsets and Mount Whitney in the background. We would all go to dinner together at the cafe, the cast and crew, and have fresh-caught trout and things like that. As I said before, there was a family sort of feeling. We only had one day off each week then, so on Sunday we would frequently drive to Independence and rent a burro pack and go up into the trout streams and catch fish. It was so beautiful up there. I loved going trout fishing.

DR: Tell me about Tim; what was he like?

Nan: He had a very engaging personality; he was a very genuine person—warm, serious, not egotistical. It was hard for him to let down and be really relaxed though. My mother adored him. She just thought he was so wonderful because he was very courteous and he had such wonderful manners. Of course, Tim and I were unofficially engaged for a year and a half or so.

DR: I heard that you two were a romantic item for a period of time.

Nan: Yes, we were; after all, he was a cowboy. (laugh) My dream at that time, and his too, was to have a ranch on the ocean where we could ride horses through the waves and on the sand. We had a lot of plans for a while; he was in the midst of a divorce at that time. I was just enchanted by him because to me he was the perfect cowboy. He knew what he was doing on a horse, and he was certainly always the gentleman off the horse, and he was very protective of me and, oddly enough, a little shy at times. He was a very special guy.

DR: What happened to the romance?

Nan: Well, I was so naive that I didn't realize Tim was going with a couple of other people at the same time he was going with me. I just thought that I was the principal person and discovered that I really wasn't—although I think he had a kind of special feeling for me. I just could see that I had been very naive—and it hurt. I just backed off. He kept in touch with my mom after we stopped seeing each other. You know, David, I still have his denim jacket that he wore in several of his films. He put a penny in the pocket of it while we were going together; he used to call me Penny. To this very day I have it hanging in my closet. In very faint detail it has on it, "Tim Holt." It was from Western Costume, I imagine. I've kept it all these years, I suppose sentimentally. You are talking to a very sentimental person.

I remember going in to see the daily rushes at the studio one night shortly after I had first met him. That used to be kind of fun, to see what you'd done that day—sometimes it was fun. Sometimes you said, "Oh, no, can't we do that again?" I remember Tim was sitting in back of me somewhere with someone else. I happened to look back as he was lighting his pipe with a match, and he looked down at me, and I looked back at him, and the flame of the match lit up his eyes and he smiled at me. And I thought, "Wow!" (laugh) A lot of charm there; that he had, yes. He was a terrific guy.

DR: Would you describe Tim as someone who enjoyed being around others or was he a loner?

Nan: Both. He loved to have the affection and support of the people around him and the feeling of friendship with them, but I also felt at times that he kind of removed himself—perhaps he wanted to be on his own for a while.

DR: Jennifer, Tim's sister, said she thought that Tim did not have a great deal of self-esteem. This came up when we were discussing his father, who, of course, had been a big star. Did you ever have that feeling?

Nan: Yes, I had it very much on the picture that we did with his father *(THE ARIZONA RANGER)*. If my memory serves me correctly, Tim had already

"I was just enchanted by him because to me he was the perfect cowboy. He knew what he was doing on a horse, and he was certainly always the gentleman off the horse. And he was very protective of me and, oddly enough, a little shy at times. He was a very special guy." (Photo courtesy of Chuck Thornton.)

Chito and Lee "Lasses" White listen as Tim confers with Nan Leslie about the receipts from the supply delivery in this scene from *INDIAN AGENT*, Nan's last film with Tim. "I wish that the leading ladies back then could have had more of the spunk they do now, but we weren't allowed to be that way then." (Photo courtesy of Chuck Thornton.)

completed *TREASURE OF THE SIERRA MADRE* at that time. In that company of such great actors and with such a wonderful part to play, his self-esteem should have been at its highest. But when we were doing *THE ARIZONA RANGER*, I sensed almost all the time that he was seeking approval from his dad—you know, in between takes while we were all sitting, waiting to do something or rehearsing our lines. I sensed it even in their horsemanship. Tim wanted to impress his father. Of course, Jack sat a horse incredibly well in a military way, as straight a posture as you ever saw. He was a little intimidating. Tim wanted very much to please him and have him enjoy what he was doing while he was making the picture. I think Tim was elated to have his father on the picture. Of course, I was awfully pleased to be in the one where the father and son were together. But he was just stern, David, is all I can say. It was just his demeanor. So I think there was always a struggle in Tim to try and prove himself. Jack was *always* very nice, very courteous to me. At that time Tim and I were still rather serious about each other, and I think Jack knew it. I was very impressed with him, and I could tell that Tim was a tiny bit nervous around him—I don't think I am betraying any confidences, because I'm sure everybody was aware of that. Jack was treated with a certain amount of deference by everyone.

I still remember Jack's boots, David. He wore alligator cowboy boots. We got all of our boots from Western Costume, of course, but his boots were custom made. They were just beautiful; they were so shiny and so supple. His whole persona was just very impressive! As I said, we were all a little bit in awe of him on that picture.

DR: *THE ARIZONA RANGER* is considered one of the best B Westerns ever made.

Nan: I'd like to see it again; I haven't seen it in years. I saw *WESTERN HERITAGE* not long ago, and I

Nan Leslie is seen here at Dana Point Harbor near her home in San Juan Capistrano, California. The photo was taken during the summer of 1993. (Photo courtesy of Nan Leslie.)

was so mortified. (laugh) I didn't think it was very good.

DR: Of the six films that you made with Tim, *WESTERN HERITAGE* is generally considered to be the weakest.

Nan: The other one that I liked very much, because I got to wear blue jeans in it, was *WILD HORSE MESA*. That's the only one where I'm not wearing a dress or a split skirt kind of thing. I really enjoyed that. The leading lady, let's face it, was a square gal in most Westerns and generally watched the hero

In fond remembrance of her many appearances as a Western film heroine, Nan Leslie recently donned Western attire for this photograph. (Photo courtesy of Nan Leslie.)

ride off at the end of the picture and gave him a feeble wave good-bye. I wish that the leading ladies back then could have had more of the spunk they do now, but we weren't allowed to be that way then. I liked the theme of *WILD HORSE MESA* too, the search for the wild horses.

DR: Do you have a favorite film from those you made with Tim?

Nan: Yes, I think I do. It's *WILD HORSE MESA;* my second favorite would be the one with Jack Holt, *THE ARIZONA RANGER*. You know, David, I was always surprised that Tim didn't continue in his career. He could have gone on a great deal longer.

DR: Yes. He left Hollywood before he was forty years old.

Nan: I lost track of him, so I don't know what happened, but, you know, he could have been in pictures for a long, long time.

*   *   *

Walter Reed Interview October 10, 1992

Sierra Film Festival
Lone Pine, California

Walter Reed's long film career began in 1942 with a picture called *ARMY SURGEON* featuring James Ellison and Jane Wyatt. An RKO contractee during the 1940s, Walter appeared in a plethora of films including two *MEXICAN SPITFIRE* films, *SEVEN DAY'S LEAVE* (1942, with Victor Mature and Lucille Ball), *NIGHT SONG* (1947, starring Dana Andrews and Merle Oberon), and *FIGHTER SQUADRON* (1948, with Edmond O'Brien and Robert Stack). By the fifties he was freelancing and appearing in such films as *YOUNG MAN WITH A HORN* (1950, with Kirk Douglas), *SUPERMAN AND THE MOLE MEN* (1951), *WELLS FARGO GUNMASTER* (1951, with Rocky Lane), *SEVEN MEN FROM NOW* (1956, with Randolph Scott), *THE HORSE SOLDIERS* (1959, with John Wayne), *HOW THE WEST WAS WON* (1962), and *THE SAND PEBBLES* (1966, with Steve McQueen). In addition to the mostly character roles in the above films, Walter starred in two Republic serials in 1951: *FLYING DISC MAN FROM MARS* and *GOVERNMENT AGENTS VS. PHANTOM LEGION*.

Walter appeared in three Tim Holt features: *WESTERN HERITAGE* (1948), *TARGET* (1952),

Walter Reed (left) appeared with Tim and Chito in three films: *WESTERN HERITAGE* (1948), *TARGET* (1952), and *DESERT PASSAGE* (1952), from which the above scene is taken.

and *DESERT PASSAGE* (1952). In *WESTERN HERITAGE* he played a nefarious character who died early on in the plot. *TARGET* and *DESERT PASSAGE* were Tim's last two Western features and Walter played despicable characters in both. In real life Walter is warm, friendly, gregarious, and not at all despicable. In recent years he has become a frequent guest star at Western film festivals and always has interesting behind-the-scenes stories to relate to fans. It was at the Sierra Film Festival in Lone Pine, California, that I visited with Walter about Tim. He was relaxing in his room at the Dow Villa after a busy day which had included a parade down Lone Pine's main street and a presentation ceremony across the street from the Dow Villa. He and his friend Richard "Chito" Martin had ridden together in a surrey-with-a-fringe-on-top which was drawn by two mules. Tired as he was from the day's activities, Walter seemed to enjoy reminiscing about Tim, and so I just let him verbally hopscotch around the topic at hand, interrupting as little as possible.

Walter Reed: Dick Martin, Tim, and I were under contract to RKO for many years. In fact, we had a good group of people like Bob Ryan, Barbara Hale, Martha Hyer, Robert Mitchum, and Bill Williams—just to name a few—under contract at RKO in the late 1940s and early '50s, and we all were quite successful.

David Rothel (DR): Tell me anything that comes to mind about Tim.

Walter: Tim was a wonderful, wonderful person. I used to needle him all the time. I'd say to him, "If you didn't have gloves on, you'd pull your wrists up." (laugh) Did you ever notice how he's constantly tugging on his gloves in scenes? At first, when I would do this, he would get very serious and maybe a little bit offended, and then he would realize that I was just kidding him, and he would laugh and make some smart remark back to me to get even.

Walter Reed (right) and Lane Bradford, playing their accustomed roles as Western film thugs, try to drive a rancher off his land in this scene from Tim's feature entitled *TARGET* (1952).

I used to needle him about his glove tugging, but I want to tell you something: that was very good "business" for his hands in a scene. It's very difficult as an actor to know what to do with your hands. I hate to see a guy just stand there with his hands at his sides, and it looks awkward for a cowboy actor to put his hands on his guns all of the time.

I also kidded him about his ability to drive a stagecoach. I'd tell him that I was afraid to ride with him because I thought he'd get us killed. As I said before, he'd usually get extremely serious when I'd needle him, then he'd suddenly realize I was just doing it to get his goat, and he'd laugh and usually call me an uncomplimentary name. The truth is that Tim was a very good stagecoach driver—and stagecoaches are very dangerous. It is very difficult to drive a four-up or a six-up because you have so many reins in your hands, and you have to know which ones to pull to keep your lead horses in line. If you are going down hill, it is particularly difficult.

Tim was a very good actor and part of his ability was due to Agnes Moorehead, who was one of the stars with him in *THE MAGNIFICENT AMBERSONS*. She taught Tim a lot about how to act. I said to her once, "Why did you bother with Tim?" She said, "Because he listens." And that is very important in an actor. Tim didn't have to do just Westerns, you know. He could have been a very big actor in A pictures. If you look at *THE MAGNIFICENT AMBERSONS*, you can see how much potential he had; he was great in it. And Agnes helped him in that picture. She took him under her wing and helped him so much.

I'm going to tell you something about Tim: he was both extroverted and introverted. He wanted to be accepted; he wanted to be liked—and that's what he got from the big pictures like *AMBERSONS* and

TREASURE OF SIERRA MADRE. But he also wanted to do what he had been doing; that is, making his popular B Westerns—so, in a way, this was the introverted side of him.

He looked wonderful on a horse. His father, Jack Holt, always looked so straight and rigid on horseback; he was an old cavalry man. Tim took after his father; he was tall and straight in the saddle too. He certainly had the stature for being a cowboy movie star.

Tim's sidekick, Dick Martin, is one of my dearest friends. We met at RKO over fifty years ago. Dick did Chito Rafferty in a picture in which I played the juvenile lead, *BOMBARDIER*. It was the first time he played the role. Thank God they saw something in that character and decided to continue it in other films. Tim and Chito had great chemistry together. Tim was kind of straight, you know, serious, as I said earlier. He needed someone for a little comedy relief, which Dick supplied in a way to complement Tim. And, you know, they personally liked each other, which is also important when you are working together in a series. If you hate each other, it shows in a performance; it shows in your eyes.

I think the Tim and Chito films hold up so well today because Tim was such a fine cowboy hero, and Chito's comedy was not hokey, not slapstick. They were just two very likeable cowboys on the screen—one serious and one with a comical sense of humor. They played their roles in a legitimate manner, no kidding around with the characters. When I did serials, I didn't play the hero characters with tongue in cheek; I played them straight too. If you accept the part, you should do it seriously—the way it should be done—not with a wink to the audience indicating that you think it's all silliness, as some actors have done. I always tried to remember that those kids were out there watching and listening to what I did with the hero character, and they could tell if an actor was being a phony. Tim and Dick never looked down on the type of films they were making for kids, and, consequently, the films are still honest today and enjoyed by today's audiences.

Believe me, Tim was an honest and extremely good actor. I don't think he had the recognition that he should have, and he left films too soon. He was still in his thirties when he left film acting in the early 1950s. My gosh, that was about the time when most of our careers began to take off and we became successful.

* * *

Popular young actor Robert Clarke looks pretty menacing in this photo from *RIDERS OF THE RANGE* (1950). (Photo courtesy of Robert Clarke.)

Robert Clarke Interview
May 16, 1993

Robert Clarke got his start as a film actor when RKO signed him to a contract in the mid 1940s and groomed him in a variety of small roles commencing with *THE FALCON IN HOLLYWOOD* (1944) and continuing in such well-remembered films as *THE ENCHANTED COTTAGE* (1945), *RADIO STARS ON PARADE* (1945, starring Frances Langford and Ralph Edwards in which Robert played the love interest opposite Langford), *SAN QUENTIN* (1946, a featured role with Lawrence Tierney starring), and *THE FARMER'S DAUGHTER* (1947 with Loretta Young starring). In addition, he had roles in such Westerns as *WANDERER OF THE WASTELAND* (1945), *SUNSET PASS* (1946), and *CODE OF THE WEST* (1947) with RKO's short-term cowboy star, James Warren. He also appeared in four of Tim's RKO pictures released between 1947 and 1951.

After a stint on Broadway in the late 1940s, Robert returned to Hollywood and by the early 1950s was playing leading roles or starring in such films as *HARD, FAST, AND BEAUTIFUL* (1951) with Claire

Trevor and Sally Forrest, *TALES OF ROBIN HOOD* (1951), *STREET BANDITS* (1951) with Penny Edwards, *THE FABULOUS SENORITA* (1952) with Estelita Rodriquez, and *SWORD OF VENUS* (1953). In addition, he appeared in many of the television drama series of the early 1950s and has the distinction of being the star of the first hour-long film made in Hollywood especially for television. It was an adaptation of *The Three Musketeers* for *Magnavox Theatre* and was telecast November 24, 1950, on the CBS network.

Robert has received recognition from aficionados of science fiction and horror films for such pictures as *THE MAN FROM PLANET X* (1951), *THE ASTOUNDING SHE-MONSTER* (1958), *THE HIDEOUS SUN DEMON* (1959, in which he not only starred but also created the original concept, produced, and directed), and *BEYOND THE TIME BARRIER* (1960, which he produced and starred in for American-International Pictures).

He is probably the only actor in Hollywood who can lay claim to working with six of the greatest horror film actors in motion picture history: Boris Karloff and Bela Lugosi in *THE BODY SNATCHER* (1945), Boris Karloff again in *BEDLAM* (1946) and *DICK TRACY MEETS GRUESOME* (1947), Lon Chaney, Jr. in *THE BLACK PIRATES* (1954), John Carradine in *THE INCREDIBLE PETRIFIED WORLD* (1959) and *FRANKENSTEIN'S ISLAND* (1982), and (not in films but on radio) Vincent Price on *Lux Radio Theatre,* and Peter Lorre on *Suspense.*

His friendship with Richard Martin, Tim's longtime sidekick, goes back to their early years as contract players at RKO. "Dick is one of my very favorite people," Robert informed me. "When I got to RKO and I saw this guy, who was about the handsomest fellow I'd ever seen, standing in the doorway of the studio, I knew he was headed for stardom. And he's still handsome today. Dick's now got a Cary Grant resemblance. When he puts on those dark horn-rimmed glasses, with that silver hair, he is striking. When Alyce and I were married, Dick and Elaine gave us a very lovely party. We've remained friends over the forty-odd years we've known each other."

Robert Clarke lives in North Hollywood, California, with his wife Alyce, who is a member of the famous singing group, The King Sisters. (Many people fondly remember their popular ABC-TV series of the 1960s, *The King Family,* for which Robert was the announcer.) Some years back Robert took the position of public relations officer with

Robert Clarke is seen here at one of his recent speaking engagements on "The Golden Years of the Movies." This particular presentation was entitled "The Magic of Sci-Fi Film Making."

the Bank of Encino, but he continues to maintain a position in the film business as a public speaker and talks on the subject he knows well, "The Golden Years of the Movies." In his speaking engagements he reminisces about (among other things) working with such stars as Clark Gable, Greer Garson, Ginger Rogers, Nelson Eddy and Jeanette MacDonald. In addition, he is presently preparing a film sequel to *THE HIDEOUS SUN DEMON*. "I have a thing about retiring; I never want to retire," Robert states with considerable gusto.

When I phoned him at the time we had earlier agreed upon for an interview, he was going through some photos from the four Tim Holt pictures in which he had appeared. "Just trying to refresh my memory. I can't believe how youthful I looked then—younger than springtime," he chuckled.

While Tim was the focus of our conversation, we also talked about the making of the pictures, the other performers who appeared in them, and Robert himself. When I asked him about his background, I was surprised to discover that he was originally from Oklahoma, where Tim had spent the last twenty years or so of his life.

Robert Clarke: I was born and grew up in Oklahoma City, not far from Harrah, where Tim lived. I went to junior high and high school with Mary Frances Heflin, who was Van Heflin's little sister. Dale Robertson also went to the same school we did, Classen High School in Oklahoma City. After high school I first attended the University of Oklahoma and then went on to the University of Wisconsin, because a teacher I had during the summer of 1940 down at the University of Oklahoma said, "If you want to be in theatre or work in radio as an actor or announcer, you should go to the University of Wisconsin and get rid of your Oklahoma twang. I used to talk like Dennis Weaver and Dale Robertson—who later used their accents very effectively as actors. I went to Wisconsin and got rid of my Oklahoma accent, and I often wonder what my career would have been like if I hadn't. (laugh)

David Rothel (DR): The first two of the four pictures you made with Tim—*THUNDER MOUNTAIN* (1947) and *UNDER THE TONTO RIM* (1947)—were made in Lone Pine, California. Do you have any special recollection of filming in Lone Pine?

Robert: Just that the nights were cool and beautiful, and the days were hot and almost unbearable during the times that we were up there filming. Mostly I remember how much I wanted to impress the producers and directors at RKO with the kind of acting I was capable of in those parts as an outlaw and as the renegade brother—playing two or three drunk scenes, gambling and all. It was an opportunity that I didn't want to let slip by, and Lone Pine provided some wonderful atmosphere for those roles.

I'll certainly never forget one Lone Pine incident from early in my film career. We were shooting a chase scene through the Alabama Hills just outside of Lone Pine. It was a single shot of me on horseback behind a camera car that was going probably forty miles an hour. Unfortunately, the horse I was riding kept stumbling and, as a result, threw his head up to keep from falling, making it very difficult for me to ride him. My job was to stay in the saddle with my left hand on the reins, fire the '45 with my right hand, and at the same time somehow try to keep my hat from blowing off. Although there were only blanks in the pistol, they contained a full load—and a full load was a real blast! To do these three things—ride the horse, keep the hat on, and fire that pistol in the direction of the camera—was difficult enough, but to add a stumbling horse was the last straw! I thought I was going to go right over that horse's head every time he stumbled! Boy, I didn't know if I was going to make it or not! At one point the horse ran off the shoulder of the road and started to slip down into a small ravine. Fortunately, it was at about the time the director called "cut!" That was my initiation into the chase car and how they filmed run-bys. I was one scared young actor! I was trying to act as if I really knew what the hell I was doing, but I'm not sure I succeeded too well. It's funny as I look back on it now, but it was scary at the time.

DR: The town scenes for Tim's pictures were shot at the RKO Ranch in Encino.

Robert: Yes, the Bank of Encino, where I work today as a public relations officer, is only about two or three blocks from a street named Louise, which leads right out to the area that was the RKO Ranch and which now has a couple of Little League baseball diamonds on it. It's barely a mile from where I work today to where we shot those sequences on the Western street for not only Tim's Westerns but all of the others for the RKO studio. It's an area where no homes have been built; it's sort of a reservoir area, and these two Little League diamonds are where the RKO ranch once had the Western street—the street, by the way, where Frank Capra and Jimmy Stewart made *IT'S A WONDERFUL LIFE* back in the late 1940s.

DR: Oh, I didn't realize it was shot there.

Robert: I was out there one night when they were shooting scenes for it. They had several night schedules on *IT'S A WONDERFUL LIFE* out at the RKO Ranch. I remember they were filming the sequence in which Jimmy Stewart is running through the streets of the town where he and Donna Reed live in the picture. It was supposed to be wintertime, so they had ice machines making ice and snow for the scene. It was the middle of summer at the time, July or August, and there they were in winter wear—overcoats and that sort of thing—with snow flying all over the place. I don't have any really special remembrances of shooting Westerns on the RKO Ranch, but I'll never forget watching the filming of *IT'S A WONDERFUL LIFE*.

DR: Did you enjoy making Westerns?

Robert: Oh, yes, very much; I guess, perhaps, because the parts were usually substantial. The roles in the Westerns were larger, and I had more opportunity as a young actor to stretch my abilities, to make it as real as possible. I guess the Westerns

Leading lady Jacqueline White pours coffee for Tim, Chito, and her ne'er-do-well brother (Robert Clarke) in this pleasant breakfast scene from *RIDERS OF THE RANGE* (1950). (Photo courtesy of Robert Clarke.)

were especially appealing to me because when I was a kid in Oklahoma, Tom Mix, Buck Jones, and others that I saw on the movie screen were my heroes. To my way of looking at it, they were the real cowboys. Although Gene Autry and Roy Rogers were extremely successful, they, to me, did not embody the "real cowboy" as much as the Buck Jones/Tom Mix type of cowboy actor. And Tim Holt fit in more with that type. He was a realistic cowboy on the screen; he made you believe he was *really* a cowboy.

DR: How long were you under contract to RKO?

Robert: I was at RKO for three years. I went there in 1944, which is the same year that Robert Mitchum did. My contract began at $250 or $300 a week, and in those days that was a lot of dough. It called for a hefty increase in salary—more, I assure you, than I was worth—at the end of the third year; it was to go up to $500 or $750, something like that, and RKO didn't exercise the option—and I, frankly, think they made the right decision. (laugh) So I was there from 1944 though '47, and *UNDER THE TONTO RIM* was one of the last roles I played before I left the studio. I remember I also did a very small role with Randy Scott, Gabby Hayes, and Anne Jeffreys in *RETURN OF THE BADMEN* at that time. It was a real nothing role. I guess they (RKO) were trying to get their money's worth before I left in July or August of 1947 and went to New York to work on Broadway. I came back from New York in 1949 and did *RIDERS OF THE RANGE* with Tim. I thought to myself at that time, "How ironic; I went to New York for two years, I come back, and I'm right back in another Western." But I had a good part in *RIDERS OF THE RANGE*, as I recall.

DR: Were you back on contract then?

Robert: No, I was freelancing. I remember going over to the RKO casting office and seeing Dick Stockton and Eddie Ryan and telling them about

In this scene from *RIDERS OF THE RANGE*, Chito excitedly explains to Jacqueline White and Robert Clarke how he lost his lucky peso in a fight. (Photo courtesy of Robert Clarke.)

being lucky enough to have been on Broadway with Louis Calhern and Faye Emerson in *The Play's the Thing* and about doing summer stock. They asked me if I would be interested in doing a Tim Holt picture. "We've got a hell of a part; it runs the length of the picture, and we'll up your salary a bit," they told me, so I said, "Sure," and it worked out pretty well. Jacqueline White was the leading lady in *RIDERS OF THE RANGE*, and she was a sweetheart. She was a lovely, lovely gal who dressed up the picture very well; she had class. I played her ne'er-do-well brother who gambled and got into all kinds of trouble.

DR: Reed Hadley was the main villain in the picture.

Robert: Yes. He came across very well on screen, I thought. He had a voice that rang very clear with authority, and he was an easy type of actor to respond to in a scene. He always gave to the scene as much sincere quality of performance as he was capable of doing. I liked working with him because his attitude was very professional.

Talking about the Tim Holt pictures reminds me of a story about Tim that I haven't thought of in years. There was a husky actor at RKO before Tim named George O'Brien, who did a lot of Westerns. I grew up on George O'Brien Westerns back in Oklahoma City. I remember Tim saying with a smile, but at the same time proud of the fact, "I'm the only actor on the lot that can fit into George O'Brien's shirts." (laugh) Well, O'Brien had a big chest; he was a real chesty guy, and Tim was a well-built husky type too, and I'm sure it was true that those shirts that were

Robert Clarke and Tim are pictured here in a tense scene from *PISTOL HARVEST* (1951). Robert Clarke: "I remember Tim saying with a smile, but at the same time proud of the fact, 'I'm the only actor on the lot that can fit into George O'Brien's shirts.'" (Photo courtesy of Robert Clarke.)

once made for George O'Brien would fit Tim. (laugh)

DR: Yes, I remember director Oliver Drake telling a story about O'Brien's chesty appearance. It seems that a kid walked up one day when O'Brien, wearing a T shirt, was washing his car in the driveway. The kid studied him for a few minutes and then asked, "Is that your real chest or is it fake?" (laugh) Oliver liked to tell that story about O'Brien, who was his friend and neighbor.

Robert: I'm looking at a photo of Tim from *RIDERS OF THE RANGE*, and he's looking so serious, which he was—as an actor and as a person. He took his work very seriously. You could always depend on Tim to know his dialogue, and he most likely knew yours as well. He was a very quick study, and he was a doggone good horseman and cowboy. He could handle his guns and horse as well as any cowboy on the screen. Tim acquired the ability to always sit in the saddle very well; you could never see forty acres between him and the saddle. And he was a very accommodating type of star. He never made you feel as if he was the "star" and that you had to conform to any certain amenities or any certain courtesies to him because of the fact that his name was in big caps above the title of the film. I must say I admired him as an actor; I admired him as a man; and certainly as a star, which he was and entitled to that position because he was doggone good at what he did.

DR: You spoke about him being very serious. Can you add anything regarding his personality?

Robert: Well, he would have a few jokes between

Robert Clarke: "I'm looking at a photo of Tim from *RIDERS OF THE RANGE*, and he's looking so serious, which he was—as an actor and as a person. He took his work very seriously." (Photo courtesy of Robert Clarke.)

takes, but my feeling is that he was most interested in keeping the picture on schedule and that he wasn't, at least in my observation, one who felt he had to be as entertaining when the camera was off as when it was on. Some actors are "on stage" to the crew almost as much as they are "on" when the camera is involved in shooting a scene. A lot of time can be wasted in the jocular fashion of some guy trying to make it known that he is also a comedian as well as an actor—making with the jokes. With Tim I got the feeling that it was a business. We were there to do a job and not to waste a lot of time. You'd almost think that Tim was a part of the production office, because he let you know that the number one job was to get the scene shot. As Dick Martin probably told you, they usually had two-week schedules.

DR: Several people have commented that Tim saw very little glamour in Hollywood; he saw his work in films as just a good job. He very likely acquired that feeling from growing up with a father who worked in the movie business.

Robert: Yes, and Jack Holt was a very fine actor. He was another favorite of mine when I was going to grade school back in Oklahoma City. He was not only a famous silent actor, but he broke into "talkies," as they were called then, and he became a successful star in his own right. And you're right; to Tim this was no glamour job. It was a job by which he made, I'm sure, a very good living and carried on the family name in a series of Westerns which did very well at the box office or RKO wouldn't have continued to make so many of them.

DR: Can you reminisce a bit about *PISTOL HARVEST*, which was released in 1951?

Robert: Wasn't that the one where Bob Wilke and I were together in a lot of scenes?

DR: Yes. You and he were bad-guy pals for much of the picture.

Tim subdues a wounded-but-fiesty outlaw (Robert Clarke) in this scene from *PISTOL HARVEST*. (Photo courtesy of Robert Clarke.)

Robert: He had a great face; he just looked mean. He wasn't mean in real life, of course. We worked effectively in the scenes for the picture. Our physical features were very different, of course. He was so tough looking, and I was playing the "kid" outlaw. There was no competition acting-wise in the scenes because we were such different types. I guess you would call him the lead heavy in the picture, and I was along for whatever purpose there was in having a younger-looking guy in the situation. Shortly after *PISTOL HARVEST* he was catapulted to fame in *HIGH NOON*, where he was so effective as one of the killers. His price went way up, and he continued to do some very good work in pictures.

DR: Mauritz Hugo was the dress heavy in *PISTOL HARVEST*.

Robert: I knew Mauritz fairly well; we worked together several times. Yes, he was the sort of city-slicker type in pictures. I know that the times I worked with him he was always looking for that next role that would get him to the point where he wanted to be. Mauritz had that on his mind an awful lot, as I recall. With Bob Wilke it happened. You know, after *HIGH NOON* everybody who had a good part for a Western heavy was after him.

DR: Tim always came across on the screen as a no-nonsense type of cowboy, which apparently he was to a pretty good degree in real life. Did you ever see any temperament from Tim? Ever see him lose his patience?

Robert: I don't think I ever did. I tell you, he commanded respect from everyone. That was my observation. You just didn't want to do anything to cross him or in any way not contribute to getting the job done. Tim was pretty private, as far as I was able to observe. He was not like Mitchum, for example, who at the end of the shooting day would go with the cast and crew down to the watering hole there in Lone Pine and have a few drinks. That wasn't Tim's style. After the day's shooting was over, he usually went to his trailer or the hotel where they had us staying, and you didn't see much of him. I never felt that we were real good pals, although he was always very courteous. As I said, he never tried to upstage you or take the star's position. He was a very democratic guy, and he realized that it made a scene better if you allowed a kind of free rein among the actors—that you'd get a greater depth in the playing of the parts by operating that way. But at the same time, he was pretty intent on making sure that the dialogue was spoken as it was written in the script, and if you and the horse were supposed to go out left to right, he made sure that you did it that way—and that you didn't goof up. (laugh) I guess that is my strongest recollection: that he was extremely conscientious about doing the best possible job.

*   *   *

"Will you stop worrying, Sis; I'm going to be all right," says Robert Clarke to Joan Dixon in this happy-ending scene from *PISTOL HARVEST*. (Photo courtesy of Robert Clarke.)

Myrna Dell

Myrna Dell Interview
May 3, 1993

Myrna Dell appeared in only one Tim Holt picture, *GUNS OF HATE* (1948), but for much of the forties and fifties she was a frequent leading lady or second lead in many B pictures and a few A's. Her credits include *RIDERS OF RED GAP* (1943, with Robert Livingston and Al St. John), *ARIZONA WHIRLWIND* (1944, with Ken Maynard, Bob Steele, and Hoot Gibson), *LUST FOR GOLD* (1949, with Glenn Ford and Ida Lupino), *ROUGHSHOD* (1949, with Robert Sterling and Gloria Grahame), and *THE FURIES* (1950, with Barbara Stanwyck and Walter Huston).

I phoned Myrna because Richard Martin had mentioned her while discussing the extreme cold winds and temperature they had experienced during the shooting of some *GUNS OF HATE* scenes outside a cabin in Lone Pine. As it turned out, Myrna remembered Lone Pine but not the specific scenes.

Myrna Dell: I hated Lone Pine! Oh, god, what an experience!

DR: Do you have any remembrance of the scenes at the cabin with Richard Martin?

Myrna: Do you know, none at all. I'll tell you the truth, David. I did fourteen Westerns, and I hated every Western I ever did. (laugh) Usually because of the heat and the heavy clothes I had to wear.

DR: What is your remembrance of Tim?

Myrna: Well, prior to being in his picture, *GUNS OF HATE*, when I applied for membership in the Screen Actors Guild, he was the person who was assigned to interview me for membership, so he was obviously on the SAG board. I remember it was in an office, and I was very young and nervous that day.

I had always admired Tim even before I worked with him. I thought he was a marvelous actor. In my estimation he could have had a much bigger career. He did very good work besides the Westerns. He was always very nice and very attractive but a kind of quiet, withdrawn person. I never could say that I really knew him.

DR: Well, you only worked that one film with him.

Myrna: Yes, but it only takes one. You get to know a person working in this business. You can get to know a person in one day working with them in a film, when in any other situation it would take you a year. Also, I'm very good with people. I like people, and, as a rule, I can draw them out, but I never could figure him out. He was kind of quiet. Tim, I think, was basically a loner, and he was rather reserved. I really can't say that I knew him, and there are very few people that I have met or worked with that I can say that about.

* * *

William Phipps is pictured here in a scene from the Tim Holt feature *RIDER FROM TUCSON* (1950).

William Phipps Interview
May 5, 1993

Bill Phipps had major roles in two of Tim's pictures, *THE ARIZONA RANGER* (1948) and *RIDER FROM TUCSON* (1950). His long career, spanning almost fifty years in films, started with the prestigious *CROSSFIRE* (1947, with three Roberts: Young, Mitchum, and Ryan), and continued in big and little films such as *DESPERADOS OF DODGE CITY* (1948, with Allan "Rocky" Lane), *FIVE* (1951), *CINDERELLA* (1950, supplying the voice of Prince Charming for Disney's animated classic), *JULIUS CAESAR* (1953, with Marlon Brando), *GUNFIGHT IN ABILENE* (1967, with Bobby Darin and Leslie Nielsen. And at seventy-one he's still working today. "I have a Bud Dry commercial that's running; I'm the only one that talks in it. In the commercial I say, 'Well, there goes the neighborhood!' (laugh) Remember that in case you see it. That's me. And I'm in a movie that's in release now, *HOMEWARD BOUND*, a Walt Disney movie. I rescue the cat from the river. I did a lot of stuff that they cut out, which I'm really unhappy about." Bill told me all of this as we chatted on the phone. Then we turned to the subject of Tim and the two pictures in which he appeared.

Bill Phipps remains active as a film actor, having recently appeared in the Walt Disney film, *HOMEWARD BOUND*.

William Phipps: I remember that *THE ARIZONA RANGER* was my second time in front of the camera. My first picture was *CROSSFIRE* at RKO, and they put me under contract. They wanted me to go into this Western, and I did my damnedest not to do it. I was too stuck up; I thought it was beneath me to do a Western. Can you believe that? I went on to do more Westerns than anything else, and I love 'em. I wish I were still doing them.

I did several movies that John Houseman produced. One of them was *JULIUS CAESAR*. When I went to see him one day before I started work on the movie with Brando, he said, "What have you been doing, Bill?" I said, "Well, I've been making a lot of Westerns. He said (with some haughtiness in his professorial voice), "You, you make Westerns? I don't believe it!" Being a character actor, I was typed in people's imaginations. The way they used me was the way they saw me. Some people saw me only in Westerns, and some people saw me only in Shakespeare. I've been able to keep that flexibility for about fifty years.

I remember *ARIZONA RANGER* was shot in Lone Pine and that on my first day of work I had to do some mounts, dismounts, and riding in and out of camera range. Tim came up to me—remember, this was my second picture; I was very new—and he said, "My god, you can ride! We get guys cast in these pictures and they don't know how to ride. You ride great!" He was very impressed and surprised that an actor could come on the set and somewhat match his horsemanship. I've never forgotten Tim's comments because they meant a lot to me then. He was very curious that I could ride horses well. Well, I'm from Indiana, and I grew up in a rural community where I had a pony when I was a kid, so I learned to ride before I ever saw a saddle. It was second nature to me.

DR: Jack Holt co-starred with Tim in that picture. Did you notice any father/son business between them?

William: It was very touching to watch them on the set. They didn't look anything alike; you wouldn't know that they were father and son if somebody didn't tell you. There was no tip-off, no special consideration or anything overt between them, but every once in a while I would catch them with a silent communication that they were father and son, and it was very gratifying to see. There was Jack Holt, the old timer, working in a Western with his kid. It was quite a big deal, but they made no outward show of it.

Very often when I was doing a scene with Tim—like one where we're facing each other and the camera is catching us in profile—he would make faces with one side of his face, the side away from the camera, trying to break me up. He would curl his lip on one side or bat his eye, wink it real fast. The camera couldn't see it, but I could see it, and it was sometimes a struggle to get a take. Sometimes we'd end up giggling and then the director and other people would wonder what was going on or wrong. (laugh) It's awfully hard to play a serious scene with someone making silly faces with one side of his face.

Popular character actor John Doucette.

* * *

John Doucette Interview
May 13, 1993

Movie tough guy John Doucette has been a menacing figure on the screen since *RIDE THE PINK HORSE* (1947, starring Robert Montgomery). Through the years audiences have come to know his face even though they frequently cannot recall his name. Alternating between hoodlum gangsters and cowboy villains, John fashioned a solid career as a character actor in films. Among his films are *SIERRA* (1950, with Audie Murphy), *HIGH NOON* (1952, with Gary Cooper), *THE BIG HEAT* (1952, with Glenn Ford), *THE FAR COUNTRY* (1955, with James Stewart), *NEVADA SMITH* (1966, starring Steve McQueen), and *BIG JAKE* (1971, with John Wayne).

According to John, his rough-house demeanor on the screen is all acting. "I usually play heavies and frequently get beat up or beat up somebody else; however, my real nature is not like that," John assured me as we began our telephone conversation about Tim. John appeared as the main heavy in Tim's feature *BORDER TREASURE* (1950).

John Doucette: Well, Tim and I had quite a few laughs on that show. I enjoyed working with him, and I found him to be a gentleman. I also worked with his father once at Warner Brothers. I didn't realize it prior to working with Tim, but he was as great a horseman as his father was. The show itself (*BORDER TREASURE*) came off rather good for a little Western. That's the kind of picture where you come to work, and, because of its low budget and skimpy story, you don't know how it's going to come out. Well, this one came out rather good, a rather entertaining show. They still show it on television. That's a good sign.

Tim was very professional and a very competent actor. *THE TREASURE OF SIERRA MADRE* is an all-time favorite of mine. I have my copy of it here at home, and every once in a while, when I feel like a *good* Western, I turn on *TREASURE OF SIERRA MADRE*. Yeah, he was wonderful in that.

* * *

Gail Davis Interview
May 21, 1993

Knoxville Western Film Caravan

Gail Davis has had a long and successful career as a Western film heroine for cowboy stars such as Gene Autry, Roy Rogers, Monte Hale, Rocky Lane, Jimmy Wakely, and—one of her special favorites—Johnny Mack Brown. In addition, she starred in one of the most successful television Western series of the 1950s, *Annie Oakley*. Gail is a frequent guest star at Western film festivals now, and she is always delighted to meet her legion of fans and to provide them with autographs, or a warm handshake and a friendly "Howdy!"

I first interviewed Gail in 1987 when I was revising my book on Gene Autry. She was gracious to me then, and she was again most gracious when I phoned her at the 1993 Knoxville Western Film Caravan and asked for an interview regarding her remembrances of Tim Holt. I was surprised when she immediately remembered the title of the film in which they had appeared together (that's impressive when you consider the number of films Gail Davis has made and that B-Western film titles all

Gail Davis: "I always admired Tim very much. He was a very special person to me even though we only did the one show together. I thought he showed so much promise as a very fine actor. Unfortunately, he didn't take the opportunity to finish his promising career."

pretty much sound the same). She even remembered the basic plot situation! We quickly agreed upon a time to get together later that evening to talk about Tim.

DR: You and Tim only made one film together, *OVERLAND TELEGRAPH*, which was released in 1951.

Gail Davis: Yes, David, and I really, truly loved it. It was one of the best scripts for a girl that I'd seen around that particular time. A lot of times in Westerns they gave the girl the part where she sits at the ranch house waiting for the cowboy to come home, or she waves to the cowboy at the end of the picture as he rides off into the sunset. But this film had a lot of story to it, which was wonderful. At one point it called for me to be hanging upside down from a telephone pole. Tim was to come along and rescue me. In addition to the picture having a great script, it was a big thrill to work with Tim and Dick Martin.

DR: That scene where you were on the telephone pole, was that really you and not a stunt double?

Gail Davis poses with author David Rothel at the 1993 Knoxville Western Film Caravan.

Gail: Oh, that was me; it certainly was. Tim was really cute. They got me up there to shoot the scene, and he yelled to everybody, "Lunch!" (laugh) They all turned around to leave, and I said, "Don't do this to me!" (laugh) So they came back and we did the scene. Tim was a great joker, you know.

DR: Tell me about him, his personality and anything else that comes to mind.

Gail: Tim was a very warm person, and it was just a real pleasure to work with him. He was a perfect gentleman; he was a very giving person. When you are working in a scene with another actor, some actors don't really listen to you when you are saying your lines. Tim was very concerned about his acting and was a very good actor *and* listener. He would say his line, and I would reply to him, and you could see the response in his eyes. You knew he was listening to what you were saying. With a lot of actors you can't read their feelings on their faces. Some will even look right at the top of your forehead and never look you in the eye—probably because they are trying to think of their next line. Well, Tim was never like this; he was very conscientious about his work, plus he was a very nice person to work with. Of course Dick Martin was the same way. He was always very funny and pulling jokes of some sort or another. They were just two great guys. I just felt that it was an honor to work with them.

*   *   *

Harry Carey, Jr. Interview
May 20, 1993

Knoxville Western Film Caravan

During my research on Tim Holt, someone told

me that Tim had gone to high school with Harry Carey, Jr., the son of the actor who starred in *THE LAW WEST OF TOMBSTONE* (1938), the film that provided Tim with his first major role (and a good one it was as the Tonto Kid).

Harry, Jr., of course, went on to a very successful career as an actor in his own right, appearing most notably early on as John Ford's resident "youth" in such films as *THREE GODFATHERS* (1948), *SHE WORE A YELLOW RIBBON* (1949), *WAGONMASTER* (1950), *RIO GRANDE* (1950), and *THE SEARCHERS* (1956). In addition, he appeared in a wide range of roles in many other outstanding Westerns from the 1950s through the 1980s, including *RIO BRAVO* (1958), *THE COMMANCHEROS* (1961), *SHENANDOAH* (1965), *THE BALLAD OF JOSIE* (1967), *BANDOLERO* (1968), *BIG JAKE* (1971), *CAHILL, U.S. MARSHAL* (1973), and *THE LONG RIDERS* (1980). And the list goes on. With the passage of years, Harry became a highly respected character actor, depicting despicable killers and crotchety "old timers" with equal aplomb.

When I heard that Harry was to be a guest star at the 1993 Knoxville Western Film Caravan, I figured it would be a good time to talk to him about Tim. Harry and Mrs. Carey (Marilyn, the daughter of prominent character actor Paul Fix) invited me to join them for lunch in the hotel dining room after he finished an autograph session for the film festival fans. After ordering, we chatted about Tim and other related matters.

Harry Carey: No, I didn't go to school with Tim Holt, but in that era all the movie stars' sons went to military schools like Black Fox and Culver Military Academy, which I guess Tim attended. At the one I attended, Black Fox, the two Chaplin boys were there, Paul Whiteman's son was there, Sam Goldwyn, Jr. was there, and a lot of others.

You know, Tim *looked* like a hero should look on screen. He was handsome, well built, and he rode good. He handled a gun good, too, just like his father. My dad went to NYU in New York, and Jack Holt was about two or three classes behind my dad.

DR: Tim was with your dad in *THE LAW WEST OF TOMBSTONE* in 1938.

Harry: Yes, and that's a great picture and Tim does a fine job in it. You know, my dad was marvelous in that too. That was so against his character, playing a blow-hard and con man like that. Even with that marvelously honest face that he had, he got it across.

DR: It's really more of a comedy than a traditional Western.

Harry: It *is* a comedy; my dad's so full of baloney in it. He made about three pictures in a row there at RKO. You know, Tim should have been in *THE LAST OUTLAW* (1936) with my dad. Hoot Gibson played the part that Tim should have had, the love interest with my dad's daughter in the picture. I love Hoot, but he was too old for the part. Tim would have been perfect for that role.

DR: Did you ever personally meet Tim?

Harry: I admired Tim through the years as a performer, but the only personal contact I had with him came just before his death. Jennifer (Holt) was visiting my mother in Santa Barbara—at the time Jennifer only lived a couple of miles south of my mother. While she was there, Jennifer called Tim in Oklahoma, and my mom talked to him for a while and then I talked to him. He sounded so warm and gracious, like we had been old friends. I remember that it was only about two weeks after that conversation that he passed away.

*   *   *

Ann Rutherford Interview
July 28, 1993

Ann Rutherford, in addition to co-starring in twelve Andy Hardy pictures at MGM with Mickey Rooney, has appeared in such well-known films as *GONE WITH THE WIND* (1939), *PRIDE AND PREJUDICE* (1940), *THE SECRET LIFE OF WALTER MITTY* (1947), and *THE ADVENTURES OF DON JUAN* (1948). In the Western genre she

Harry Carey, Jr. poses with author David Rothel at the 1993 Knoxville Western Film Caravan.

had been a leading lady for such cowboy stalwarts as Gene Autry in *COMIN' ROUND THE MOUNTAIN* (1936) and John Wayne in *THE LAWLESS NINETIES* (1936), *THE OREGON TRAIL* (1936), and *THE LONELY TRAIL* (1936).

Ann was a guest star at the Lone Pine Sierra Film Festival in 1992, and, in a chat with Berdee (Mrs. Tim) Holt, she commented on a long-ago romance that Tim had had with her friend, actress Bonita Granville. Later, Berdee mentioned the comment to me during my interview with her.

When I called Ann to talk with her about the Tim/Bonita romance, she quickly emphasized to me that she hadn't really known Tim very well, but she remembered Bonita's infatuation with him.

Ann Rutherford: I never worked with Tim myself, but I knew him, and he was just a darling kid. He couldn't have been more attractive. He had lovely manners; his parents had done an exemplary job of raising him. My mother, too, thought he was darling! Bonita Granville was my close friend, and she had a big crush on Tim. Bonita, of course, frequently fell deeply in like or love (laugh); she fell in love very easily. (laugh) She was in puppy love with Tim, and they couldn't have been more attractive together. As I remember it, this was around the time of *HITLER'S CHILDREN*.

We were all working kids in those days (early 1940s), and we didn't have much time to socialize. Believe it or not, we worked six full days a week at the studio. We were all too tired at the end of the day to go out. Our only day off was Sunday. When all of us were working, our way of entertaining used to be Sunday brunch. Everybody would sleep late and then we'd gather at somebody's kitchen and scramble eggs and cook bacon.

I remember that Bonita brought Tim with her to some of the brunches. Bonita was probably the brightest young person I had ever met. She had total recall for everybody's name; she took a little notebook with her, and, when she was introduced to somebody on the set, she'd scribble the name down to refresh her memory.

Oh, yes, Tim and Bonita had a big crush on each other for a time. But one of their problems was that Tim was frequently gone on location for a picture, and Bonita was always bereft because he was out of town. I think that their romance eventually died of its own weight because they were both working on pictures that required a location.

I met Tim's wife and children in Lone Pine last October (1992) at the film festival. His wife is darling, and I was very impressed with his children and grandchildren that I met there. I thought they were all delightful. Obviously, Tim was a good father.

* * *

There is an interesting addendum which can be added to Ann's remarks about Tim and Bonita. When I later interviewed Jennifer Holt, I commented to her that I almost never heard a bad word about Tim, to which she replied with the following.

Jennifer: I think you'd have to talk to a couple of ladies that he dumped to get anything ugly. That's about the only time you're going to hear anything negative about Tim. I know of a few ladies that weren't too happy with him, particularly Bonita Granville, who would just barely talk to me because I'm Tim's sister.

DR: Ann Rutherford has told me about Bonita's crush on Tim, but I don't know the details of how it ended.

Jennifer: Disasterously for Bonita. I crossed the ocean with her once sometime in the late sixties, and she said, "Well, I hate to say it, but I like you in spite of the fact that you're Tim's sister." We saw quite a bit of each other in London and had quite a good time. She said, "He really was a—unprintable word!" (laugh) Bonita had been going with Jackie Cooper, you see, but Jackie began to fool around with Tim's girl, June Horne. Tim said, "Okay, Jackie, I'll just move in on Bonita." And he did!

* * *

Budd Boetticher Interview
July 30, 1993

Budd Boetticher, respected film producer/director/writer and former bullfighter, has been a member-in-good-standing of the film industry since he served as technical director for *BLOOD AND SAND* back in 1941. Western fans are probably most familiar with his direction of a series of Randolph Scott pictures in the 1950s, which are generally ranked as the best of the Scott Westerns. Titles include *DECISION AT SUNDOWN* (1957), *THE TALL T* (1957), *BUCHANAN RIDES ALONE* (1958), and *RIDE LONESOME* (1959). Though he has been less active as a director in recent years, age seems to be no deterrent to this hard-working seventy-seven-

Ann Rutherford and David Rothel posed for this photo at the 1987 Memphis Film Festival.

year-old director. As of this writing, he is prepping a new Western film which is scheduled to go into production within the next few months.

My friend Ken Taylor had the opportunity to visit Budd Boetticher and his wife Mary at their home in Ramona, California, a little northeast of San Diego. While there he discovered that the director had known Tim quite well.

Budd Boetticher: We were at Culver together. Tim and Hal Roach roomed together. My last year in Culver I was captain of the football team and captain of track, and we became very good friends at that time. Hal ran interference for me. Tim was so bowlegged, having been such a horseman all of his life, that he was captain of the polo team and about third string on the football team. He wasn't a very good football player.

I remember he used to walk around in our suite of rooms there (at Culver), and he often had on his '38 revolvers and holster. He'd walk up and down the hall in his bathrobe and practice drawing his guns. He'd say, "I'm going to be a Western star some day." And we'd say (derisively), "Sure! We'd sure take a bet on that!" And I was really thrilled when he made it. In my opinion, Tim and Joel McCrea were the two

Mary and Budd Boetticher pose with Ken Taylor (left) during his visit to their home in Ramona, California. (Photo courtesy of Ken Taylor.)

best horsemen we ever had in pictures. And he didn't just look good; he could really ride. He was a great horseman and a delightful guy.

Look at the pictures he made: *THE MAGNIFICENT AMBERSONS;* you can't do a better job. *THE TREASURE OF THE SIERRA MADRE* is still my favorite picture of all time. Tim should have been a big star—not a Western star, not a featured player. He had everything going for him: the curly hair and the cherub face, and he was so nice. I always respected and liked him. I used to date his sister, Jennifer, a wonderful gal.

* * *

When I later talked with Jennifer, I mentioned to her that Budd Boetticher had said he had dated her. She remembered the director with fondness.

Jennifer: I think Budd was my first crush. Yes, he *was* my first crush. We used to go to the Bel Air Bay Club when I was still not allowed to date, but I was allowed to go with Tim. As long as Tim was there, I could go to a dance at the Bay Club. Let's see, I guess I was about fifteen or sixteen. I would think that would have been the summer after Tim graduated from Culver.

When Tim died, Budd went to all the trouble to find where I was working in Santa Barbara and to call me to express his sorrow. We had a nice long talk, and that was the only touch point that I have had with him in all these years.

* * *

Orson Welles Comment

Orson Welles: (Referring to Tim's performance in *THE MAGNIFICENT AMBERSONS*) Extraordinary... One of the most interesting actors that's ever been in American movies, and he *decided* to be just a cowboy actor. Made two or three important pictures in his career, but was very careful not to follow them up—went straight back to bread-and-butter Westerns. He was the most marvelous fellow to

Orson Welles, director of *THE MAGNIFICENT AMBERSONS*.

work with you can imagine. We ran every picture you can think of before we found him. And then we ran all kinds of six-day movies Tim made before we were absolutely certain. It was a lucky decision. (From *This is Orson Welles* by Orson Welles and Peter Bogdanovich.

*   *   *

Tim relaxes for a few minutes with issue No. 1 of his comic book.

Chapter 9
A Tim Holt Scrapbook

Comic Books

The Tim Holt comic books were a favorite among kids in the late 1940s and well into the 1950s. All of them featured Tim on the cover, either in an artist's rendering or in a photo cover. Many of the issues had color-photo back covers as well, and on the inside covers there was a feature entitled "Tim Holt's Western Album," a series of black and white photos of scenes from Tim's movies or photos of Tim on rodeo or personal-appearance tours. Lengthy captions explained the montage of photos on these inside covers.

The first issue had a black and white cameo

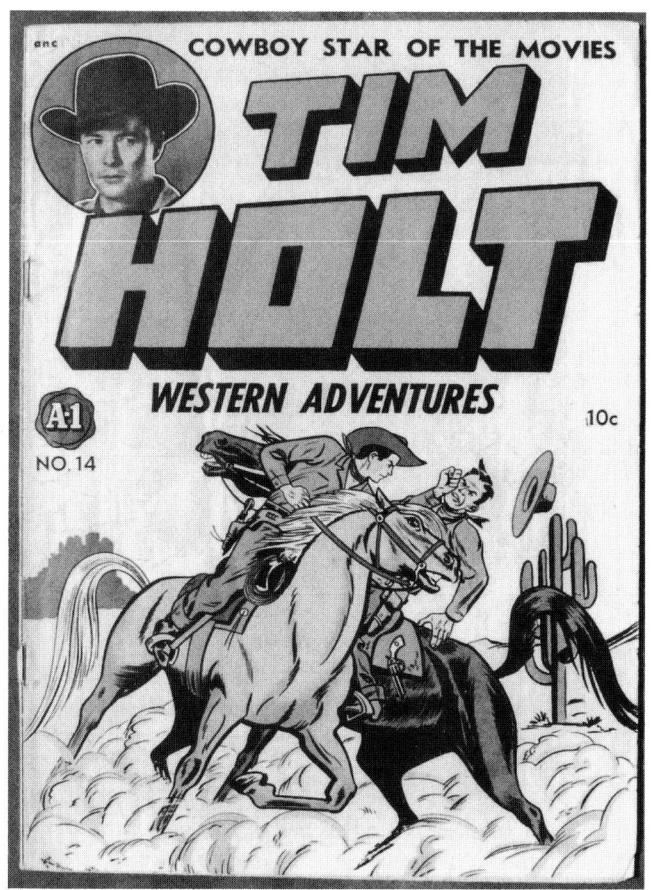

Issue No. 1 of "Tim Holt Western Adventures" appeared in 1948. Today a near-mint copy is worth around $285. (Comic book courtesy of Ed Shetterly.)

photo of Tim in the upper left corner with exciting artwork elsewhere on the cover which depicted Tim clobbering a bad guy while both were on horseback. From issue two through eighteen, color-photo covers of Tim were the rule, and these issues are generally the most sought after by Tim Holt fans.

In 1991 *AC Comics* editor and publisher Bill Black revived the Tim Holt comic book, publishing the first "Tim Holt Western Annual." The book, fifty-six pages in black and white, consists of reprints of stories which appeared in the original Tim Holt comic book series of the forties and fifties. In addition, Bill has enhanced the book with photos of Tim on the outside covers, a publicity photo of Tim and Chito on the front inside cover, and a movie ad and still on the inside back cover. Inside the issue there are other publicity ads for various Tim Holt movies and several reprints (again from the original Holt comics) of a one-page feature entitled "Western Range Book" (Artwork by Dick Ayers), which contain interesting tidbits of information on our Western heritage:

> The great "Buffalo Bill" Cody once served with General Custer in one of the most famous hand-to-hand fights of the early West. Cody met in single combat and killed a mighty chief of the Indians, Yellow Hand. This initial victory disheartened the redmen, and the cavalry under Custer swept on to victory.

Also featured in this *AC Comics* publication is a brief history of the Tim Holt comic books which was written by Bill Black, who has been kind enough to let me present excerpts herewith:

> *TIM HOLT* Western comics made its debut in 1948 as published by Magazine Enterprises [ME], Vincent Sullivan, publisher. The stories were based on the fictional adventures of RKO film star, Tim Holt. The series ran for a decade, the final issue appearing in 1957. All stories were illustrated by FRANK BOLLE, an excellent illustrator whose development can be followed through this series. The first issue

Full-color photo covers started with No. 2, the September-October issue for 1948. (Comic book courtesy of Ed Shetterly.)

Many of the early issues of the Tim Holt comic book had color back covers. This photo appeared on the back of issue No. 5. (Comic book courtesy of Ed Shetterly.)

contained crude art that showed potential. By 1953, he was a top-notch professional, as good as they come.

In earlier issues, Tim was accompanied by Chito Rafferty, an Irish-Mexican woman chaser based on the character played in the film series by RICHARD MARTIN. The stories were well constructed, good solid Western adventures. The characterizations of the two leads paralleled their screen counterparts.

In issue No. 20, editor RAYMOND KRANK added a new dimension to TIM HOLT comics. In that issue, Tim donned a crimson outfit and became REDMASK OF THE RIO GRANDE....The origin of the character, with its setting in Mexican legend, owes much to ZORRO.

Most of the comic book stories were located near the fictional town of Bullet, Arizona. Tim made his secret headquarters in REDMASK's cave, located by the T-Bar-H Ranch. REDMASK proved very popular and soon Tim became the crimson cavalier every issue.

Writer GARDNER FOX did his research well, endeavoring to mix the real West with his fictitious West. In the first story in this issue, Fox has Tim and REDMASK competing with such real life characters as Wild Bill Hickok and Billy Tilghman.

Another fascinating aspect of TIM HOLT comics was the back-up feature, THE GHOST RIDER, brilliantly illustrated by DICK AYERS. This feature started in No. 11 and ran through No. 50. It told of traveling marshal REX FURY who donned a skull mask and white cape to become a spectral lawman. It was a very popular feature.

During the ten-year run, Tim and REDMASK ran into dozens of colorful villains...THE STRAWMAN, MAN IN THE

IRON MASK, BLACK DOMINO, and THE CAPE among them. Most often the villain was a beautiful woman such as THE WILDCAT, BLACK RIDER, and WHIP WOMAN. The most popular of these was a beautiful blonde masked outlaw called THE BLACK PHANTOM. REDMASK reformed her and she became a deputy in the Bullet sheriff's office along side of Tim Holt. She became a regular co-star, replacing Chito. She was even given a chance at her own title, but it failed after the first issue.

With issue No. 42, the title of the ME book changed from TIM HOLT to REDMASK. Eventually, Tim Holt was dropped from his own book. The character became REDMASK all the time. This was no doubt due to the fact that the RKO Tim Holt film series concluded in 1952. ME owned REDMASK and did not have to pay a licensing fee on that character as they did on TIM HOLT.

"Tim Holt's Western Album," on the inside covers, was a popular feature for Tim's fans. It provided background photos and information on Tim's film and rodeo appearances. (Comic books on this page courtesy of Ed Shetterly.)

Censorship in the form of the Comics Code Authority forced ME to drop the GHOST RIDER feature because of its horror overtones. REDMASK No. 51 saw the creation of a new character, one that the Comics Code smiled upon because he carried no guns. This was THE PRESTO KID, also created and illustrated by Dick Ayers. PRESTO was cover featured on the last 4 issues of REDMASK. *AC* has also reprinted a PRESTO KID comic.

Despite the popularity of the Tim Holt comics for about a decade, the series was by no means a financial bonanza for Tim or for Richard Martin, whose character of Chito appeared in the earlier issues. I asked Richard about the comic book series during my long interview with him regarding Tim. His only comment was a terse, "Frankly, that was a rather poor and mismanaged operation. Neither one of us came out well on it. I blame that on the agent who handled it."

Today the Tim Holt comics are, like most cowboy movie star comics of that period, quite valuable if they are in mint to near-mint condition. In the current Overstreet price guide, the No. 1 issue of Tim's comic book in near-mint condition is listed at $285; in fine condition at $122; and in good condition at $41. The three condition grades for issue No. 2 are valued at $175/75/25. With issue No. 11, where The Ghost Rider appears, the price range again jumps dramatically to $200/85/29. Even the later issues with Tim as REDMASK have a price range of $45/22.50/7.50. Don't you wish your mother hadn't thrown out those comics when you grew up and left home!

* * *

In 1990 *AC Comics* published "REDMASK of the Rio Grande" and followed it up in 1991 with "Tim Holt Western Annual." Both are part of *AC's* Collector Classic series and consist mainly of reprints from the original comic books. These comics are highly recommended for the Tim Holt fan who has no access to the original publications—and that's a large part of the reason for their existence; the originals are hard to find and expensive. For information on these and other comic books published by *AC*, write to *AC Comics*, Box 1216, Longwood, FL 32752. Bill Black is the editor and publisher.

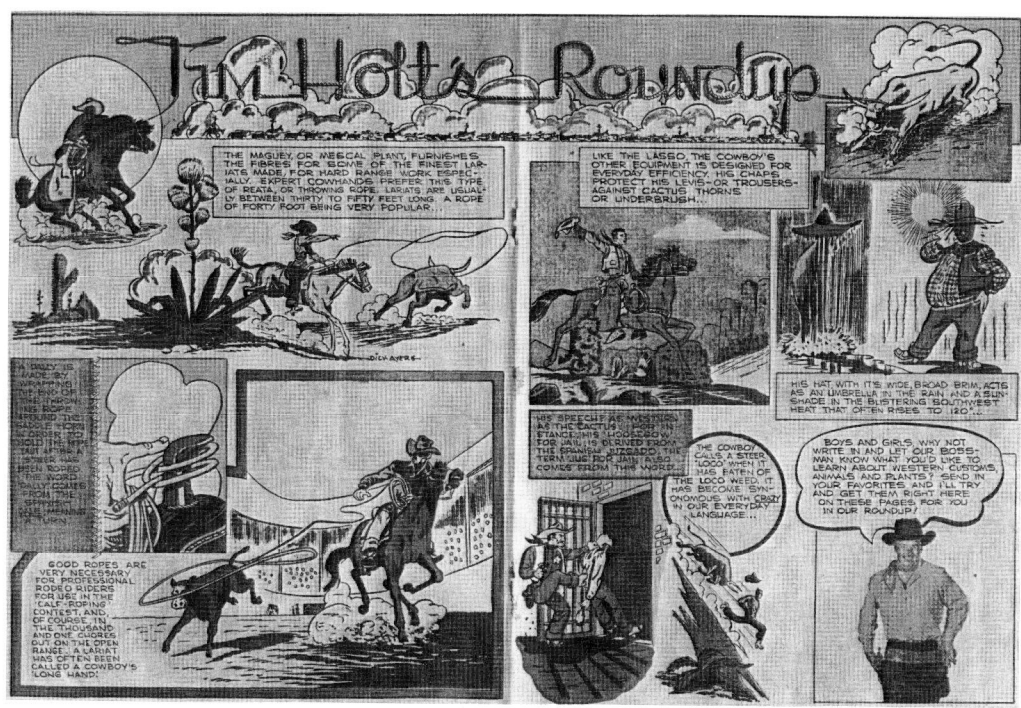

Dick Ayers, who illustrated several supporting features for Tim's comic book through the years of its publication, drew this "Tim Holt's Roundup" of Western lore for issue No. 1. In later issues Ayers would have a similar feature entitled "Western Range Book." (Comic book courtesy of Ed Shetterly.)

The artwork for the Tim Holt comics was done by Frank Bolle, who capably demonstrates his skill as an illustrator in these pages from issue No. 14 (1950). It can also be seen here that the basic elements of Tim's RKO film series were utilized in the comic book: Tim, Chito, and Tim's trusty palomino horse, Lightning. And what about Chito in that last panel? Trust me; he escapes from that angry Grizzly.

Although Chito appeared as a character in the early comics, he only rarely appeared on the covers. Here we see him with Tim on the covers of No. 9 (September 1949) and No. 14 (February 1950). The two shots were originally publicity photos for Tim's RKO film series. (Comic books courtesy of Ed Shetterly.)

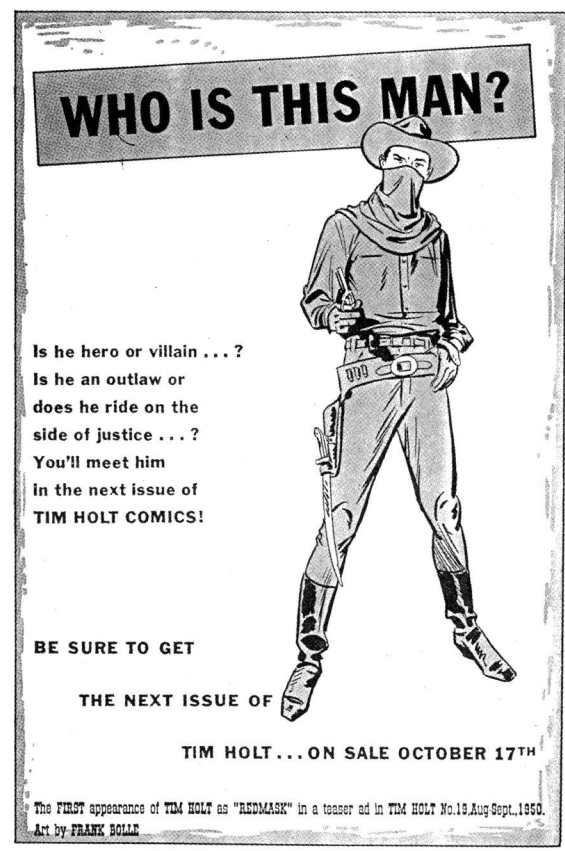
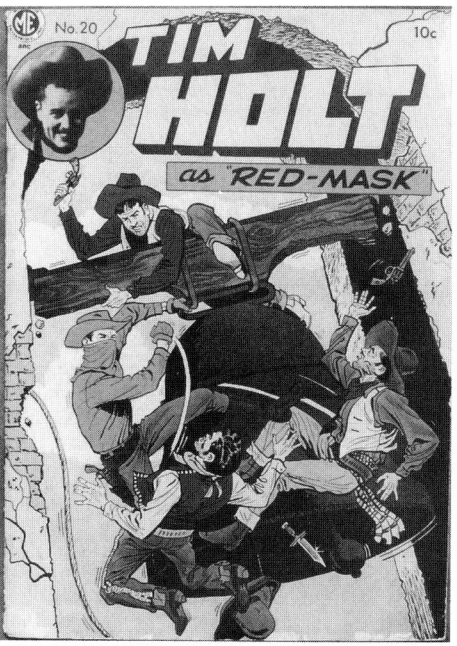

It was with this issue (No. 20) that the character of REDMASK was introduced. [The title character's name is shown printed in various ways: as two words, hyphenated, and as one word. For the sake of consistency, the one-word version will be used here.] (Comic book courtesy of Ed Shetterly.)

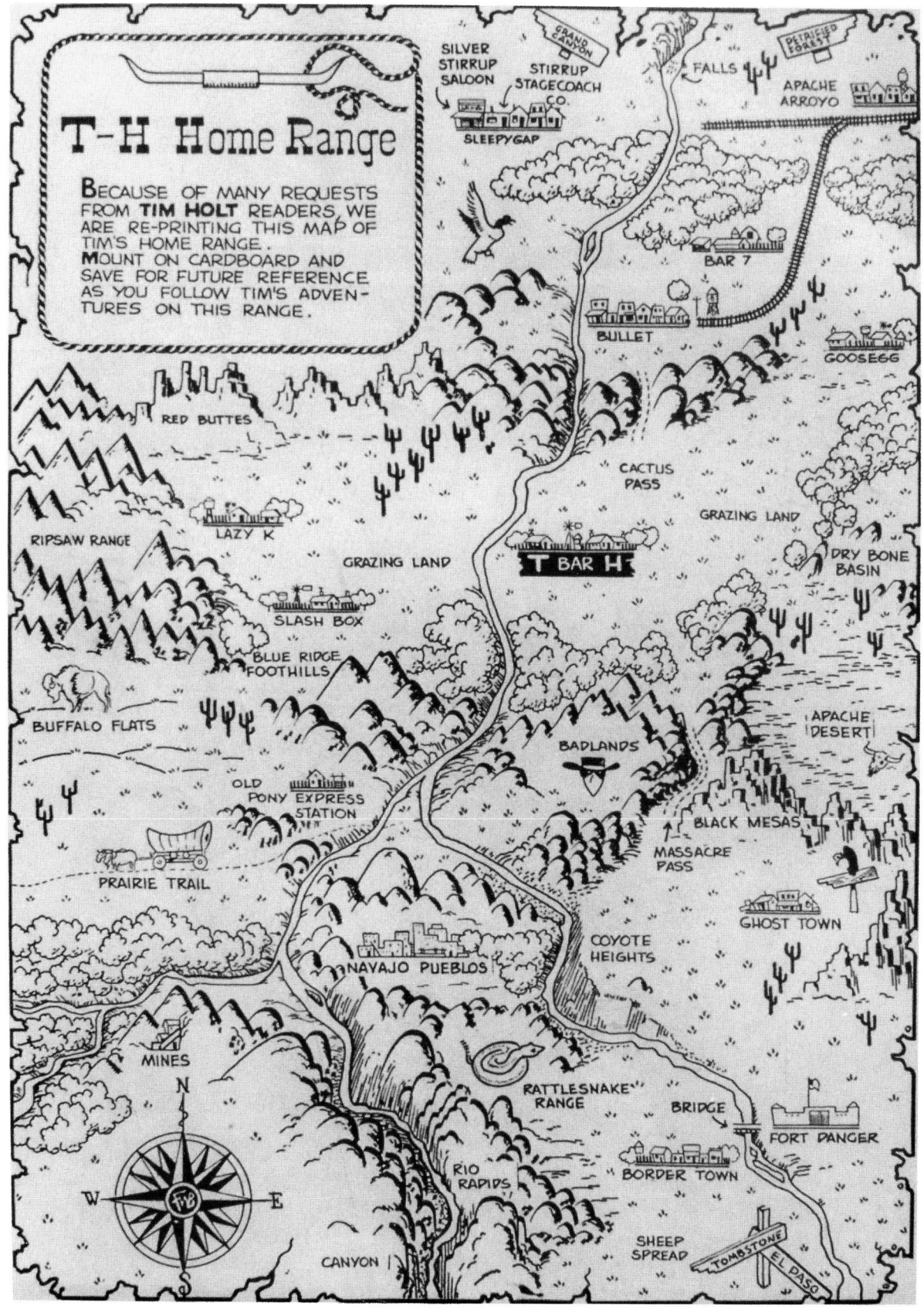

"T-H Home Range" for the comic books was Tim's T-H Ranch and the area around it, which included the town of Bullet. This map of the area was printed in two different issues and young readers were instructed to "mount [the map] on cardboard and save for future reference as you follow Tim's adventures on this range." (Comic book courtesy of Ed Shetterly.)

In issue No. 11 a back-up feature entitled "The Ghost Rider" was introduced. Frequently thereafter the covers displayed a small insert promo of the character's story. These two covers (No. 16 and 18) have such promos for "The Ghost Rider." (Comic books courtesy of Ed Shetterly.)

"The Ghost Rider" was brilliantly illustrated by Dick Ayers, as this two-page spread clearly demonstrates. Unfortunately, the character eventually ran afoul of the Comics Code Authority because of its horror overtones and was dropped after issue No. 50. (Comic book courtesy of Ed Shetterly.)

Although Tim and Richard were happy with the quality of the Tim Holt comic book, according to Richard, it did not turn out to be very beneficial for them from a financial standpoint.

No. 3 (November-December 1948). (Courtesy of Ed Shetterly.)

Tim appeared on the cover of "Crack Western" for issue No. 72 (May 1951). There was no illustrated Tim Holt story in the issue; inside there was only a plug for Tim's then-current movie, SADDLE LEGION. (Comic book courtesy of Ed Shetterly.)

No. 5 (March-April 1949). (Courtesy of Ed Shetterly.)

No. 8 (August 1949)

No. 12 (December 1949)

No. 10 (October 1949)

No. 13 (January 1950)
(Comic books on this page courtesy of Ed Shetterly.)

These two illustrated covers (No. 19 and 36) provide good examples of Frank Bolle's artwork. (Comic books courtesy of Johnny Efird.)

OTHER MEMORABILIA

Unlike the two leading cowboy stars of the forties and fifties, Gene Autry and Roy Rogers, Tim never had much of a chance to merchandise his name and likeness in the form of lunch boxes, cowboy outfits, cap pistols, and other merchandise. Autry and Rogers pretty much had the corner on the market. In addition, they also had radio shows and, later, television shows to boost their visibility and sales.

Tim got in on the comic book market, of course, albeit not with the lucrative deals of the aforementioned cowboy stars. In the toy market the only Tim Holt product uncovered by this writer was the "Tim Holt 2-Dart-Games-in-1 Rodeo and Pistol Range" put out by the Bar Zim Toy Company of Jersey City, New Jersey, in the late 1940s. The game consisted of a double-sided tin target (one side the "Tim Holt Pistol Range" and the other side the "Tim Holt Rodeo"); a red plastic dart gun, holster and belt; three feathered magnetic darts; and a stand for the target. When the darts were not in use, they could be attached by magnetism to the metal studs on the gun's holster.

The instructions for the dart gun informed the player that "to shoot a dart, first push the projector all the way in the gun until it catches. Then place the dart, magnet end first, against the metal piece on the end of the projector. When the trigger is pressed, the projector will shoot out and release the dart which will turn around and continue toward the target." Scoring instructions stated that "if dart touches any part of the figures, score amount marked in center of circle. If dart touches two figures, take higher score. If dart touches any part of numbered circle, double the score."

During these same post-war years, Tim's photo and name were also to be found on writing tablets and "Movie Star Notebook filler Paper" wrappers. Both items bore a small printed autograph. The writing tablet and one of the notebook paper wrappers had a photo of Tim in his typical Western outfit—shirt, neckerchief, and hat. Interestingly, the other notebook paper wrapper had a very youthful shot of him—definitely pre-war—wearing what appears to be a suit coat and smoking a pipe. Since

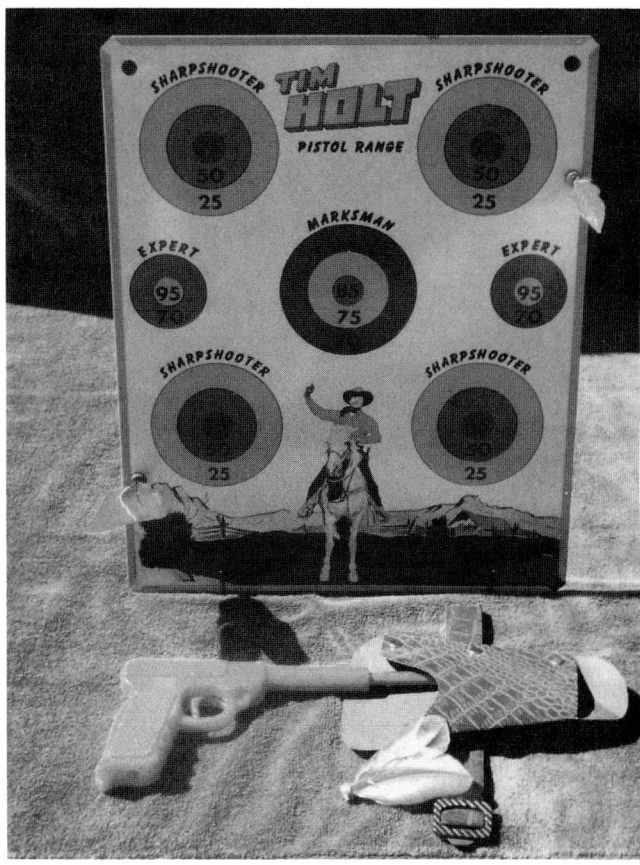

Additional magnetic darts could be ordered from the Bar Zim Toy Company. A set of four darts was fifty cents. (Photo courtesy of Boyd Magers.)

The Pistol Range target had a photographic likeness of Tim and Lightning on it, while the Rodeo target utilized an illustrator's artwork. (Photo courtesy of Boyd Magers.)

The Tim Holt Dart Games came in this eye-catching box. (Photo courtesy of Boyd Magers.)

The Tim Holt writing tablet. Notice the autograph on the rock. (Photo courtesy of Boyd Magers.)

(Photo courtesy of Boyd Magers.)

Tim was primarily known as a cowboy movie star during this period of his career, his appearance "out of costume" is surprising, and one has to wonder about the use of such an old photograph.

During the late forties and early fifties, Tim was usually on the rodeo circuit when he wasn't filming his Western film series. Sometime during that period, Tim commissioned the Edward H. Bohlin Custom Leather & Silver Works Company in California to make him two silver show saddles with accessories for his personal appearances—one with a square skirt and one with a rounded skirt, but both with essentially the same style and trim. During 1949, most likely, Tim posed with the square-skirted, silver-trimmed saddle for several publicity pictures, which eventually turned up on the cover of a comic book (No. 13, January 1950) and as a publicity still to promote his film, HOT LEAD (1951).

Now we jump ahead in time to 1987—fourteen years after Tim's death—and the showroom of the Bohlin Company in Burbank, California, where the Tim Holt round-skirted, sterling silver saddle (and related accessories) was on display. At some point in time the saddle had come back into the hands of the Bohlin Company, the circumstances not entirely clear, and it was for sale. Western film fan Ernie Worthington from Aurora, Indiana, entered Bohlin's

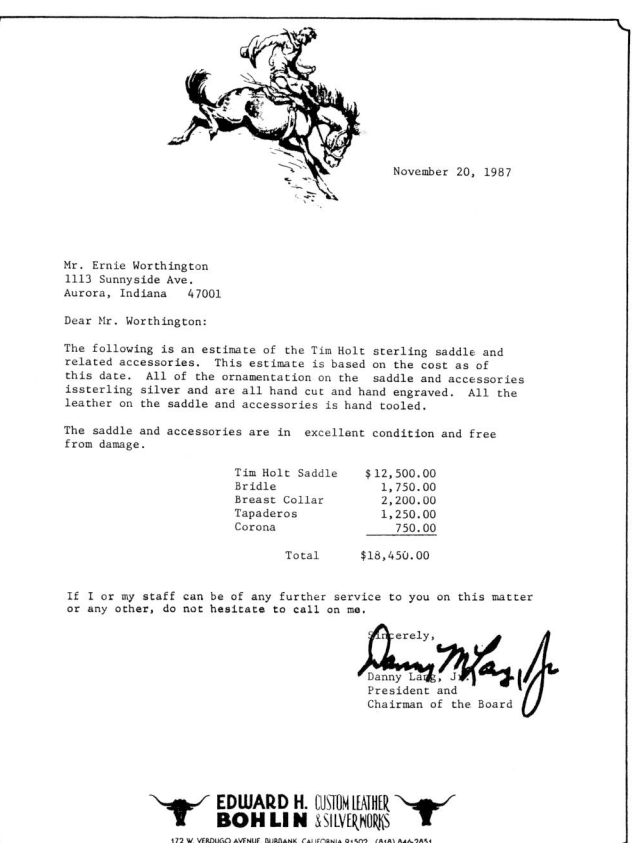

(Letter courtesy of Ernie Worthington.)

Tim is seen here with his silver-trimmed show saddle. (Photo courtesy of Chuck Thornton.)

shop one day in 1987, admired the saddle, and asked that a breakdown of costs for the various items be sent to him for his consideration. On November 20, 1987, the letter was sent which outlined the costs totaling $18,450; Worthington made an offer to the Bohlin Company and, ultimately, purchased Tim's saddle with all the trimmings—but not necessarily at Bohlin's asking price. Today, Ernie Worthington, known to many who attend Western film festivals, owns Tim's silver show saddle and has it and its accessories prominently displayed in his home.

*   *   *

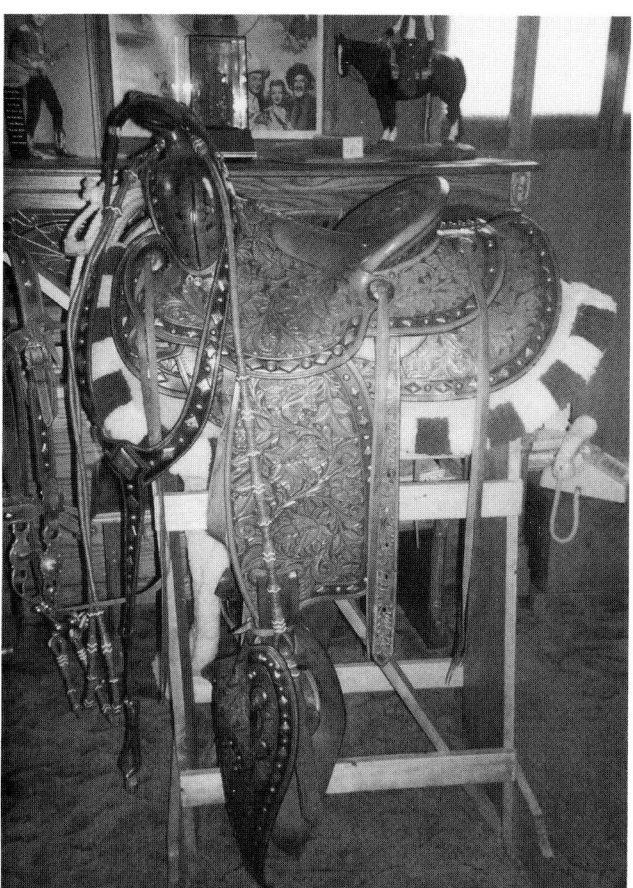

Top left: Ernie Worthington poses with the Tim Holt round-skirted sterling silver saddle that he purchased from the Edward H. Bohlin Company. (Photo courtesy of Ernie Worthington.)

Top right: This close-up of the saddle reveals that it has the same basic design as the square-skirted saddle pictured with Tim. (Photo courtesy of Ernie Worthington.)

Tim Holt Scrapbook Clippings And Photos

What follows is a collection of fan magazine and newspaper clippings about Tim which were published from the 1940s until his death in 1973. Interspersed with the clippings is a gallery of photos from his career and personal life.

* * *

Bottom right: Tim enjoys his pipe during a relaxed moment at home. (Circa 1940s)

THE LIFE STORY OF TIM HOLT

Our Postcard Series.   *Tim Holt.*

The picture above is intended to be cut out and pasted on a postcard. In this way you can add to your postcard collection.

TIM HOLT most assuredly belongs to the screen. Son of Jack Holt, one of the most popular male stars of the silent days and just as popular to-day, he was born in Beverly Hills where many of the stars live. He played in Hollywood, and grew up in Hollywood, so it was only natural that he should choose the screen for his career.

He was born on February 5th, 1918, and he was only ten years old when he made his film debut. A youngster was needed to play the part of Jack Holt as a boy, and the studio failed to find one who was suitable. The elder Holt arranged a leave of absence from school for his son, and gave his consent for Tim to play the part, so long as he returned to school afterwards.

Tim demonstrated his ability as an actor, but that was the end of his career for the time being. The promise made to his father was kept, and Tim went back to the grammar school he was then attending. His father sent him next to a public high school for one year, and after that he allowed him to select his own school.

Tim talked the matter over with his friend Hal Roach, Jun., and they found that they both wanted to go to the same type of school.

"I want to go in the army—the cavalry," Tim announced to his dad, so Culver Military Academy was chosen as his next school. He did not realise it then, but it was not the idea of going into the army which appealed to him so much as the idea of combining education with a good deal of horseback riding.

There were amateur dramatic shows at Culver, and Tim, who was drawn to them naturally, turned out to be a good actor. He soon found that he was longing for schooldays to be over, so that he could start on his career. When he told his father of his decision to become an actor instead of going into the army, Jack did nothing to make him change his mind. Very wisely he had always intended to allow the boy to follow his own bent.

Walter Wanger "Discovered" Him

Immediately he graduated from Culver, Tim joined the Westwood Theatre Guild, situated just outside Hollywood, and he was given the juvenile lead in a play, opposite Mae Clarke and Bodil Rosing.

Walter Wanger happened to be in the audience, and he immediately arranged for Tim to have a film test, and it proved to be so good that he placed him under contract straight away.

His first part was that of a radio operator in *History is Made at Night*.

He had his first important role when Samuel Goldwyn borrowed him from Walter Wanger, and, oddly enough, it was the same part that launched the son of another famous star to screen stardom several years before. That other young fellow was Douglas Fairbanks, and the role that of David Grosvenor in *Stella Dallas*. Mr. Goldwyn made both the silent and talkie versions, so he was responsible in helping both the sons of famous fathers to attain success.

A Polo Accident

Tim has always been very keen on polo, and early in his career he suppressed the news of an accident he had because he was afraid Mr. Wanger might forbid him to play any more. Several weeks went by, and then at last he did confess. A member of a famous polo team, he was playing against another strong team at Santa Barbara when his horse crossed his front legs and fell, throwing Tim to the ground. While the actor was stunned and helpless on the turf a horse from the opposing team struck the back of his head with his hoof, cutting a deep gash, and he was unconscious more than half an hour.

As it happened he need not have worried about telling Mr. Wanger of the accident.

"Don't worry, it's all in the game," the producer said, "and you might have been struck by a car crossing the street." Mr. Wanger understood such things, being a keen polo player himself and only a short while previously a similar accident had occurred to him.

Tim Holt's next film after *Stella Dallas* was *Gold is Where You Find It*, and since then he has played in *Sons of the Legion*, *The Renegade Ranger*, *The Law West of Tombstone*, *Man's Heritage*, *Stagecoach*, *Swift* Vengeance, *The Girl and the Gambler*, *Fifth Avenue Girl*, *Swiss Family Robinson*, *Laddie*, *Back Street*, *The Magnificent Ambersons*, *Along the Rio Grand*, *Cyclone on Horseback* and *Hitler's Children*. He has given up his career for the time being, as he is now serving in the American forces.

A Good All-round Sportsman

Tim has light brown hair, brown eyes, and is five feet eleven inches in height. He is one of the best all-round sportsmen in Hollywood. Besides being a crack polo player he also excels at swimming, badminton and tennis. His hobby is raising cocker spaniels. He has always hated wearing formal clothes, and feels dressed at his best in slacks and a polo shirt. He has always been an outdoor enthusiast, and when he drove his car he always had the top down, with the result that he had a complexion like an Indian. Closed cars are, as a matter of fact, one of his special dislikes.

In December, 1938, he married Virginia May Ashcroft, and they have a little son, Lance.

Would Not Be A Copy of His Father

Tim is a great admirer of his father, but when he started on his career he was quite determined not to copy him in any way.

"Copies never have a chance," he says. "Acting is a lonely job, for every actor must be a law to himself."

He was very glad, however, of his father's advice. Jack would watch him rehearse a scene, and then offer suggestions, but they were only general suggestions. He, too, wished Tim to interpret roles in his own way and not to imitate him. They both agreed that although imitation is the sincerest form of flattery, it is no way to get along if you wish to be successful as an actor.

Tim has always watched the prop boys and the electricians in the studio to see if he is playing a scene well. If they take no notice and talk to one another in dumb show he realises that the scene is not going so well.

"But if they turn round and look at me, I know that I am probably getting along all right," he says.

This publicity release originally appeared in *Picture Show*, a British publication, circa 1943. (Article courtesy of Nick Nicholls.)

Twenty-three-year-old Tim is seen here with first wife Virginia and his long-tongued dog, Tell. (Photo courtesy of Chuck Thornton.)

This shot was taken shortly after Tim returned from service in World War II.

Tim is set for some no-nonsense action in this scene from *UNDER THE TONTO RIM* (1947). (Photo courtesy of Chuck Thornton.)

tim holt

Famous son of a famous father, he's a rising young star.

Tim Holt, who has just turned 30, started in life with a birthplace which most people would consider a handicap for a rough-riding Westerner. He was born in Hollywood, almost in the shadow of a movie studio. This glamorous birthplace was justified, however, by the fact that his rugged father, Jack Holt, was then acting in Westerns himself. In fact, he is still acting in them. He co-starred with Tim in a picture recently released, "The Arizona Rangers."

Tim, unlike most sons of movie actors, learned to ride almost before he could walk. Today he is one of the finest horsemen in the West. Before returning to the movies, Tim spent nearly a year with a rodeo to take the wartime kinks out of his legs. Last year, he bought an interest in that same rodeo, and appears with it when he is not making pictures.

His post-war career got a quick shot in the arm when he appeared in "Treasure of Sierra Madre," a hard-bitten movie about gold-miners and their greed. Since his great success in that film (see next page), Tim has won a big following as an action star. Signed by RKO, he now makes six Westerns each year, to the delight of his large fan following.

AN EXPERT SHOT, Jack Holt's son Tim is also good at juggling his weapons, a trick he's often performed in his Western movies and on tour with the rodeo of which he is part-owner.

tim holt

In "Treasure of Sierra Madre," Tim won wide acclaim for his portrayal of a tough miner.

Tim was doing well as a Western star at RKO, but it was not until he appeared on loan-out in Warner Brothers' "Treasure of Sierra Madre" that the public became aware that Tim was a fine actor as well as a man of action. Playing a disillusioned young American on the bum in Mexico, Tim gave depth to a difficult role.

Tim, Humphrey Bogart, Walter Huston, and other members of the cast spent two months in Central Mexico, and another two weeks in the grueling heat of California's Mojave desert. Yet, the toughest work often brings the best results. The hot sun, the desert air, and the grimy sweat added a realism which went a long way toward making the film the year's best outdoor story.

DISHEVELED, weary, and suspicious, Curtin (Tim Holt) worries about losing his share of the gold which he and his partners have dug out of the Mexican hills. He rightfully distrusts his greedy partner, Dobbs, whose nerves have snapped under strain.

  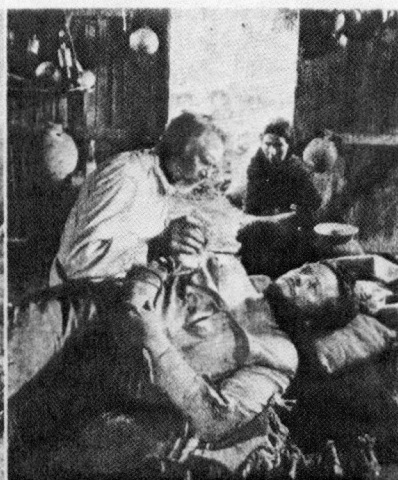

CONFIDENT of riches, Dobbs and Curtin bear great hardship. But as their cache grows, their mutual distrust becomes hatred.

GUNPLAY is the outcome of Dobbs' greed. Believing Curtin wants more than his share, Dobbs fires, leaves him wounded.

CURTIN'S WOUNDS are treated by his other partner. Later, they find Dobbs' body robbed of their gold by bandits.

brothers in the saddle

Tim is called upon to rescue his renegade brother, Steve, from a lynching party. Believing his brother innocent, Tim rides into Mexico to find the only witness who can clear him. While Tim is away, Steve robs a stagecoach and kills a passenger. Tim is heartsick to learn that he has been wrong in defending his brother and personally brings him to justice. After a savage gun-battle in the hills, Tim shoots Steve in self-defense.
→

the arizona ranger

Tim plays the son of his real father, Jack Holt. Commissioned to command the first company of Arizona Rangers, Tim tries to clean up the territory by legal methods. His father, Rawhide, a tough rancher, believes that rope is the only law for outlaws. They conflict when Tim stops his father from lynching the outlaw leader. Only when his stubbornness jeopardizes his son's life does Rawhide respect the law. Tim and Jack (right).
→

guns of wrath

Tim Holt and his saddle partner, Chito Rafferty (Dick Martin) find themselves falsely accused of murder. Escaping from jail, they discover that the murder is linked with a plot to steal a valuable mining property from a friendless girl. Tim and Chito pick up a trail that leads to the real killer, Morgan, the owner of the town saloon. After a rough-and-tumble fist-fight, on a runaway wagon, Tim forces Morgan to confess his guilt.
→

outlaw valley

Looking for jobs, Tim and Chito stop off at a prosperous ranch. The owner has lost 400 prize steers to rustlers. They are not long in discovering that the local sheriff is the ringleader of the cattle thieves. The sheriff tries to kill them in a staged jailbreak. But Tim and Chito escape and, after an uneven gun-battle, bring peace to the rangeland. In a thrilling climax, Tim rides down the crooked sheriff and bulldogs him from his saddle.
→

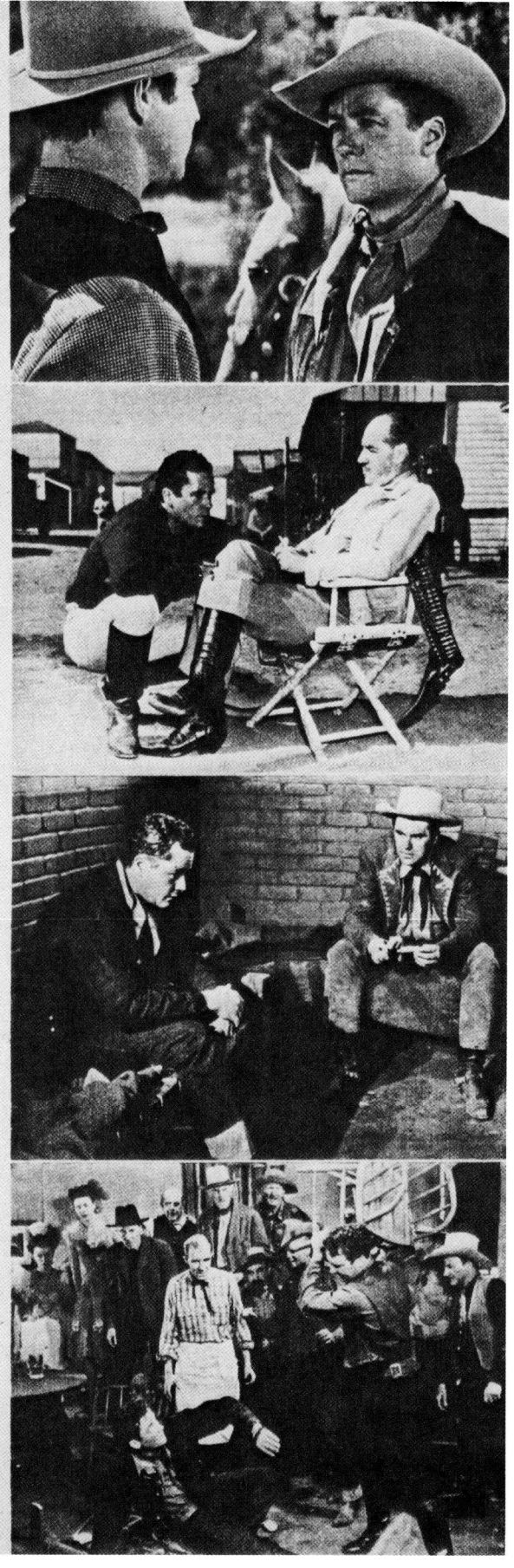

tim holt

In his latest film, Tim Holt displays the talent that has made him a Western star since his discharge from the Army.

In "Indian Agent," Tim Holt and his sidekick, Chito Rafferty (Dick Martin), encounter a tough frontier problem. While riding into the town of Boulder, they are called upon to rescue an old printer and his niece from an attack by marauding Indians. Normally peaceful, the tribe has been driven to robbery by hunger. When Tim and Chito learn that the Indians are being victimized by a crooked Indian agent, they undertake to solve the mystery of their missing food allotments. Their search leads Tim and Chito to many adventures fraught with danger and the threat of imminent death.

THE FRONTIER PAPER of Ellen Wheeler (Nan Leslie) and her uncle stirs up trouble in the town of Boulder when it exposes the mysterious robbery of food sent by the government, intended for Indians of the neighboring territory.

TIM CONFRONTS the crooked wagon-train operator and his partner-in-crime, the Indian Agent. He attempts to argue and persuade them into stopping their theft, but gets nowhere with peaceful tactics.

REDFOX, Indian Chief, is angered at the white man's double-dealing and plans a bloody revolt. But Tim is able to persuade him to defer his attack until his plan can work.

243

TAKING SHORT-CUT, Tim and Chito ride over the hills and cut off wagon-train loaded with war supplies and ammunition for the Indians. Concealed behind rocks, Tim and Chito are able to hold back wagons for a short time but, greatly out-numbered, they are finally encircled. Fortunately, the sheriff and the Indians ride up just in time to save them from an ambush—and certain death.

REALIZING that Tim is closing in on his gang, the crooked wagon-train operator (Harry Woods) mercilessly shoots the Indian Agent and frames the innocent Tim for his murder.

IN JAIL FOR a crime he did not commit, Tim's anger turns to fury when he hears that Indians are being incited to outbreak. He is released from jail when Ellen proves his complete innocence of the crime.

The preceding publicity release originally appeared in *Western Stars*, Volume 1, No. 1, November 1948-February 1949. (Article courtesy of Ed Shetterly.)

WESTERN, HO!
Continued

FOLLOWING in his famous father's footsteps Tim Holt has won the fans' favor for his sharp shooting, good looks, and expert riding. Practically born in the saddle, Tim finds a barbed-wire fence and post an ideal easy chair while on location for his sagebrush film *Renegade of the Rancho* for RKO. Tim favors a pipe over other Western stars' hand-rolled cigs.

The *RENEGADE OF THE RANCHO* film referred to in this item was changed to *THE MYSTERIOUS DESPERADO* (1949) prior to release. The source of the clipping is not known. (Courtesy of Nick Nicholls.)

Tim prepares to take dead aim at the bad guys in this scene from his Zane Grey period (1947).

TIM HOLT and his pal Chito Rafferty (Richard Martin), stopped by pretty Martha Hyer who means business with that Winchester.

DECIDING that the threat calls for drastic action, Tim dismounts and, in a flying tackle, knocks the rifle out of Martha's hands.

help! help!

Tim Holt, who's a normally mild-mannered man, knows exactly what to do when a pretty girl pulls a gun on him. The code of the West, like the code of ancient chivalry, is based on a deep respect for womanhood. But there are times when even a nice girl can get out of hand. A Winchester in the hands of an angry female can be just as deadly as if a man were pulling the trigger. It doesn't matter that the girl's anger is based on a misunderstanding. How to discourage the shooting habits of otherwise genteel young ladies no longer bothers Tim. In "Outlaw Valley," RKO Western, he finds that a good spanking is just the thing.

SHE KICKS and squirms and struggles to keep from screaming against the outrage of the spanking that Tim firmly intends to administer.

TIM COULDN'T be more intent if he were trying to tame a wildcat and, in fact, he's thinking the comparison is completely accurate.

HE TIPS her upside down, asks her if she'll be a good girl now, but Martha is no in-name-only cowgirl. She fights to get free.

When brunette Martha Hyer draws down on Tim with a Winchester, he dismounts, knocks the gun from her hands, and administers resounding whacks right where nature intended they should be placed. Tim doesn't advocate spankings as a general practice, but says that, in the case of Martha, it did her a world of good.

ONE LAST good smack, and Tim figures he's proved his case. Chito's horse looks scornful. Tim's, naturally on his side, is unperturbed.

OPERATION Object Lesson completed, Tim lets Martha drop. The tale has a happy ending. Believe it or not, she finds it was for her own good!

UNDER orders from his renegade brother Steve, Danny suggests short-cut to military post while riding Army wagon, carrying guns. Colonel's daughter Judy is with him.

THE WAGON is held up; the driver killed and escort wounded. Judy succeeds in driving off the bandits with her marksmanship. The boy leaves with bandit gang.

When Tim Holt and his friend, Chito, find a mere boy being used as a gun runners' pawn, they take the law by the horns!

gun runners

Acting under orders from his renegade brother, Steve Reeves (Douglas Fowley), Danny (Gary Gray), ten years old, tricks Sergeant Hasty Jones (Paul Hurst) into taking a short cut to the Army post with a consignment of guns. The outfit is ambushed by Reeves and his gang, who kill the escort, wound Hasty and escape with the wagons. Judy (Martha Hyer), daughter of Colonel Davis (Robert Warwick), Commandant of the Post, who was in the party, escapes injury. She had unwittingly helped Danny trap the wagon train.

Tim Holt (Himself) and his side-kick, Chito Rafferty (Richard Martin), riding to Hasty's ranch, are attracted to the scene of the holdup by the gunfire and take Judy and the wounded Hasty to a nearby town. Then, accompanied by the Sheriff (Don Haggerty) and a posse, Tim and Chito start out in search of Danny, the crooks and the guns.

Returning from a cold trail, Tim and Chito spot Danny and follow him to the bandit hide-out, where they capture the boy and Steve. Dodge (Robert Bray), another of the gang, gets away and goes to the spot where the rest of the gang have hidden the guns.

Back in town, Steve is put behind bars, after being identified as a gun runner wanted by the Mexican government. Danny is put in the care of Tim and Chito, in the hope of getting him to reveal the hiding place of the stolen wagons, but they have no luck.

gun runners

As a result of the holdup, Hasty is court-martialed and dishonorably discharged from the Army, but Judy writes to the Secretary of War, revealing her responsibility in the affair. She wins a promise that Hasty's case will be reviewed. In the meantime, Hasty has succeeded in winning Danny's affection and regenerating him. He even recovers the boy's beloved dog and pony from the bandit hide-out, which, of course, is final proof to the boy that Hasty is really sincere in all his dealings.

Then, one day, while Danny is out riding, he is cornered by Dodge who tells him that Steve is being taken to Mexico and will be shot. If Danny wants to say goodbye to his brother, he can have that chance by flagging down the Nogales stage at a certain point on the highway.

He will run no risk by doing this, Dodge adds, and it will please Steve to know that Danny cares that much about him. Steve, says Dodge, is a good guy who got a bad break.

Unsuspecting, Danny follows Dodge's suggestion and is instrumental in enabling Dodge and others of the crooks to hold up the stage, wound the driver, and rescue Steve. Panic-stricken at what he has done, Danny decides he will have to go back to the bandits' hide-out, because he couldn't face his new friends now.

While searching for Danny, Tim finds the barn where the ammunition and guns are hidden, but he is trapped in one of the out-buildings. Danny saves Tim's life by blinding one of the bandits with a sling shot. Although injured, he then goes for help.

The sheriff and Chito refuse to believe Danny's story and think it is a trap. But Hasty discovers that Danny has been wounded, and this substantiates his story. So a posse heads for the hills, kills or captures all the gun runners and recovers the Army property. When Hasty is reinstated in the Army and Danny enrolled in a military academy, all's well, with law and order on their side once again.

ARRIVING at scene, Tim Holt and Chito Rafferty learn story, help get wounded sergeant to post; sergeant is dishonorably discharged from the Army. Judy feels guilty for the unwitting role she played.

HENCHMEN tell Danny Steve will be killed when he's turned over to Mexicans. Danny stops stage, and henchmen save Steve from law.

WOUNDED, Danny goes for help. But Sheriff and Chito think his story is only a trap. Sgt. Hasty discovers boy's wound; trusts him.

IN ORDER to help clear Sergeant Hasty's name, Tim and Chito mount their horses and set out on trail of Danny, the crooks and the guns. Having no idea where to look, they will have to fake a cold trail.

SPOTTING Danny, they follow him to hide-out, where they capture boy and brother. Steve is taken to jail; Danny is given spanking, but it's the kind that hurts spanker much more than the spankee.

PANIC-STRICKEN, Danny goes back to bandits' hide-out. Searching for Danny, Tim finds barn where guns are hidden, walks into trap.

IN FINAL showdown, Tim kills one bandit, rounds up the others. They celebrate Danny's breaking clean with gang by a soapy bath.

TRAPPED in one of the outbuildings, Tim and Steve fight a tough battle. Danny saves Tim's life by injuring one of the bandits.

WHEN Sgt. Hasty is reinstated in the Army, and Danny has started a new life as a military student, Tim decides all is well again.

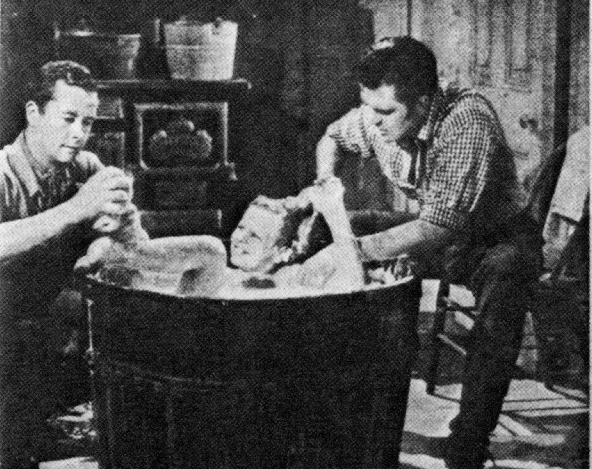

The preceding publicity release originally appeared in *Western Stars*, Volume 1, No. 2, March-June 1949.

1. Thatcher's orders are to kill Arnold before he can discover thievery.
2. Collins and Rafferty deliver their passengers safely, in spite of hold-up attempt en route by Thatcher's gunmen.
3. Dave's next assignment is a shipment of gold; Jessie, disguised as a boy, goes along without her father's knowledge.
4. This time Thatcher's men succeed in their ambush, but Arnold is no longer on board.

stagecoach

7. In her unaccustomed men's boots, poor Jessie has a hard time, but refuses any help. She's only too happy, though to douse her burning feet in a soothing bath.

Strange things had been happening at the Rainbow Ranch. Shadows that moved in the dead of night, and cattle missing in the morning where footprints spread through the tell-tale loam. These were the things that Peter Arnold, who owned the ranch, should know—and would know—now that he was returning home with his daughter, Jessie. But there were three men who wanted Peter Arnold uninformed. One was the ranch foreman, James Thatcher, the others: Clint Carter and Jack Parnell. For they knew more than anyone else about the missing cattle. They were stealing them. There was only one way to keep Arnold from finding out, and Thatcher sent his two henchmen out to seal his lips forever, before he could discover their treachery. Arnold and Jessie were arriving on the stagecoach, owned and driven by Dave Collins. Thatcher forgot to reckon with Dave Collins, and when Carter and Parnell went out to intercept the stage they ran into a hail of rifle bullets. Collins brought his two passengers safely into town and found himself up to his ears in one of the most dangerous adventures of his young life. Playing the role of Dave Collins in this rapid-fire thriller is Tim Holt, who handles the coach with a professional assurance—assurance that would make some of the famous old Concord drivers take notice.

5. Jessie is unrecognized, but she is able to spot Parnell, when his mask is accidentally dislodged.

6. The coach horses bolt in the excitement and all its occupants are forced to hoof it to Dave's ranch. It's tough on Jessie.

western stars MOVIE preview

There were two passengers in the lonely stage —a wealthy cattleman and his beautiful daughter marked for death

kid

CAST: *Dave Collins*—Tim Holt, *Chito Rafferty*—Richard Martin, *Arnold*—Thurston Hall, *Jessie*—Jeff Donnell.

more →

stage coach kid,

continued

8. Leaving the others at the ranch, Dave and Chito go to town looking for Parnell. They find him quickly . . .

9. . . . and Dave convinces him that it would be the wisest thing to come along to meet the folks at the jail.

13. Back at the ranch, Jessie is discovering that a boy's life is not all peaches and cream. Dave is called upon to inflict a little masculine punishment.

14. After the spanking, Jessie runs away. Dave follows her, and both run into Carter. In escaping Jessie is unmasked as a girl.

The preceding publicity release originally appeared in *Western Stars*, Volume 1, No. 3, October-December 1949.

Tim utilized the Alabama Hills of Lone Pine, California, as the location site for thirteen of his films.

Tim takes time out for a cup of coffee at the mobile lunch counter while working on *BORDER TREASURE* (1950).

TIM HOLT AND THE Masked Raiders

western stars  preview

ROBIN HOOD—there's a legend that has fascinated people the world over! When bold Robin stole from the rich and selfish to help those who were in need, it gave hope to the poor. It made them feel that they were not powerless against overwhelming odds of wealth and influence. And this sort of thing happened often in Western towns where ambitious men conspired to gain control of all the land and its resources, attempting to build private empires, which would assure them a constant supply of riches. Often they accomplished this at the point of guns in the hands of their hired gang of ruthless hoodlums and killers. Sometimes they operated a financial squeeze-play, using banks to foreclose on mortgages. But it was always at the expense of the ordinary citizen and the small landowner. The only defense the victims had, usually, was to take the law in their own hands. That's what happened in Willcox, Texas. When the town marshal and banker teamed up to gain control of the whole area, they did fine until their plans were upset by a rancher called the Diablo Kid and a group of masked raiders. Every time the bank foreclosed on a mortgage, the Diablo Kid "foreclosed" on the bank and gave the money back to the people. But any kind of stealing is bad—even when it's for a good purpose. So Texas Ranger Tim Holt is sent to Willcox to capture this modern Robin Hood. It's a tough job for Tim because he's the kind of a guy who can sympathize with the poor ranchers, but to a Ranger, duty comes first.

CAST: *Tim Holt*—himself. *Chito*—Richard Martin. *Gale*—Marjorie Lord. *Artie*—Gary Gray. *Banker Corthell*—Frank Willcox. *Doc Nichols*—Charles Arnt. *Marshal Barlow*—Harry Woods.

■ *Tim and Chito, with orders from the Colonel of the Rangers, are riding the trail toward Willcox, Texas when they are set upon by four men (1) and taken at pistol point to the Trevett ranch. The men accuse them of being part of a masked gang which has been terrorizing the area. Tim tells them they are from a town named Glenbar and proves it to the Trevetts—and niece Gale—by the mud on Chito's boots. (2) The ranchers warn Tim against going to Willcox, not knowing that he has orders to put an end to the masked gang. The moment Tim and Chito reach Willcox, their guns are taken by the marshal (3). As Tim begins his investigation the masked gang is on its way to town (4). The gang rips into Willcox without warning, firing their guns while the Diablo Kid robs the bank (5). Plunging into the battle . . .*

The Masked Raiders

continued

6. ... Tim tries to stop Diablo Kid but is met with bullets. He's nicked by shot fired from ambush by Doc Nichols who then ...

7. ... patches Tim up without admitting he'd done the shooting. A few comments, however, make Tim believe Doc's in gang.

8. Back at the hide-out, Diablo Kid—Gale!—divvies up loot, gives it to ...

12. Doc won't confess. He tells Tim the Diablo Kid is like Robin Hood—the banker is the real crook.

13. But orders are orders. Using Doc as "bait," Tim figures on luring Diablo Kid into rescue attempt.

14. This is precisely what Gale—the Diablo Kid—intends to do. She tells her gang she'll go by herself.

15. The marshal, however, has plans of his own. Knowing that Tim carries the looted money with him, he and his gang lay in ambush. But when he strikes, and Tim hands over the money, Doc yells a warning. He's recognized the marshal's horse, cries out that this is a fake Diablo Kid. With

9. ...Artie. He has to bring it to Doc— who'll deliver it to bankrupt ranchers. But accidentally package opens up. Fleeing...

10. ...to Doc's office, Artie leaves money there, then scoots. The marshal tracks him, third-degrees Doc on Diablo Kid's identity.

11. In steps Tim to give marshal a dose of his own medicine. Revealing himself as a Ranger, Tim fires marshal, jails the Doc.

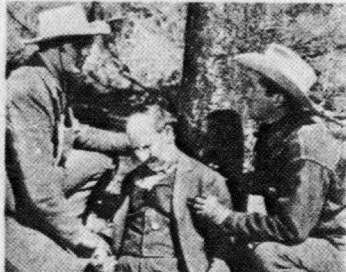

16. As soon as Tim checks and finds the Doc not seriously wounded, he tells Chito to stay behind and he takes off in a hurry.

17. Along the trail he runs into the real Diablo Kid. Tim battles her gently as he can, wins by ripping off her black mask.

18. Gale confesses, tells Tim how the marshal killed her father and how she became The Diablo Kid to defend herself and others.

19. Together they return to Doc. Gale is left to tend his wound while Tim and Chito pick up the marshal's trail, follow it...

...that, the marshal and his gang blast away, wounding Doc, and then they gallop off with loot, firing as they go to keep Tim and Chito pinned down.

20. ...to banker's house. In the gun battle that follows, the banker is killed and the marshal captured, ending their iron rule.

21. Chito is assigned task of taking the marshal and Doc to Glenbar for trial. Tim remains behind to take care of "things."

The preceding publicity release originally appeared in *Western Stars*, Volume 1, No. 4, January-March 1950. (Article courtesy of Ed Shetterly.)

It's about time to settle the score in *LAW OF THE BADLANDS* (1950). (Photo courtesy of Chuck Thornton.)

Pre-Vues

Dynamite Trail

With: Tim Holt
Richard Martin
Lynne Roberts
Regis Toomey

★ Cheers for a slight switch in the old formula, contributed by Tim Holt's latest RKO film! This time, neither a stolen herd nor a gold cache is the bone of contention. All the pioneers want now is a simple way to get from one place to another: a road on which they won't have to pay tolls to a pair of rogues (John Dehner, Robert Shayne). Tim and the Mexican-Irish pal of his movie adventures, Richard Martin, hire out to protect the builders of a new road, as employees of Lynne Roberts and her amiable, no-good husband, Regis Toomey. Not only guns but charges of dynamite come into play as the heroes of the tale strive to push the road through against the bitter opposition of the toll-collectors and their henchmen. The action-packed plot, which takes place in a New Mexico locale about sixty years ago, is well built up to a thrilling climax, with a daring rescue and explosion. Tim Holt's performance holds up his reputation for fine work, and Regis Toomey is convincing in the role of a weakling. Lynne Roberts is as lovely as ever. Credit for direction goes to Lew Landers, who has a deft touch with action scenes, as his past pictures have proved.

The preceding publicity release originally appeared in *Movie Thrills*, May 1950. (Article courtesy of Ed Shetterly.)

"Hands up!" Tim gets the drop on the desperados in this scene from *SADDLE LEGION* (1951).

Tim poses for this publicity photo in his typically conservative Western garb. Notice the incongruous bus way back by the tree on the right.

25 TOP COWBOYS

tim holt: fastest man with a six-gun in films!

a k.o. punch without a single boxing lesson!

Although Tim Holt has never taken professional boxing lessons, he is one of the best sluggers in the business. While stunt men often take over for other actors in a fight scene, Tim does his own work, and does it with gusto. Mishaps have occurred only when the other actors have stepped before the cameras and lost their heads in the excitement. Tim's nose has been broken four times, and always by actors who threw punches not called for in the script.

■ Tim owns a 160-acre ranch near the Mexican border where he lives the life of a ranch hand, training his horses and working his land. Thirty-three years old, he has been married twice, has one son, and does much work for underprivileged children, appearing at benefits and visiting bedridden kids. As a boy, Tim rode a horse before he could walk, and even today finds riding more natural than footwork. He has put his Palomino Lightning out to pasture and replaced him with a fiery stallion named Sun Dance. Tim has an excellent war record, having been decorated several times, is an expert with both pistol and rifle, and is probably faster on the draw than any other movie cowboy, having practiced since early boyhood. He goes to Hollywood only for picture work, and then stays with Dick Martin, his screen side-kick who plays Chito Rafferty. They are close pals and photography fiends, preferring the wildest possible country for camera subjects, and for hunting and fishing. A tall, stocky young man, Tim always wears boots and seldom puts up with a hat. Like his father before him, he scandalized his Virginia family by deciding to become an actor, and although he started off with tear-jerkers like **Stella Dallas**, he soon switched by preference to Westerns, and with a great sense of loyalty, makes sure that old buddies of his father, the late Jack Holt, always get work in his pictures.

Tim and Chito, played by Richard Martin, fight side by side for law and order

more→

The above publicity still from *HOT LEAD* served as the inspiration for the Ivan Jesse Curtis painting which adorns the cover of this book.

Arizona rocks to bandit gunfire as Tim Holt avenges a murder and wins a fresh start for a reformed convict.

"hot lead"

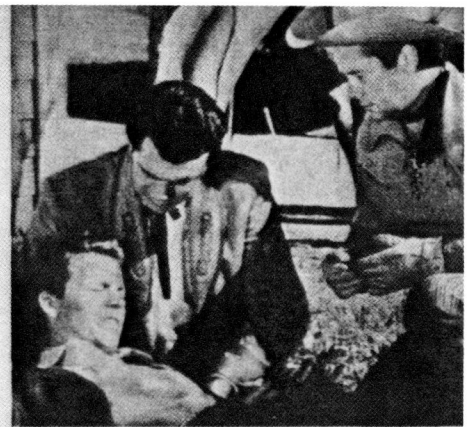

1. Tim and his buddy Chito find a fellow cowhand Bob dying after trading lead with gunmen robbing a train at Trail Head. The train safe was empty.

4. Accidentally rescued by Tim and Chito, Dave is signed on at the ranch of lovely Gail Martin. He writes to his mother back East that he owns the ranch—and falls hard for Gail.

5. Turk having killed the former telegrapher as part of his scheme, his men Dakota and Stony run off Gail's herd to get Dave fired. But Tim checks their stampede and pursues them.

6. Out-gunned, Dakota is made prisoner. A reluctant sheriff agrees to Tim's plan to trap the gunmen by having Dave made new telegrapher and tip off Turk on a phony gold shipment.

7. A suspicious Turk kidnaps Dave and Gail. When Dave fails to appear as promised, the sheriff threatens Tim and Chito. Only Tim's sixgun keeps them free to hunt the missing pair.

2. Tim chases the empty-handed bandits, who scatter and escape. Their chief, Turk Thorne, remembers telegrapher David Collins is due for prison parole.

3. Lured west on promise of a decent job, reformed Dave is forced from the stage. Turk wants him to replace the Trail Head operator and relay news of gold shipments.

8. Trailing them to an abandoned cabin, Tim knocks out the guard left with Gail. But Turk, Stony and a helpless Dave are bound for Trail Head to flag down the train supposedly carrying gold. Since the sheriff now is hunting Tim, the station is clear.

9. Tim and Chito reach town in time to slug it out with the bandits, caught red-handed in the baggage car. They turn Turk over to the returning lawmen.

THE END. A wedding is not far off at Gail's spread —and when his mother pays her visit to Trail Head, Dave will indeed be the top man on his own ranch.

The preceding publicity release originally appeared in *Who's Who in Western Stars*, Volume 1, No. 1, 1952.

tim holt: pop's boots are big—

Tim Holt's biggest recent thrill was provided by the school children of Ada, Oklahoma, who gave him a miniature Shetland pony named Whisper of Ada, who is to be trained for visits to children's hospitals and orphanages. Tim, as a matter of fact, makes scores of such tours each year and his appearances cheer thousands of lives which are bleak and lonely. Born Charles John Holt, Jr., in Beverly Hills, Tim seldom speaks of his father, Jack Holt, for whom he was named because he doesn't want to seem boastful. Tim adored his dad. Almost as soon as Tim could walk, Jack taught him to love and respect a good horse and to play polo. For years, in addition to his string of polo ponies, Tim owned a Lippizan (ballet horse) acquired from the Austrian Royal Stables. The horse, a magnificent white stallion named Pluto, has been given 14 years of training as all Lippizans are. It was Pluto who starred in the 20th Century-Fox production "Florion." When Pluto began to age (he is now over 30), Tim found a good home for him at pasture near Garden Grove, California, where Pluto still does ballet leaps across the meadows on fine mornings. Tim visits him regularly. Tim also loves dogs, now owns an Australian sheep dog, a boxer, and a Doberman Pinscher. Thanks to his father, Tim is an expert shot, and—to this day—always bags his limit within a few hours when he goes hunting for geese on the Colorado River. One of his proudest possessions is the gun collection which Tim inherited from his dad. Another inheritance was respect for the western heritage and a determination to live up to its ideals. Tim uses perfect English even though the flavor is western, and he never endorses a product that he hasn't, personally, tested and found to be of honest quality. For 4 consecutive years a Tim Holt comic book has been issued with enormous success. The adventures are always constructive in nature, stress the importance of clean living, kindness, and integrity. A natural born fighter, Tim is a cagey boxer, does his own movie fights and in real life served notably during World War II. He was bombardier in 22 B-29 missions over Japanese oil fields, crash landed on Guam the last day of the war with 175 flack holes in the plane's fuselage. To date he has owned 3 ranches, is in the market for the fourth. Once he has an outfit running smoothly and making money, he likes to sell it, buy a spavined spread and work it into shape. He always smokes a pipe and owns a fine collection of Briars. Drinks his coffee black, eats his eggs sunny side up, likes his bacon crisp. He will never die with his boots on because they are the last items of clothing he dons before leaving the house, the first things he removes when he hits carpet. His Tim Holt's Ranch Review has played thousands of Midwest towns. The act includes Chito Rafferty (Dick Martin), Ray Whitley on guitar, and Jack O'Shea. Tim has already taught his 12-year-old son, Lance, to ride, and would eventually like to include him in the Ranch Review, as well as possibly feature him in his pictures. Tim's wife, Alice Harrison, travels with him whenever possible. His latest pictures are "The Marshal of Pecos" and "Desert Passage."

he's quick on the shutter

Tim Holt is a shutterbug, nearly always carrying a camera in his saddlebag when he is riding fences at his ranch. He likes to try different filters to get spectacular cloud effects which are seen over California's rangeland, hopes to experiment with stroboscopic lens during rodeos in order to catch some of the furious action. Buys every new camera that is marketed (for instance the Polaroid Land camera which produces a print in 60 seconds, and the stereo-realist which takes 3-dimensional shots in color) and keeps up-to-date in the camera gadget department. Hopes to be able to enter some of his western subjects in camera competition in time to come.

desert passage

The dust of time had not dimmed the lure of the lost treasure, when a thief crept from behind prison walls to claim it

1. Lavic, Arizona, echoes to sudden gunfire as sinister strangers Langdon and Allen trade lead with a third new arrival, John Carver, who just has been released on parole from prison and who comes after a long-hidden cache of money which he had once stolen from the Lavic Bank.

6. Driving back their wrecked coach, they find Carver's girl Roxie has shown up also wanting the loot. Locating it in the barn, Tim turns it over to Emily for return to Lavic's bank.

7. Bronson, Langdon, Allen and Roxie's new admirer, Warwick—having overcome Carver—now join forces to take back his money. At Roxie's tip about Tim, all converge upon Emily's locked door with guns ready.

2. A badly hurt Carver seeks help from bankrupt stage drivers Tim Holt and Chito Rafferty, who agree to transport the sick stranger south of the Border in their aged coach for one thousand dollars.

3. On the road they find Emily Bryce, daughter of the bank's dead founder. Stranded while seeking a Sheriff after she recognized Carver back at Lavic, Emily denounces the ex-thief.

4. Aware of riders following them, Tim and Chito uneasily turn in after dark at Burley's way-station. Its old owner is missing; but Carver's lawyer Bronson is waiting, eager to take over the money.

5. Carver's ex-cellmate Langdon steals the coach and rips it apart hunting the money—which Carver actually has sewn in the team's harness. Chito and Tim interrupt this vandalism.

6. But Tim helps Emily's escape by the window. With Chito also aboard they whip up the coach for Lavic. In the race which follows, the pursuing riders are out-gunned and Bronson (who, it is found, killed old Burley) dies.

THE END. Back at Lavic, their reward for the return of the long-hidden bank loot is sufficient to keep Chito and Tim in business. Emily promises a happy Tim an even greater reward.

The preceding publicity release originally appeared in *Who's Who in Western Stars*, Volume 1, No. 2, 1952. (Article courtesy of Ed Shetterly.)

Bring Back the White Hats
Cowboy Hero Says It's Time For Return of Cowboy Heroes

By JAMES PURDY

OKLAHOMA CITY — (UPI) — Tim Holt, twin six-guns blazing, rode the range in 140 movies as the good guy in the white Stetson to a generation of popcorn-chomping youngsters.

And in these days of the disreputable hero he thinks the movie industry is missing a financial bet by not bringing back the traditional knight of the purple sage who rarely drank anything stiffer than sarsaparilla and only petted his horse.

Holt, whose father Jack Holt was a thriller hero in the silent movie days, is sales manager for a radio station here. Now 52, he's perhaps best known to the younger generation through TV reruns of "The Treasure of Sierra Madre," in which he appeared with Humphrey Bogart and Walter Houston.

Holt thinks the kind of movie he played in for 22 years could be the shot in the arm the movie industry needs.

"It's real simple," he said in an interview. "The type of picture that we made was family entertainment, and when television first started it then became the family entertainment.

"Our market left us. It just wasn't economically feasible to make the pictures.

"I think they could be made now, however," he added. "I think people are tired of staying home and watching television all the time."

• • •

HOLT is enthusiastic about the rating system, which he describes as "a necessity."

"What other protection have I got for my kids?" he asked.

"In the old days, when you had Gene Autry and Roy Rogers and Hoppy (William Boyd), you would see kids out on the front lawn, playing. They identified themselves with those characters.

"Nowadays, kids don't have anybody to identify with. Clint Eastwood and Lee Marvin are two real good friends of mine, but I sure wouldn't want my kids identifying with them.

"When you get the sex and violence and things like that, it's so far outdone that it just becomes absurd," he said, then added, "I think just like any other pendulum, it's going to swing the other way."

• • •

HOLT occasionally returns to Hollywood for short acting roles. However, he says he has no interest in returning to movies fulltime.

"The business has changed to such an extent I don't want to anymore," he said. His movie star father died in 1951 at age 62.

"I just got back from doing The Virginian out there," said Tim Holt. "The people are lovely to work with, except they have to do it all too fast. I don't see how they can perfect their work going at the speed that they have to go."

One of the changes in movie making is the use of stunt men.

When Holt started in movies in 1935, at the age of 17, stunt men weren't very common.

"You were your own stunt man then," he recalled, adding that during his career he "broke both arms, both shoulders, one leg, seven ribs and I don't know how many times my nose has been broken.

"They always used to leave the stunts and the fights until the last day of the picture so that if you did get hurt you wouldn't hold up the production," he said.

TIM HOLT tries out his old six-guns he used as movie cowboy.

United Press International article, circa 1971. (Article courtesy of Nick Nicholls.)

Tim Holt, Western Star During '40s Bemoans Immorality in Today's Films

TIM HOLT blazed many a trail across the screen in the 1940s.

Tim Holt, whose singing six-guns blazed a Hollywood western trail in the 1940s, believes today's cowboy pictures sound a sour note.

"Yesterday's films were a lesson in morality. Today's films are a lesson in immorality," he says.

Holt regrets the passing of the family western—the kind he made, sometimes at the rate of eight a year.

"Today, the hero is a dishonest carouser, who would rather shoot an opponent in the back than arrest him."

AS FOR the idea that times have changed, Tim blows a big six-gun hole in that, too.

"What's the difference between children then and children now? They still have to earn to eat and dress themselves, and go to school.

Tim Holt ...A quiet heroism

THE NATIONAL TATTLER

"The difference is just in what their parents tell them.

"Reality? What's so real about today's films?

"In today's movies, they'll beat a man up, kick him down a flight of stairs, break a board over his head, and then shoot him, and he'll still get up fighting. Now is that realism?

"Just how much punishment do you think a human body can take?

"I THINK I know, having to go through these cobalt treatments every day. And that's no picnic."

The real-life Tim Holt displays a quiet heroism that's as tough as anything the Hollywood Tim Holt ever did on the screen. He's a cancer victim.

But he hasn't given up on life. His throat is so painful it's difficult for him to speak. Nevertheless, along with those cobalt treatments, Holt keeps a full schedule as manager of a country music radio station in Oklahoma City, Okla.

"I've been here since 1947," he says, "but a lot of Oklahoma people are surprised to find a Hollywood movie star in Oklahoma.

"ACTUALLY, I never did like Hollywood. I never did feel there was anything mystic about it."

This from a man who was born to the tinsel, if anyone was. Tim's father, Jack Holt, was a Western star in his day, too.

Tim, now 54, spent 20 years in the film business before moving to Harrah, Okla., population a few dozen. He likes it there.

"After all, Dale Robinson is from Harrah. Used to own the home right next door to mine. And Spanky McFarland lived in Oklahoma City until a couple of years ago."

IN 1947, he came to Oklahoma to help run a rodeo, and met a girl who worked for the local school board. He married her and has been an Oklahoman ever since, except for a college study stint at Ames, Iowa.

He's Cancer Victim, But Hasn't Given Up on Life

Tim Holt isn't the big guy you'd expect to see slamming a villain around in a Western. He wears hornrims and a business suit nowadays, and about the only thing he retains from the film days is his cowboy boots and the way he moves. Fast.

If you want to get in touch with him, try the radiotelephone in his car. That's where you'll usually find him—moving around the city, meeting people, planning advertising campaigns and TV commercials.

But he's never too busy to talk about the old days.

"REMEMBER Jack O'Shay?" he asks. "He was the bad guy in most of my pictures. I must have shot him behind the same rock a hundred times.

"We'd wind up the film. Then we'd make the next one and I'd chase him again. The kids never did seem to mind that I was after the very same badman over and over."

The tactics of the Jack O'Shay-type badmen were a far cry from the cowboy in today's movies, says Holt.

"Sure, a cowboy's closest friend was his gun. But he didn't use it to shoot people. He used it against rattlesnakes and coyotes, and for food for the table. All that shooting in the cowboy pictures is exaggerated. But when we used it, we'd never show a man fall in the street if he was shot.

"WE SHOWED a killing to be a terrible thing, not something exciting. Unlike today, blood and gore and sadism were carefully avoided."

But Tim Holt, who made 149 Family Westerns, sees new hope for this kind of entertainment today.

"Marty Robbins just signed a contract to do four films of that type—with singing. If it sells, there could be a whole string of them."

Which would be very pleasing to family man and ex-cowboy Tim Holt. —WES BRANCH

The *National Tattler* article, circa 1972. (Article courtesy of Mrs. Tim Holt.)

Hot on the trail! Tim and Chito traverse the rocky terrain of Iverson's Movie Location Ranch in search of rustlers in this scene from *PISTOL HARVEST* (1951).

CANCER CLAIMS ACTOR

Tim Holt Dead at 54

Former western movie actor Tim Holt died Thursday in Shawnee Memorial Hospital after a lengthy bout with cancer.

The 54-year-old Holt's problem with the disease began last August when he began experiencing a great deal of pain. He was admitted to the hospital in late November.

Holt, whose movie career began in 1935, was noted for his portrayals in westerns, including "Stagecoach" with John Wayne and "My Darling Clementine" with Henry Fonda.

Of the approximately 150 pictures he made, he was probably best known for his role as an itinerant American searching for gold in Mexico in "Treasure of the Sierra Madre."

"I think 'Treasure' was his favorite role," his wife, the former Berdee Stephens, said, "because of working with Humphrey Bogart and the two Hustons, Walter and John."

Holt was also known for an out-of-character role as a Nazi officer in "Hitler's Children" in 1943. The highly successful anti-Nazi picture was made shortly before Holt entered the U.S. Army Air Corps.

He served in the South Pacific as a lieutenant and flew several missions over Japan as a bombadier on B-29s.

Holt was born in Hollywood and was the son of silent film western star Jack Holt. He came to Oklahoma in 1947 when "I met a girl who worked for the school board . . . and decided to stay here," he said.

He commuted back and forth to California until 1954 when he gave up motion pictures for good.

Holt was never known for his love of the limelight. "I never did feel there was anything mystic about Hollywood," he once said. "I never really did like it."

In recent years Holt, who made his home in Harrah, concentrated mainly on radio work in the Oklahoma City area, with occasional side trips to California to appear in television shows.

He originally started with KLPR AM in 1961 and went to KEBC AM last year as advertising manager.

Holt was elected to the National Cowboy Hall of Fame and was a member of the Screen Actor's Guild.

Services are tentatively planned for 2 p.m. Monday at the Harrah United Methodist Church with burial in Memory Lane Cemetery in Harrah directed by Wilson Funeral Home, Harrah.

Other survivors include three sons, Lance, Roseland, N.Y.; and Jack and Jay, both of the home; a daughter, Bryanna, of the home, and a sister, Mrs. Jennifer Holt Cardinal, Santa Barbara, Calif.

Tim Holt

Tim Holt, Popular Western Star, Dies

SHAWNEE (P)—Tim Holt, 54, a popular star in western movies during the World War II era, died Thursday in Shawnee Medical Center Clinic.

Gov. David Hall said of the Oklahoma actor-rancher, "Oklahoma has lost a beloved son. His courage the past months in a losing fight against cancer was an inspiration to all of us."

Holt also served as sales manager of Oklahoma City radio station KEBC-FM before his death.

He is survived by his wife, Birdie, and three teen-age children.

His father was the late Jack Holt, a star of silent pictures.

Tim Holt played the good guy in Westerns. He succumbed on February 16 He was 53.

The preceding articles were published on February 16, 1973, following Tim's death on February 15. (Articles courtesy of Boyd Magers.)

Tim Holt's Last Days

By Kathy Garner

SHAWNEE — Although former movie star Tim Holt appeared thin and pale during one of his last public appearances, his audience was unaware that he was fighting the terminal illness which claimed his life here Thursday.

Holt, who took delight in telling stories of his Hollywood career and his humorous moments with some of movieland's famous stars, appeared happy and quipped with his listeners when he made the appearance.

It was at a workshop on the American West late last year at Central State University in Edmond.

He covered the full range of his good times, his favorite memories, his feelings about various types of movies and some of his fellow actors during the session.

Director John Ford and actors Humphrey Bogart and Walter Huston were among those who had his respect and admiration. He liked to talk about them and things that happened behind the scenes.

Holt described John Ford as a colorful character who would make an excellent subject for a book.

The well-known director, Holt told the audience, had his own unique way of doing things.

Once while on location for a film, Ford received word from the studio that they were three days behind in their shooting schedule.

He said the director calmly ripped three pages out of the script, saying: "We're not behind now."

One of Holt's best-known pictures was "Treasure of the Sierra Madre," in which he co-starred with Bogart and Huston.

Bogart and Huston were enjoying a wave of popularity at the time, Holt recalled, and could get away with temperamental behavior without fear of being fired.

Holt took part in several of their pranks, he conceded, including a scene in which the three actors clowned their way as "wall flowers" instead of the rugged "he-men" called for by the script.

"Jack Warner almost had a heart attack when he saw that one," Holt chortled.

The actor had still another story about Bogart.

"One day Bogie was not in a very good mood," Holt said. "Here came Ronald Reagan bounding up in white slacks and sweater and about 14 inches of white teeth."

When Reagan slapped Bogart on the back, he continued, "Bogie didn't even look up. 'Blankety-blank all-American boy,'" he growled.

Questioned about his attitude toward contemporary movies, including the so-called "spaghetti westerns," and those rated X, Holt said he felt there was room for different types of films.

The cowboy star noted that in most appearances the audience usually asked two classic questions: Why the six-guns never needed re-loading, and why the cowboy hats never fell off.

"Those guns are a military secret," he joked, and added: "The hats stayed in place because they were designed that way. After all, a real cowboy can't stop roping a steer to chase his hat."

Holt, asked about his favorite role, named "The Ambersons," directed by Orson Welles. "I liked it because it was a serious part and different from the western roles I usually played."

His memories of Hollywood seemed to be happy ones, although he has been known to disparage the glamor usually associated with it.

He grew up in show business, following the footsteps of his father, and began his motion picture career when he was still a young man. His sister, Jennifer, also appeared in many western films. She is now married and living in Chicago, Holt said.

Holt and his wife made their home in Oklahoma City and Harrah in recent years.

The preceding article appeared in February 1973. (Article courtesy of Mrs. Tim Holt.)

Holt Rites On Monday

HARRAH—Services for Tim Holt, 54, popular star of western movies during the World War II era who died Thursday in a Shawnee hospital, are tentatively set for 2 p.m. Monday in Harrah where he had made his home in recent years.

Holt, son of silent film western star Jack Holt, died of cancer after an illness of several months.

Services will be in the Harrah United Methodist Church with Wilson Funeral Home directing.

Holt had been a Harrah area rancher in recent years and served as sales manager for Oklahoma City radio station KEBC-FM. He also was active in sports programs for youths.

Survivors include his wife, Berdee; a daughter, Bryanna, of the home; three sons, Lance of Roseland, N. Y., Jack and Jay, both of the home, and a sister, Mrs. Jennifer Holt Cardinal, Santa Barbara, Calif.

(Article courtesy of Mrs. Tim Holt.)

INTO THE SUNSET

Tim Holt enjoyed being a cowboy, whether he was up there on the silver screen portraying the cowboy hero; chatting with a fan before riding at breakneck speed into the rodeo ring, waving his Stetson to the cheering fans; or during later years in Oklahoma just donning his western-cut suit and cowboy boots before heading off to work at the radio station. He was a cowboy. It was ingrained, part of his life, and he was comfortable with this persona he had nurtured most of his life.

His daughter Bryanna commented to me, "I remember the Wranglers. That was his favorite way to dress, the Wranglers." And then son Jay thought for a moment and said quietly to me, "He didn't own a pair of shoes that I know of. He was buried in his cowboy boots."

I was curious about how these things got started that continued throughout his lifetime and remained intact as he rode off into his final sunset. From where did this cowboy state of mind come, this longing to be a cowboy? Certainly he was influenced by his father, the man who taught him his love of horses and took him onto Western movie sets when he was barely old enough to walk.

Yes, the mind set was there early on. Culver schoolmate Budd Boetticher recalled teenaged Tim parading up and down the halls of their dorm clad only in a bathrobe, with holsters and guns strapped to his hips, proclaiming, "I'm going to be a Western star some day." And he was right, of course!

Let's end this treatise on Tim Holt by going back to the moment, the precise moment, when he knew he wanted to be a cowboy for life. He wrote about it, of that inspiration, in a article for *Western Stars* magazine back in 1950:

With the oom-pah-pah of the band booming in my ears and my pony shaking his head like the most fierce of Arabian stallions, I rode down the main street of Fresno one wonderful day in 1924, and no kid in the whole world could have been happier than I was at that moment.

I was five years old, and I was the Crown Prince of Rodeo! At the head of the parade rode my father as King of Rodeo, and the crowd was cheering him and throwing paper confetti over his broad shoulders as he led the glittering procession toward the rodeo grounds. I tried to sit up straight in the saddle as he did, and every once in a while I'd look down at my new cowboy boots with their tooled leather designs, and I made up my mind that I'd never wear regular shoes again as long as I lived. *I was going to be a cowboy for the rest of my life.*

*   *   *

SELECTED BIBLIOGRAPHY

Black, Bill, Editor. *Red Mask of the Rio Grande,* 1, 2, 3, Longwood, Florida: AC Comics, Circa 1991.

_____. *Tim Holt Western Annual,* Longwood, Florida: AC Comics, 1991.

Copeland, Bobby J. "On the Festival Trail with Richard 'Chito' Martin," *Westerns and Serials,* No. 38, Circa 1991.

Dellinger, Paul. "Tim Holt—One of a Kind," *Under Western Skies,* (No. 38, 1990).

Garfield, Brian. *Western Films,* New York: Rawson Associates, 1982.

Jewell, Richard B. with Vernon Harbin. *The RKO Story,* New York: Arlington House, 1982.

Maltin, Leonard. *TV Movies and Video Guide,* New York: Signet, 1989.

Mathis, Jack. *Republic Confidential, Volume 2—The Players,* Illinois: Jack Mathis Advertising, 1992.

Pitts, Michael R. *Western Movies,* North Carolina: McFarland & Company, 1986.

Place, J. A. *The Western Films of John Ford,* New Jersey: Citadel Press, 1974.

Rainey, Buck. *The Fabulous Holts,* Tennessee: Western Film Collector Press, 1976.

_____. *Heroes of the Range,* North Carolina: World of Yesterday, 1987.

Rothel, David. *An Ambush of Ghosts, A Personal Guide to Favorite Western Film Locations,* North Carolina: Empire Publishing, 1990.

_____. *Those Great Cowboy Sidekicks,* New Jersey and North Carolina: Scarecrow Press and World of Yesterday, 1984.

Thornton, Chuck. *The Western Adventures of Tim Holt,* Privately published, 1987.

Welles, Orson and Peter Bogdanovich. *This is Orson Welles,* New York: HarperCollins Publishers, 1992.

*   *   *

FILMOGRAPHY INDEX

Along the Rio Grange, 62, 64-65
Arizona Ranger, The, 23, 86, 92-93, 177, 184, 196, 199, 209-210, 241
Avenging Rider, The, 81-83
Back Street, 45, 55-56
Bandit Ranger, The, 62, 76-78
Border Trail, The, 69-70
Border Treasure, 114-115, 211, 257
Brothers of the Saddle, 86, 97-100, 187, 241
Come On, Danger, 51, 73-75
Cyclone On Horseback, 67-68
Desert Passage, 130-131, 200, 272-273
Dude Cowboy, The, 62, 70-72
Dynamite Pass, 26, 32, 111-114, 263
Fargo Kid, The, 62-64
Fifth Avenue Girl, 18, 45, 53
Fighting Frontier, The, 79-80
Girl and the Gambler, The, 52-53
Gold Is Where You Find It, 47, 150
Gun Smugglers, 86, 95-97, 157, 186, 246-251
Gunplay, 123-124
Guns of Hate, 25-26, 86, 93-94, 187, 209
His Kind of Woman, 133, 136
History is Made at Night, 17, 45-46
Hitler's Children, 46, 58-59, 156, 214
Hot Lead, 26, 124-125, 231, 267-269
I Met My Love Again, 47
Indian Agent, 94-95, 193, 198, 242-243
Laddie, 45, 53-54
Land of the Open Range, 62, 72-73
Law of the Badlands, 25, 117-119, 262
Law West of Tombstone, The, 18, 45, 48, 61, 213
Magnificent Ambersons, The, 16, 20-21, 23, 32, 45-46, 56-57, 59, 133, 152, 156, 158-159, 173, 201, 216-217
Masked Raiders, 86, 105-107, 121, 187, 258-261
Monster That Challenged the World, The, 27, 133, 136-137, 177-178
My Darling Clementine, 18, 25, 32, 85, 132-134, 152, 173
Mysterious Desperado, The, 104-105, 244

Overland Telegraph, 125-126, 212
Pirates of the Prairie, 78-79
Pistol Harvest, 26, 121-123, 206-208, 275
Red River Robin Hood, 83
Red River Valley, 15
Renegade Ranger, The, 51, 61, 74
Rider from Tucson, 110-111, 160, 162, 165, 184, 186, 209
Riders of the Range, 107-108, 187, 189, 205-207
Riding the Wind, 72
Rio Grande Patrol, 115-117
Road Agent, 26, 71, 128-129, 184
Robbers of the Range, 66-67
Rookie Cop, The, 18, 45, 52
Rustlers, 100-101, 187
Saddle Legion, 120-121, 187, 227, 264
Sagebrush Law, 20, 80-81
Six-Gun Gold, 68-69
Sons of the Legion, 48
Spirit of Culver, The, 51
Stagecoach, 18, 20, 32, 45, 49-51, 85, 152, 156, 158
Stagecoach Kid, 101-104, 252-255
Stella Dallas, 17, 41, 46, 150, 156
Storm Over Wyoming, 108-109, 187
Swiss Family Robinson, 45, 54-55
Target, 129-130, 199-200
This Stuff'll Kill Ya!, 27, 133, 138-139, 178
Thunder Mountain, 86-87, 186, 204
Thundering Hoofs, 19, 75-76
Trail Guide, 126-128
Treasure of the Sierra Madre, The, 23-24, 32, 59, 133-136, 152, 156-158, 173, 198, 202, 211, 216, 240
Under the Tonto Rim, 24, 87-88, 193, 195, 204-205, 237
Vanishing Pioneer, The, 13, 23, 45-46
Wagon Train, 62
Western Heritage, 90-92, 198-200
Wild Horse Mesa, 25, 86, 89-90, 185, 199
Yesterday Machine, The, 27, 133, 138-139, 178

Author David Rothel in the Alabama Hills of Lone Pine, California.

ABOUT THE AUTHOR

David Rothel's lifelong fascination with show business began with frequent visits to his local movie theater, where he followed the adventures of his favorite screen heroes. He has since gone from youthful observer to performer, theatre producer/director, teacher (thirty-year career as instructor of drama, speech, and language arts), and published authority on various aspects of popular entertainment (ten books in twenty years). His first book, *Who Was That Masked Man?: The Story of The Lone Ranger*, received enthusiastic reviews, was a main book club selection, and was expanded and revised. Mr. Rothel's second book was *The Singing Cowboys*, an informative, back-in-the-saddle examination of the B musical Western films. Next came *The Great Show Business Animals*, a charming work that reflects Mr. Rothel's ability to capture the spirit and analyze the impact of show business phenomena. *Those Great Cowboy Sidekicks* provided an in-depth examination of such fondly remembered comic character actors as George "Gabby" Hayes, Smiley Burnette, and Andy Devine. *The Gene Autry Book* and *The Roy Rogers Book*, both reference-trivia-scrapbooks, have been popular with Mr. Rothel's readers. He co-wrote with Chuck Thornton the revised editions of *Lash LaRue, The King of the Bullwhip* and *Allan "Rocky" Lane, Republic's Action Ace*. In 1990 Rothel's *An Ambush of Ghosts, A Personal Guide To Favorite Western Film Locations* was published and received excellent reviews. Film historian Leonard Maltin devoted two of his *Entertainment Tonight* segments to the book, including an interview with Mr. Rothel. Mr. Rothel's writing is characterized by thoroughness of research, warmth, wit, and understanding.